SERVING THE PEOPLE?

The Need to Reform
the Irish Legal System

Michael Williams

D1513222

The Liffey Press

Published by
The Liffey Press Ltd
Raheny Shopping Centre, Second Floor
Raheny, Dublin 5, Ireland
www.theliffeypress.com

A catalogue record of this book is
available from the British Library.

ISBN 978-1-908308-42-9

Contents

In memory of Barney and Peter

and for

Ruth, Judith, Louise,

Laura, Rebecca, Max and Tansy

Acknowledgements

A few years ago, I wrote some articles about legal issues for a Dublin magazine. In 2011, when my association with it ended (in a way that charity suggests I should not go into), my friend Tom Kilroy said that what I had to say about law in Ireland needed the space of a book, and could not be accommodated in a series of articles. That comment was the genesis of this book. Another old friend, John Horgan, read an earlier draft of this book, and offered encouragement and helpful comments. I am grateful to both of them.

I did not ask any of my lawyer friends to comment on it. I thought my views might be unpopular among lawyers, and, if so, for me to ask one of my lawyer friends to align himself with views that his other friends and colleagues rejected might be asking of them more than was fair. If I was wrong not to trust them, I hope they will understand and forgive me.

Jonathan Williams, my literary agent, read this book in an earlier draft, helped me to develop it, and was consistently helpful, encouraging and patient in bringing it to publication. I could not have had a kinder or more generous guide.

My thanks also to my editor and publisher, David Givens, who was a pleasure to work with.

As an apprentice solicitor, years ago, I fretted at not being allowed the freedom my contemporaries enjoyed. I now realise that when my Master, the late D.R. Pigot ('Senior') insisted that I keep office hours when not studying, he was giving me my first lesson as an aspiring lawyer. By accepting me as an apprentice he undertook to teach me my trade, and he intended to honour that commitment, just as he would honour any other he might make. I was lucky to be introduced to the practice of law by an honourable, upright, conscientious gentleman, who brought those qualities to the service of his clients as well as to the education of his apprentice. Without realising it, I absorbed from him lessons that I hope have stood to me.

My education was continued by my one-time employer, later partner and always mentor and friend, the late Alexis FitzGerald, who, among other things, taught me that to understand the law we need to go to its primary sources. I also learnt from him that you can become an effective and successful lawyer by taking care of your clients, but to be a really good one you must care for them. My gratitude to both continues.

Introduction

What this Book is About

This book looks critically at the Irish legal system and the people who operate it, argues that neither serve us as well as they should and suggests how both might be improved. Why should anyone, except maybe a few lawyers and civil servants in the Department of Justice, spend time reading it? Well, one reason is that the legal system, operated by lawyers and controlled by judges, affects citizens' lives, in more ways than they may recognise.

Indeed, 'affects' may not be strong enough. 'Controls' may be more accurate. Judges decide what standard of care you are entitled to expect from your doctor, whether the way you drive your car is dangerous, and if you have driven dangerously whether you should be allowed to continue to drive, or even be sent to prison. They decide how much protection you are entitled to expect from other people, and how much protection other people are entitled to from you. If your reputation is attacked, protecting it is their responsibility, and if you damage someone else's reputation, they may intervene to protect him. If you are accused of a crime, they may decide whether you are guilty or not, and if a judge doesn't actually make that decision he will certainly influence it. If you are found guilty, a judge will decide whether you should be fined or sent to prison, and how big the fine should be or how long you should spend in prison. Judges decide how long violent criminals should spend in prison, and to that extent they have a major role in protecting citizens from violent crime.

Judges in the higher courts can cancel legislation and decisions of the government. If the Constitution is right in describing the powers of government as being 'legislative, executive and judicial' – and it clearly is – then the judicial is probably the most powerful of the three. Unlike the game of stone, paper and scissors, where each of the three has equal power – scissors cuts paper, but is broken by stone – judges can set aside decisions of either the legislature or the executive, but decisions of higher courts may not be countermanded by either of the others. So, a book that describes the legal system, shows what aspects of it operate to our benefit and which do not, and goes on to suggest how it could be improved, may be worth reading.

Another reason this book may be worth reading is that it will argue that at the highest level and on important issues judges have made decisions that the Constitution specifically prohibits, and have extended their powers in a way that threatens our democracy.

Readers should not be put off by a fear of unfamiliar jargon. Legal language will be kept to a minimum, any unusual words will be explained when they first occur, and again in a Glossary at the end of this book. Nor should they worry that they will have to grasp subtle 'lawyer-type' distinctions. There is nothing in this book that an intelligent layperson cannot grasp with a little effort.

Judges will be referred to as 'he'. Nowadays, there are a number of women judges, and when you read 'he' rather than the more cumbersome 'he/she', that is for simplicity, and does not imply that law is a unisex profession. Some legal documents include tedious definitions, often including the formula 'words importing the male gender shall be deemed also to include the female gender'. Or, as law students used to say years ago, giggling at their naughtiness, 'male shall embrace female'. This book adopts that concept.

This may be a good point to say something about 'legal jargon'. If you own a home and are not its first owner, the document by which its previous owner transferred it to you will have said that he did so 'as beneficial owner'. If you went to the trouble of reading that document, your eye probably passed over those words, or you thought of them as a piece of 'legal jargon'. In fact, your lawyer insisted on using them because if a seller tells the buyer he is the 'beneficial owner' of what he is selling, the buyer gets legal rights that he would not have if those words had not been used. So, using those words was valid and useful, and they are not jargon, though they may look like it.

Before you got to that point, you might have noticed that the entire text was one long sentence with no punctuation. That is increasingly rare in modern legal drafting but is still used in traditional 'conveyancing' – the process of transferring ownership in land and buildings – and it does not make for easy reading.

If you own your home under a lease, you will have seen that the document described how the lease was granted, maybe many years ago, and then, instead of listing its various owners over the years, it said that by 'divers mesne assurances acts in the law and events' it came into the ownership of the person who sold it to you. Those words 'divers mesne assurances' are an example of legal jargon. They mean 'various transfers since then', no more and no less. Lawyers will tell you they are used in such documents because they are accepted usage, and they are. But there is no good reason not to use simpler words that you would understand without needing to have them explained.

Why is simpler language not used? Lawyers would say their vocabulary is 'traditional' but that is a label, not an explanation. Fear is probably a big factor. A young lawyer on one side of a 'conveyancing' transaction would hesitate to suggest to his senior on the other side that simpler words would be better. He would be afraid of being thought a presumptuous young puppy, trying to change a system that has worked for years to the satisfaction of older and wiser people. Moreover, he probably likes to use 'legal language', for a reason that is not entirely discreditable. Many a young lawyer's life is dominated by fear. He knows his clients, and maybe his employer, expect from him a level of expertise that he is not confident he has. Using language that shows he has mastered at least some of the tricks of his trade may help. If it is language the clients do not understand, so much the better. In the words of the song, 'if you say it fast enough, you'll always sound precocious'. By the time he has overcome his panic, he may be so accustomed to the language that he will no longer notice that it is archaic. At that stage, he might be disposed to shoot down a younger lawyer who had the temerity to suggest simpler words could be used instead of those that lawyers have used for generations. (Temerity is another of those words lawyers tend to use.)

So, such language continues to be used, almost unnoticed by lawyers, irritating some clients but maybe impressing others. You may have noticed that lawyers tend to use pompous language in their letters, too, like writing 'same' where most people would write 'it'.

So, there are two different kinds of 'legal language'. There are words and phrases like 'beneficial owner' that have a specific, technical meaning, because they have been defined by Statute or interpreted by judges. Not to use those words would mean losing precision, which people reasonably expect from law, and lawyers rightly try to deliver. There is also what might fairly be called flim-flam. Unfortunately, very few laypeople are able to say which is which. Indeed, some lawyers may not be. If you find flim-flam in this book, it is the author's fault.

There is another problem with legal language. Judges decide cases and very often as well as making an order ('the Defendant is to pay the Plaintiff €100,000') they deliver an explanation of their decision, called a 'judgment'. So they should. People who go to court want not only to get a decision but to be told why the judge decided as he did. That is part of the process of trying to ensure that, as lawyers say, justice is not only done but is seen to be done. Such judgments explain the principles the judge followed in reaching his conclusion. (They may also show grounds for the loser to appeal.) They are usually expressed in technical legal language (though not in flim-flam) and for a good reason.

4

Judges do not want a single sentence from their decision to be detached, quoted out of context and given a misleading interpretation, so they try to ensure that if they articulate a principle and there may be exceptions to it, or it needs to be restricted or interpreted, the restriction or interpretation will be included in the same sentence, not in a later paragraph, even though the sentence thereby becomes unwieldy and hard to follow. (The foregoing sentence is a fairly restrained example.) Someone unaccustomed to legal prose is in danger of becoming lost in subordinate clauses.

Precision is important if the judgment lays down legal principles lawyers may want to quote in the future, and the wording may be carefully parsed by another judge on appeal, or by lawyers in years to come who will quote the judge's words in support of their arguments in other cases. So, judges cannot altogether avoid technical legal language. But they could put more effort into making their judgments accessible to non-lawyers.

Is it acceptable that citizens untrained in law cannot understand judges' decisions because the language is so opaque? Judges' powers derive from the Citizens of Ireland, and should surely be expressed in a way most of those citizens can follow. This book aims to avoid lawyers' language that others cannot understand, and perhaps even to contribute to combating its use. Later, in the Appendix, we will see examples of how judgments might set out legal principles using language that laypeople could follow.

One final thing to be said about legal language is that lawyers use a capital letter at the beginning of a word that has been defined or is used in a technical sense. This can be useful, as we will see later, for example, when discussing a 'Statement of Claim', a document a Plaintiff (again, a defined word with a capital) has to produce in the High Court as part of the litigation process. When a word starting with a capital letter appears, it is a technical term and will be found in the Glossary.

This book is critical of aspects of how law is administered and may at first sight seem anti-lawyer. It is not. Law is important in any society, and we need lawyers to ensure the law serves us efficiently. This book was written by someone who trained and worked for more than thirty years as a lawyer, in the company of conscientious hard-working colleagues, devoted to serving their clients to the best of their ability. I believe lawyers as a group, like many of us, have been infected by greed, no longer have the respect of the community, and need to recover their focus. (Anti-lawyer jokes, some quite nasty, are a symptom.) I see the legal profession as like a car that needs servicing, but certainly should not be replaced. Or, perhaps better, like a person whose body has got a bit out of alignment, but can be cured by a few sessions with an osteopath, and by adopting a healthier posture and lifestyle. It is significant and encouraging that consistently in surveys where the question has been asked, people who had a low opinion of lawyers made an exception for their own lawyer.

The Shape of this Book

This book will be a tour of some of the less satisfactory aspects of a legal system that has developed in a haphazard way, like a rambling old house, over centuries. Like an old house, it reflects the tastes of the people who have occupied it, not the likely preferences of visitors. A book that offers a tour of its outlines is likely to be rather shapeless. However, there is a pattern, if not a shape. It is divided into two parts. The first part, Chapters 1-7, looks at the delivery of legal services and how it could be improved. The second part, Chapters 8 and 9, examines some recent decisions of our Supreme Court, and their consequences.

In the first part, the first three chapters will focus on the legal system as it is. Chapter 1 examines the services available to someone who is unlucky enough to be involved in litigation, the lawyers who provide those services, and the pitfalls clients face in bringing their grievances to court. Chapter 2 looks at alternatives to the litigation process, shows that they are largely dominated by lawyers, and argues that this does not serve the community well. Chapter 3 focuses on judges, how they are appointed, how they perform, and the difficulties they face.

Chapters 4, 5 and 6 propose how unsatisfactory aspects of our legal system identified in the earlier chapters might be reformed. Chapter 4 suggests reforms among the judges. Chapters 5 and 6 propose reforms among practising lawyers, including reforms in their charges and a redefinition of the duties lawyers owe to the public. They also propose a way of identifying the issues a judge has to decide that would be simpler and cheaper than the current process of 'Pleadings'.

Chapter 7 looks at two attempts already made at reform. One is the report issued in 2006 by the Competition Authority, some of which this book welcomes. The other is the Legal Services Regulation Bill, which is currently before the Dáil.

Chapter 8 summarises some recent Supreme Court decisions. It argues that there is an emerging pattern or trend of the Court exceeding its constitutional authority and interfering unduly with the other organs of government. That argument is pursued in greater depth in the Appendix. Chapter 9 examines consequences of this trend.

This book focuses only on how the 'civil courts' operate, and does not look at the criminal courts or prosecutions for crimes. It does not discuss lawyers' work not directly related to the court system, such as 'conveyancing', administering wills, trust work and so forth.

Since the focus is on judges and practising lawyers, there is very little on Statute Law, the laws passed by the Oireachtas, and then only in the context of judicial intervention in Statute Law, or, indeed, interference with it. Legal principles laid down by the judiciary are also outside the scope of this book, except, again, where judges have delivered judgments that set aside Statute Law.

It will examine the High Court and Supreme Court, and look only in passing at the lower courts, the District Court and the Circuit Court. More cases are processed through those courts, and taking a claim in either of them costs a lot less, but their limited jurisdiction means that they do not often deal with major issues.

As mentioned earlier, this book also includes a Glossary of terms, including Latin phrases, that may not be familiar to some readers. It also gives references to reported cases and quotes Articles of the Constitution mentioned in the book.

This book represents the views of one former lawyer. It is for the reader to decide whether he agrees with all or some of them.

Chapter 1

How the Court System Operates

Some laypeople complain that Britain and Ireland are unusual in dividing practising lawyers into two branches, barristers and solicitors, and say this artificial distinction should be abolished. But it recognises that people in different situations need different kinds of legal services, some of which are likely to be best provided by one kind of lawyer, and some by a lawyer with other gifts and temperament. It may have the additional advantage that since barristers are sole practitioners and do not carry the big overheads solicitors must, they should be able to offer a cheaper service. Rather than spend time on it, I propose to focus on things I think are more important.

Lawyers often object when people say that the difference between solicitors and barristers is like that in medicine between GPs and specialists, but for readers of this book it is a reasonably accurate description One example of the parallel is that a client who wants the advice of a barrister will usually have to approach him through a solicitor, not directly, just as a patient usually contacts a specialist through GP referral.

Solicitors work in offices and need people to staff them. In general, barristers do not need more than one room or even a table in a shared room, access to a legal library and the services of a typing pool.

Solicitors are divided into self-employed and salaried solicitors. Solicitors on salary may work for another solicitor, a partnership, a state body or a commercial entity. Under current rules, a barrister who takes a salaried job ceases to be a 'practising barrister', and will not be allowed to appear in court on behalf of a client, so we can ignore employed barristers. There is a distinction among barristers between 'Juniors' and 'Seniors', which we will examine later.

The first important thing is that lawyers – barristers and solicitors – have a monopoly. They are the only people allowed to appear in court on behalf of litigants, the only people entitled to give legal advice and charge for it, and the only people entitled to prepare a wide range of documents and to charge for doing so. They have that monopoly because their education and training should enable them to do such work competently. It exists to protect the public from being badly served by untrained people. That is, it is for our benefit. It is probably to our advantage, too, that the process of becoming a lawyer is long, and requires a good deal of study as well as practical training. Lowering standards, and increasing the number of practitioners, might bring down prices in the short term. But the long-term result would be a market of ill-trained lawyers, many delivering a poor service – perhaps for some clients disastrously so – and all hoping to make a living.

A monopoly given for the public benefit surely imposes a duty on those who have it to use it for the public good. One of the themes of this book is that this duty has too often been forgotten or overlooked, and too many lawyers see their monopoly simply as a means of enriching themselves. First, though, let us look at another question. If we need the services of a lawyer, how available are those services?

There is a saying in England that 'The Courts are open to all, like the Ritz Hotel'. It is usually credited to a nineteenth century English Judge, Sir James Mathew, though it is much older. Of course, it means that justice is not available to people who cannot pay for it. In general, it does not apply in Ireland.

In the criminal courts, where people accused of a crime are tried, poor people get free legal representation. A Criminal Legal Aid Scheme provides that someone accused of a crime who shows he cannot pay for lawyers is entitled to retain solicitors and except in minor cases a barrister to defend him. He gets to choose his lawyers, and they are paid by the state.

In the civil courts, people look for compensation if they believe they have suffered as a result of something someone else did, which they should not have done, but which may not necessarily have been a criminal act. Genuinely poor people in that situation can get advice and representation, though not in a systematic way. Someone with limited resources who has been injured and has a good claim for compensation will find lawyers to bring his claim to court on the understanding that they will be paid for their work by the Defendant if their client wins, if his claim is settled the settlement terms will cover their fees, and if he loses they will not be paid at all. Lawyers call these 'no foal, no fee' cases. In years gone by, most lawyers who agreed to represent poor Plaintiffs were satisfied to accept whatever fees the Defendant paid, but nowadays some look for additional payment from their client.

If the claim fails, presumably the unsuccessful Plaintiff will be ordered to pay the successful Defendant's costs of defending an unjustified claim, but since he could not pay his own lawyers, it is unlikely that the lawyers on the other side will be able to get money from him, and that risk will not deter him. So, if a person can show lawyers a reasonably strong case, his poverty will not prevent him from advancing it in court. If it fails he will not be much worse off. So, both the criminal Ritz and the civil Ritz are open to him.

But what about a member of the so-called 'middle class', someone with a steady, reasonably well paid job, probably with a home and a mortgage? If he was injured in a motor accident and his case seems strong, lawyers will probably agree to represent him in making a claim, without insisting on being paid in advance. But he will have a real disadvantage over a poorer person when trying to negotiate a settlement, or if he decides to refuse a settlement offer and bring his claim to a hearing. A genuinely poor Plaintiff knows that if he loses his case, he will not have to pay his lawyers and will not be worse off. If he is shrewd enough, he will guess that even if he rejects his lawyers' advice to settle, they will continue to represent him, because walking away from his claim at that point would mean abandoning any prospect of being paid.

A better-off person knows that if he loses in court, he will have to pay his own lawyers unless he has made a deal with them – and it is hard to see why they should agree to make one. He also knows that successful Defendants, or their insurance company, will see a prospect of collecting their legal expenses from him. They may force him to sell his house to pay their bill, or look for payment by instalments out of his salary. He has something to lose, and is under much more pressure to compromise than someone who is broke would be. He is more likely to settle, maybe on disadvantageous terms, because he is afraid not to. Of course, insurance companies and their lawyers understand this and pitch any compensation offer accordingly.

The better-off person has another problem. Companies, including insurance companies, have to finance litigation as part of the cost of carrying on their business. But they have two important advantages over personal litigants. First, their lawyers' charges are a cost of running their business, and are deducted before arriving at the figure on which they will pay tax, so that the Revenue Commissioners part-finance their litigation. Secondly, the Value Added Tax that their lawyers add to their bills does not much affect them since they can claim it back on their next VAT return. Private citizens, on the other hand, do not get the VAT back, and it is between one-fifth and one-quarter of the total. This means that VAT on legal fees is a tax levied only on individuals, with commercial entities effectively exempt.

If consulting a lawyer was what is called 'discretionary spending', meaning something we choose to do, that might seem fair enough. But who consults a lawyer by choice?

But suppose our middle-class litigant wants to go to court with some other type of complaint; for example, if he believes he has been libelled in a newspaper and the only way to restore his reputation is through the courts. He can probably afford to pay lawyers to write to the newspaper demanding a retraction and apology, but if the newspaper refuses, he knows that the cost of suing them will be astronomical, and even if he wins and gets an award of damages, he may still be out of pocket. He also knows that if he loses he could be bankrupt, or equivalent. So it is unlikely he will take the risk involved in trying to protect his good name. And, of course, the people who run the newspaper know his weakness and factor it into their decision-making. They may calculate that they can get away with denying him the correction that he and justice both demand. If they calculate correctly, he will suffer injustice.

So, we can say that the Irish courts are like the Ritz Hotel, but with a hostel in the basement. They accommodate the rich and the poor, and of course provide 'corporate suites', but have no room for people who are neither very rich nor really poor – that is, most of us.

Clearly, it is a major flaw in the legal system of any country if some of its people do not have access to justice. In order to see how to cure it, we have to understand why it is so. Two reasons emerge. One is an unnecessarily cumbersome, and therefore expensive, system of preliminaries before a legal claim comes to a hearing. The other is excessive charges for lawyers' work.

An Example

Perhaps a good way to illustrate the first problem, the cumbersome system, is by describing a piece of litigation some years ago. A company sued the firm of accountants that had acted as its auditors, claiming that the accounts the auditors had approved some years earlier did not present a 'true and fair view' of the company's position. The company claimed that it had been losing money, although the accounts showed a profit, and said that if the auditors had done their job properly the losses would have been recognised and corrective action taken. It claimed the auditors should compensate it for the losses it had sustained in the meantime. The company's lawyers issued a High Court Summons claiming damages. They then followed up with the next document in the process, called a Statement of Claim, describing how they claimed the auditors had failed them, how this had led to loss, and how they calculated the huge compensation they demanded.

If litigation claiming negligence against auditors winds up in court, it will be decided by reconstructing how the auditors did their job, to see if it was done adequately. This is done principally by examining their 'audit papers', the record auditors generate showing how they went about the job, what they checked, how they checked it and whether they failed to check and confirm figures they ought to have examined. The hearing would turn on an examination of these 'audit papers', and other evidence would probably not count for much.

But the process of litigation is governed by Rules of Court, which lay down the steps each party should follow before a claim goes before a judge, and the sequence they should follow. That sequence includes a step called, rather oddly, 'Discovery of Documents', in which each party must list the relevant documents they hold and make them available to be inspected by the other side. In this case, of course, 'Discovery' would require the auditors to produce their audit papers for inspection. Rationally, the Plaintiff company should have sought 'Discovery' at the beginning and, having studied the audit papers, been able to say, 'Here is where we say you blundered', or 'Having seen your audit papers, we admit that you did the job adequately, and we withdraw our claim'.

However, the Rules of Court say that 'Discovery' is to take place only after the issues to be decided have been set out in the Statement of Claim and other documents, collectively called 'Pleadings'. So, the Statement of Claim in this case ended with a warning that it might have to be amended later on, after the Plaintiff company's lawyers had seen the Defendant auditors' records.

What the company was in effect saying was, 'This is a game of Snakes and Ladders. After we have gone through the Pleadings and eventually got to inspect your audit papers, and just when we should be ready to go into court for a hearing, we may insist on rewriting our Statement of Claim. If so, the pre-trial process will slide back down the Snake from the finishing line to the beginning.'

This problem was not caused by folly or incompetence on the part of the company's lawyers. The Rules gave them little choice, and, to be fair, the Rules are not pure folly either. The thinking behind them is that until the issues between the parties have been clearly identified in the Pleadings, it is not possible to look at a given piece of paper and say, 'Yes, that document is relevant to the issues' or, 'No, it is irrelevant'. If documents are relevant, each party must produce them (unless they qualify for legal privilege, a technical concept we need not go into) but neither party should be allowed to paw through the other's papers in order to try to construct a claim. But however rational that approach may seem in theory, its effect was absurd in this case.

Indeed, the case illustrates how legal rules can produce the effect of Procrustes' bed. In Greek myth, Procrustes offered hospitality to travellers, including a bed. But he insisted that the visitor must fit the bed. If he was too tall, bits at either end had to be lopped off; if he was too wide, he had to be trimmed. If too short, he was stretched, painfully. Visitors had to accommodate themselves to the bed, instead of the other way around. For these litigants, the Rules played that role.

In theory, the next step in the process should have been for the auditors to file their 'Defence', a written statement of their response to what the company's Statement of Claim had said. They did not do so, for the following reason.

One purpose of all this exchange of paper between parties in litigation is to ensure that both can prepare for the hearing, knowing what case they have to answer and that the other will not be able to spring any last-minute surprises. If the lawyers for the company wanted to take a different line when the case came into court, the lawyers for the auditors would point out that they had not given notice of it in the Pleadings and the judge would refuse to let them pursue it. That seems fair. Neither party should be allowed to produce a surprise that the other was not warned of.

If the story that unfolds when witnesses on both sides have been heard is significantly different from the preview of it in the Plaintiff's Statement of Claim, the judge may dismiss the claim on the ground that the Statement of Claim did not give the Defendants adequate notice of the claim they would have to meet. Lawyers use the shorthand 'not pleaded' for this situation, meaning that the Pleadings have not given the other side adequate notice of the claim they will have to rebut. (We will look at this further in Chapter 5.)

But lawyers know that what emerges in court when one of their witnesses is cross-examined by lawyers on the other side will not always be identical with what they were told when they interviewed that same witness. So, when a Plaintiff's lawyers draft their client's Statement of Claim, which must include a forecast of the story they hope will emerge in court, they word it as broadly as they can, so that their wording will be wide enough to cover a set of facts somewhat different from what they expect, if the case develops in that way. Similarly, the Defendant's lawyers want to define the Plaintiff's claim as narrowly as they can, both to make it easier for them to prepare a rebuttal and also in the hope that when the action comes to a trial, they may get it thrown out of court by claiming 'not pleaded'.

In this case, since the Plaintiff's lawyers had to produce a Statement of Claim without knowing what the audit papers would show, they had to express their complaints as widely as possible. Equally, the Defendants' lawyers wanted to limit the scope of their accusations. So, instead of filing their written 'Defence', setting out what they hoped to prove in order to defeat the claim, they sent a 'Request for Particulars', seeking to force the Plaintiff company away from generalities and pinning it down to specific allegations – which, of course, the auditors' lawyers hoped to be able to disprove. Each request was numbered and in this case there were ninety-nine – yes, ninety-nine. When, after several months, the lawyers for the Plaintiff company furnished Replies, the Defendant auditors' lawyers retaliated with a 'Request for further and better Particulars'.

Predictably, the litigation became bogged down in paper. One exchange went like this:

> *Question by auditors' lawyers:* 'What steps does the Plaintiff allege the Defendants ought to have taken and failed to take?'

> *Reply from company's lawyers:* 'The steps a prudent auditor would have taken.'

As an example of elaborate time-wasting between intelligent people, that would be hard to beat. Obviously, each set of clients was paying their lawyers to participate in this exchange and, equally obviously, the process had no connection with achieving justice. The lawyers on both sides were engaged in a pre-trial contest. The Plaintiff's legal team hoped to get a tactical advantage over the Defendants', while not allowing the Defendants' to steal a march on their client. The Defendants' lawyers were engaged in exactly the same game – and 'game' is a fair description of the process.

If each set of lawyers is competent, the result will be a scoreless draw; neither will gain any advantage and the only result will be to inflate the cost of the litigation and postpone the hearing, probably for months, perhaps for years. It may occasionally happen that one set of lawyers is craftier than the other, and their client may gain an advantage that he should not have. If so, justice may not be done.

Of course, lawyers who work in that environment must play that game, because their job is to do the best they can for their client. If there is a possibility that they can help him to win his case by exercising skill in pleading it, they must try to do so, and they are equally bound to protect him from being wrong-footed by a crafty manoeuvre on the other side. That is how an adversarial legal system works. The fault lies not in the lawyers but in a system that requires them to behave in this way.

It will hardly come as a surprise that the litigation between the company and its former auditors never got to a hearing. As it happens, justice was eventually done, but not through a route any lawyer could be proud of.

Pleadings

The above is an example, admittedly a rather extreme one, of the process of bringing a claim before a High Court judge. Historically, one of the purposes of Pleadings was that before hearing the case the trial judge could get a clear picture of what it was about, and what issues he would have to decide, by spending half an hour or so reading them. But in modern litigation, if the judge were to read the Pleadings filed in court, plus all the Requests for Particulars and Replies and other documents, it would take him several hours. The basic Pleadings are Summons, Statement of Claim, Defence and Reply, but as well as Requests for Particulars, there are:

- Interrogatories, where one party gets permission from a judge to put a series of questions to the other, who must answer them.

- Notices to admit facts – which are self-explanatory.

- Notices to produce documents – which may be 'general', meaning 'produce all the documents you have', or 'specific', requiring the other side to produce listed documents.

- Discovery of documents, mentioned above, which can require both parties to disclose in a very long and detailed affidavit (a) what documents they have in their possession relevant to the issues, (b) what documents they used to have but do not have any longer (usually consisting of originals of letters they have sent out, keeping a copy for their records, (c) what documents they have that may be relevant but which they object to being required to produce, on the ground that they are entitled to claim legal 'privilege'.

Each of these produces another mound of paper. One serves a 'Request for Particulars'. The other must reply to each question. One side serves 'Interrogatories'. The other must reply to them, one by one. 'Discovery' often generates not just a mound but a mountain of paper on each side, which they then have to exchange.

A judge wading through that lot before the case started, in order to get a sense of what it was all about, would probably waste his time. Nearly every piece of litigation turns on one issue, or at most two. The issue at the core of the dispute is often so obscured by all the documentation that even an experienced judge might miss it.

So when a judge comes into court to hear a claim, he seldom has a clear picture of the issues he will have to decide. That means that before he hears any evidence, one of the lawyers representing the Plaintiff will start by explaining what the case is about. This will take a minimum of half an hour, and in a complicated case a full day or perhaps even more. During that time, all the lawyers are in court, clocking up fees. Eventually, one of the litigants will have to pay them.

In times past, Requests for Particulars were comparatively rare. Nowadays, they are almost inevitable. They and the Replies they require represent a substantial addition to the weight of work done by lawyers on both sides before a complaint gets heard. That means a substantial addition to the amount people have to pay if they seek justice through the courts. The number of solicitors and barristers making a living from litigation (and in some cases a lot more than a living, as we will see in Chapters 5 and 6), has increased dramatically over the last half-century. So has the number of judges, which suggests that the volume of litigation – the number of disputes that are brought to court – has also increased. Courts nowadays move more slowly, and individual cases are taking longer at hearing than they used to, but that by itself would not explain the dramatic increase in the size of the pool of lawyers, including the number of judges.

Lawyers will tell you that this elaborate Pleadings process is needed in order that, as they say, 'the issues are knit', meaning that the Defence lawyers know exactly the case the Plaintiff will advance and they will have to answer, and the Plaintiff's lawyers know what defence they will have to try to rebut.

Accordingly, lawyers say, settlement negotiations cannot usefully start until after Pleadings are complete. It is certainly true that the end of the process of Pleadings brings some certainty about what the issues are – at least in the sense that neither party will be allowed to introduce some claim that cannot be found, somewhere, in the Pleadings. But it seldom does more than confirm what the parties knew from the beginning, when the lawyers first investigated the facts. Competent lawyers who have checked the facts, know the relevant law and apply it to the facts should be able to see at the outset what the crucial issues are. The argument that settlement discussions should not start until the 'issues have been knit' with the close of Pleadings is rarely justified, but postponing settlement discussions until all these documents have been generated protects a source of income for lawyers. It means they can tell their clients it is impossible to settle their dispute without first going through the process of Pleadings, which is financially rewarding for the lawyers, and draining for their clients.

Who Pays?

Something else needs to be said about the process. All of it has to be paid for, and the side that loses in the eventual hearing usually has to pick up the bill. Now, with that in mind, let us look again at 'Requests for Particulars', in general, not in the context of the claim against the accountants. If the Plaintiff's lawyers have produced an adequate Statement of Claim, you would think that the Defendant should have no need to ask for further information, and the Plaintiff should be entitled to refuse a Request for Particulars, saying, perhaps in more polite language, 'We have given you all the information you are entitled to, and you are not getting any more.' If the Plaintiff's legal team's response was justified, then the Defendant's lawyers should be censured for wasting time and putting the Plaintiff to unnecessary expense by making an unjustified demand for more information. Alternatively, if the Defendant's Request for Particulars was justified, that would mean that the Plaintiff's lawyers had failed to produce an adequate Statement of Claim, putting the Defendant to the unnecessary expense of seeking more information.

Either way, you might think the lawyers on one side or the other must be at fault. If so, you might go on to say that they should not be paid as if their work was adequate, and they should pay whatever expenses the other party had incurred because of their failure.

But of course that is not what happens. The only question that judges decide about lawyers' fees is which of the litigants should be ordered to pay the other's 'costs', and they usually decide it in favour of the winner on the main issue. So, the losing party not merely has to pay his own lawyers for the work they have done, including work that may have been inadequate or unnecessary. He also has to pay the other side's lawyers for the work they have done, including any unnecessary work they may have done, plus any inadequate work that required his own lawyers to incur expenses that should not have arisen.

So, lawyers engage in the time-wasting process described above, knowing that they will be paid, irrespective of the outcome. The system not only fails to encourage lawyers to be careful with their clients' money, but actually does the reverse. Other professionals expect to pay for any mistakes they may make. Only lawyers have the benefit of being able to pile up their bills knowing that they will be paid for their work, without regard for whether it was necessary, and irrespective of its quality.

Lawyers' Immunity from Claims

Moreover, lawyers engaged in litigation are probably the only professionals who know that even if they do their job incompetently, they will not be answerable to their client. Judges have decided that issue in advance, in their favour. The route they followed is instructive.

The first line of defence for incompetent advocates was based on the concept that a barrister may not sue for his fees.

That did not mean he would be left unpaid, because his instructing solicitor was bound to see the barrister paid (except, of course, in 'no foal no fee' cases), but it did mean he was not retained under a contract that would require him to do a decent job in return for his fee.

However, the argument that a barrister who could not sue for his fees was not required to give a competent service broke down because judges decided in other cases, not involving barristers, that someone who did a job of work for another person without payment, but did it so incompetently that the other person suffered loss, must pay compensation. That is, what is technically called a 'volunteer' must either do the job competently or pay compensation for any loss caused by his incompetence. That line of decision scuppered any argument that a barrister-volunteer need not show competence.

The next line of protection for lawyers shows ingenuity, though not much realism. It takes as its starting point an argument – perhaps it would be more accurate to call it an assumption – that public policy does not allow a court decision to be re-examined, except in an appeal permitted by the Rules of Court. If someone who had lost a case in court wanted to claim this was because his legal representation was incompetent, he would have to show, first, that his litigation was handled incompetently, and, secondly, that if it had been handled adequately he would have won. But judges have decided that this second part, showing he should have won with competent representation, would involve re-examining the original decision in which he had lost, and should not be allowed. To a large extent, this artificial approach operates to protect lawyers who work in litigation from professional negligence actions. Of course, it protects both solicitors and barristers, unlike the previous excuse that someone who cannot sue for his fees need not show competence. We cannot say that it has led litigating lawyers to have less concern for their clients than they otherwise would, or to be less competent than they should, but it certainly removes an incentive that motivates other professionals.

Having seen something of how Ireland's High Court system works and how it seems to fail to meet the reasonable needs of citizens, we will look at how the process of preparing for a court hearing could – and should – be made swifter and cheaper for litigants. But first we will look at another question. What remedies for injustice exist for people who cannot afford to go to court or who are afraid to because of the expense?

Chapter 2

Alternatives to Litigation

What options exist for people who believe they have a right to recompense, but have too much money to qualify for a 'free ride' and not enough courage to risk all they have in pursuit of their claim? Asking that question does not assume that it is acceptable to exclude middle-class citizens from access to the courts if their grievances can be satisfied in another way. In a healthy democracy, access to justice is the right of every citizen. Moreover, people who pay the salaries of judges and court officials out of their taxes have a reasonable complaint if those same courts operate in a way that excludes them. However, if adequate alternatives to litigation were available, the fact that the courts are effectively closed off to some citizens might seem a less urgent problem. What are the alternatives, and are they adequate? This chapter considers four: the Personal Injuries Assessment Board, arbitration, lawyer negotiation and mediation, which is negotiation using a neutral third party.

Personal Injuries Assessment Board

If someone has suffered a 'personal injury' (which usually means physical harm), for example in a road accident, and the prospective Defendant or his insurance company accepts full responsibility, so that the only issue is how much money should be paid by way of compensation, the claim will not go to court. Instead, the Personal Injuries Assessment Board will adjudicate.

This is a useful substitute for the courts, but only in a limited range of cases.

Arbitration

People who have a dispute of the kind they might expect to bring before a judge can instead ask an impartial expert to decide it, agreeing in advance that they will be bound by his decision. Obviously, that means employing and paying an arbitrator, because, unlike a judge, he is not paid by the State. Arbitration can have an advantage for people who value their privacy, as the courts sit in public and their decisions are reported in the newspapers (except for 'family law cases') and arbitration is a private process. Some disputes were arbitrated under informal arrangements for years before the first Arbitration Act was passed in Ireland in 1954. After the Act came into effect, many commercial agreements provided that if a dispute arose it would be dealt with by arbitration, rather than through the courts. This was particularly common in construction contracts.

But over the years, two things happened that made arbitration less attractive. The first was that the original concept of presenting the arbitrator with a single document setting out the issues for decision was eroded. The process of preparing for arbitration became almost as complicated as the process of Pleadings in High Court litigation, as described in the previous chapter. Secrecy was still an attraction for some people, but arbitration has ceased to be a fast, cheap way of getting an outside decision on an intractable dispute.

The second thing that diminished the attraction of arbitration was that arbitrators' decisions ceased to produce the finality that a court decision carries, and that most litigants want. A party dissatisfied with an arbitrator's decision (and any decision, whether of an arbitrator or a judge, is going to produce at least one dissatisfied party) can apply to the High Court for an order setting it aside. The dissatisfied party may not claim that the arbitrator got the facts wrong, but there are various technical grounds for applying, including that the arbitrator's decision was wrong in law. This means that arbitration does not necessarily conclude a dispute. The winner in an arbitration (so far as anyone who emerges from litigation or arbitration may be described as a 'winner') should pause before he celebrates. If the other party issues proceedings in the High Court to set aside the arbitrator's award, the 'winner' will at best face long delay and further legal expense before the issue is finally determined. At worst, the High Court challenge may succeed, leaving him at the starting line again. It is hardly surprising that arbitration clauses are less common in commercial contracts nowadays, and fewer people choose arbitration. If a claim goes to arbitration rather than being litigated, it is usually because neither party wants the publicity that a court case would attract, or because it arose under an agreement that made arbitration compulsory.

Lawyer Negotiation

Over 90 per cent of claims in which a Summons has been issued are settled by negotiation and do not go to a hearing. So you might assume that people who cannot afford the legal process can get their lawyers to negotiate a settlement for them, and should not suffer because they are afraid of the cost of litigation? Unfortunately, it doesn't work like that. A convention operates in settlements, too. Lawyers do not normally engage in serious settlement negotiations until 'the issues have been knit', and they say that situation is not reached until the parties have completed the process of Pleadings. That is, the Statement of Claim, Defence, Reply, Requests for Particulars with Replies to them, Discovery of Documents, Notices to Produce, Interrogatories, Notices to Admit Facts and so forth that enrich lawyers, delay the litigation process and inflate its cost.

If a lawyer representing a prospective Plaintiff, someone who believes he has been wronged and wants justice, were to propose to the lawyer representing the person he holds to blame that the claim should be settled without Pleadings, the prospective Defendant's lawyer would read that proposal as a sign of weakness. He would assume that the Plaintiff's advisers lacked confidence in the claim, or that the Plaintiff lacked the financial muscle to see it through, and reduce his offer accordingly. A prospective Plaintiff's lawyer would face an uphill struggle in negotiating with a colleague who had made such an assumption, and it is unlikely that a satisfactory settlement would emerge. The only way to dispel such an assumption in the mind of the defending lawyer is, unfortunately, to prove it wrong by showing willingness to spend money on litigation. So, a person with a complaint who shows himself unwilling to push it into court or to pay for the expensive preliminaries will start with a major disadvantage in trying to negotiate fair settlement terms. Instead of settlement negotiations focusing on the merits of the Plaintiff's case, they may turn on the views of the lawyers about his ability and willingness to fund litigation.

For most litigants, agreeing a settlement is much more attractive than taking a chance in court on what a judge may decide. (One lawyer used to describe litigation as 'a game for two losers'.) But the need to go through the protracted – and expensive – process of Pleadings beforehand greatly reduces its advantages. It is not coincidence that more personal injuries claims are settled coming up to Christmas than at any other time of year.

Mediation

That leaves mediation as a means of getting justice for someone who has a grievance but cannot afford to bring it to court. The story here is depressing, too. Professional mediation is a fairly recent arrival in Ireland, though for centuries third parties have intervened in quarrels and tried to compose them. In the mid-1980s, when professional mediation first became available in Ireland, the process was usually simple and informal. Two people in dispute met 'off the record' with a neutral third party to discuss the issues that separated them. If the parties in dispute were not individuals but companies or groups of people, each appointed a representative, usually someone with authority to finalise a binding agreement. Meetings would last for an hour or two. There might have to be three or four, spread over a few weeks. This would allow space to explore the issues and the needs of the different parties. It also allowed people who had recently been at each other's throats to adjust to the idea of making peace, and the time to make a constructive one. If after two or three meetings there was no sign of progress the mediator would usually end the process.

Time between meetings might bring another advantage. People faced with a new idea or fresh information often need time to get used to it. And one of the functions of mediation, practised in this way, is to encourage people to produce information that they might previously have been keeping to themselves, and to produce new ideas about how to resolve conflicts constructively. A mediator might say, 'It seems to me, A, that when B did such-and-such, it really upset you?' This might be followed by, 'And, B, you had no intention of upsetting A, and didn't realise you had?' (Mediators of this school were trained to ask questions more than they made statements.) B's response might well transform the atmosphere and make a resolution much more likely. Or a mediator might say, 'Has an approach to this problem come up today that none of us thought of before? Do you – or indeed do we all – need time to think it through, and see where it might lead?'

If legal or other issues arose, the process gave an opportunity for each party to take advice between meetings. Instead of each consulting separate advisers, they might agree to accept the view of one expert they both trusted. This might mean, for example, both consulting the same estate agent for a property valuation, or retaining one psychologist in a parental 'custody dispute'. If they needed legal advice, they might agree to consult an independent legal expert rather than have each consult his own lawyer and risk being stuck with contradictory advice. Agreeing on one adviser was usually a sign of progress towards co-operation and suggested that a constructive outcome might be on the way.

Lawyers seldom attended mediation sessions, but if they did it was not to speak for their clients but to give legal advice if need arose. Because the process was 'off the record' and nothing said in mediation could be quoted in court, the parties generally felt free to say what was on their minds and did not feel the need to have lawyers present, and most lawyers accepted that.

If an agreement emerged, a responsible mediator would not write it down on the spot for the clients to sign. Instead, he gave them space to have second thoughts and to take advice. If either party had second thoughts, the process would accommodate them, and there would be a further session at which both parties would discuss the reason for one of them having doubts. There were two reasons for this. People in mediation were likely to be more open to the idea of change if they knew they would not be tied down. And an opportunity for second thoughts improved the prospects that any agreement that might emerge would work in practice.

The only cost was for the mediator's time, unless the parties agreed that they wanted their lawyers present. Well-trained mediators exercised constant vigilance to try to avoid influencing the outcome, so that any bargain the parties might evolve would be theirs and theirs only. Mediators focused on trying to ensure that each client listened constructively to the other's concerns, on helping to create an atmosphere of co-operation, and helping their clients to envisage an expanded range of options. They did not try to steer their clients towards agreement, or in any direction. If the process led the clients to resolve the conflict that brought them to mediation, their mediator would be pleased. But if the clients decided after going through the process that they should not resolve the issue and needed an outsider's adjudication, their mediator accepted that decision. His focus was, consistently, on his clients, and on maintaining and protecting their autonomy. Practised in that way, mediation was and is skilled work, requiring dedication and self-discipline.

Although I have used the past tense to describe it, that style of mediation is still available. However, starting in the 1990s lawyers began to enter the field of conflict resolution. Most

Irish lawyers who wanted to mediate took training from a British organisation run by lawyer-mediators – one, incidentally, that offers both training and accreditation, which I think is a questionable combination.

Most lawyer-mediators learnt a different model of mediation. An Irish lawyer-mediator usually holds only one, open-ended, session. That is, it may start on a Monday morning and continue into the small hours of Tuesday. The full teams of lawyers on both sides are present throughout. During the greater part of the process, instead of talking to each other, the disputants are kept in separate rooms, with the mediator shuttling from room to room, passing on (or editing) the messages entrusted to him. If they reach a settlement, the mediator immediately prepares a written record of their bargain, and it is signed on the spot, essentially in order to prevent second thoughts. As with litigation and lawyer negotiation, the process assumes that 'the issues have been knit' before it starts. That is, either the disputants have gone through the Pleadings process described earlier, or their lawyers have met beforehand to summarise the issues.

Four things will be evident. One is that in lawyer-mediation the parties have very limited opportunities to talk face to face. Secondly, since most communication between them passes through the mediator, he may influence the content of any bargain that may emerge. Thirdly, the process is dominated by lawyers, with their clients, the people actually in dispute, taking a back seat. (This is underlined by the fact that the training body mentioned above also offers training in advocacy for lawyers representing clients in mediation, the assumption being that the client will sign whatever agreement the lawyers reach, but will have little active involvement in the process.) Fourth and last is that a process that requires the presence of two – or more in a multiple-party dispute – teams of lawyers, perhaps for many hours, is going to be expensive.

A fifth issue, less obvious, is that since lawyer-mediation keeps the principals apart for most of the time, and allows them little opportunity to communicate directly, it is unlikely to help the parties move towards genuine healing or reconciliation. It can be useful to litigants who will be strangers to each other after the litigation has been settled, but if people in conflict will need to collaborate in the future, that style of lawyer-mediation may not serve them well. It may settle the current dispute, but the lawyer-mediator may not even become aware of any underlying conflict, and if he does he will probably classify it as irrelevant and ignore it.

It does have a practical advantage over the older style that since a lawyer-mediator keeps the principals apart for most of the time he does not need to bring to the work anything like the capacity for empathy or interpersonal skill that clients need from the type of mediator described earlier. Accordingly, lawyer-mediators need less rigorous training, and fewer hours of it, than the other kind.

This style of mediation, embraced by the legal profession, is designed to produce a settlement, and the form puts pressure on the clients to settle, in a way that the other, consciously non-directive, style of mediating does not – or should not. Moreover, a lawyer-mediator trained in this school knows that he was appointed by his colleagues. He also knows that they are less likely to appoint him again if the process 'fails'. So, he must be tempted to put pressure on the parties to settle. If so, the fact that he talks to each party separately and not much to both together, makes it easier for him to yield to that temptation. This means that to people who measure the value of the two kinds of mediation by the proportion of each that reach agreement, lawyer-mediation will seem more effective than the other kind.

In a report published in November 2010, the Law Reform Commission issued a recommendation that would lead to these approaches to conflict resolution being labelled differently. The shuttle process that most lawyer-mediators practise would be called 'conciliation', and the slower approach, where the service-provider holds a succession of meetings with the parties together, and avoids 'caucusing' and influencing the content of his clients' bargain, would be labelled 'mediation'. The different labels should enable people in dispute to choose the kind of service best suited to their needs. So far, there is little sign of this sensible recommendation being adopted. 'Shuttle-mediation' conducted by a lawyer-mediator, and with the clients kept apart and in the background, is the only kind people are likely to be offered if they enter mediation on legal advice.

In fairness to some mediators who come from a legal background, not all have adopted the second approach described above. Some grapple with the harder work of keeping warring parties engaged in conversation, or in a series of consecutive dialogues, helping them to evolve from confrontation to collaboration. But the norm for lawyer-mediation remains having the legal teams assembled, and the mediator shuttling between hostile groups, while keeping them apart. It is hard to see this as a genuine effort to expand the range of services clients need. It looks more like an attempt by lawyers to protect what they see as their turf from competition by encroaching peacemakers. And, of course, there is competition, since the kind of non-lawyer mediation described earlier has the effect of side-lining lawyers.

An outsider looking at the limited alternatives to litigation that lawyers offer might again be reminded of Procrustes and his bed.

Chapter 3

Judges

Having looked at how a citizen might experience contact with the Irish system of litigation, and with practising lawyers, it seems sensible next to examine the judges, who sit at the top of that system. I worked as a lawyer from 1952 to 1986, when I moved to a different line of work, and during that time, and particularly the first ten years or so, when most of my work involved litigating in the High Court, I got to know quite a lot about the judges of the day, though I rarely met any of them. It was important to know their foibles, in order to do the work properly, as I am sure it is today. I know some of the current judges of the High and Supreme Courts, having worked with them in my time as a lawyer. There is none that I know that I do not respect, and even admire, but I have little knowledge of their foibles.

In my day, most of the Superior Court judges were intelligent, conscientious people who strove to do their work well, and largely succeeded. There were some who failed to shed the biases they had had as advocates, and were famous for being 'Plaintiff's judges' or 'Defendant's judges'. The performance of a few was flawed by addiction, mostly to alcohol, and two seemed almost pathologically unable to make up their minds. That mattered a lot with one, who sat in the High Court. When he had finished hearing a case, he 'reserved' his decision, that is, postponed giving it, and then the postponement became indefinite. Justice delayed, as the old saying goes, was justice denied. The indecisiveness of the other mattered less because he sat in the Supreme Court, and when his colleagues were ready to deliver their judgments, he usually chose the decision of one of them, said that he had read it and agreed with it, and did not deliver a separate judgment. (A story went the rounds that one day after he had said 'I have read the judgment of the Chief Justice, agree with what he says and don't think there is anything I can usefully add', one of his other colleagues said, promptly, emphatically and ambiguously, 'I agree!')

More seriously, one High Court judge, now dead, became so difficult and unpleasant that most practising lawyers would have described him as a full-blown sadist. He enjoyed humiliating lawyers who had to appear before him, to the point where it seemed to be more important to him than his job of administering justice. He reduced some lawyers who appeared before him to tears by his bullying. When he had to, he could apply a keen intelligence to legal issues, but in my view his personality made him unfit to serve as a judge. As an advocate, he had been a bully. That tendency became more pronounced over his years as a judge until it reached the level described. With guidance and help, most of his contemporaries whose performance was below par could probably have become more effective, but his defects as a judge were rooted in his personality. His history illustrates a view developed later in this book about how the comparative isolation in which judges work, and the deferential and obsequious treatment they receive, can have a corrosive effect on them.

Lawyers regularly working in the courts knew about the personality traits of different judges, because we needed to, but we did not talk about them, except among ourselves. Non-lawyers were left in ignorance of weaknesses and flaws among the judges. Undoubtedly, some of us were afraid that if judges were criticised in public they would know who had 'blabbed' and the lawyers and their clients would suffer. Ireland is notoriously a country where it is hard to keep a secret, and lawyers are great gossips. A lawyer who might not be personally afraid of antagonising a judge would be bound to recognise the risk that if the judge became hostile to him, his clients might suffer.

I suspect another reason why the foibles of judges were discussed only among lawyers was the clubby relationship that existed and still exists between judges and barristers, which we will look at later.

The Dáil has a tradition against criticising judges and judicial decisions, and that is as it should be. The Dáil has its constitutional role and for a TD to criticise a judge or a judicial decision would be to trespass into an area from which the Constitution excludes him. Such rules do not bind a citizen. In a healthy democracy, the judiciary should be as open to critical comment from their masters – the citizens – as the other organs of government. Any criticisms of judges offered in this book are intended to improve Ireland's democratic health – which the last chapter argues is under threat from recent trends in judicial decision-making. Some judges may resent criticism, and feel it is ill-informed and out of place. That is understandable. Judges are not used to public criticism. But it does not affect our right to criticise what they decide in their exercise of the powers that derive from us.

Chapter 8 criticises five decisions of the Irish Supreme Court. Each comment I consider valid – otherwise I would not have made it – but, like the judges themselves, I am fallible, and it may be that some or all of my criticisms can be refuted. If so, I have exercised my citizen's right to hold the judiciary to account, validly but mistakenly – which is what a judge does if he decides a case and an appeal court later reverses his decision. That I may err does not affect my right, as one of the 'people', to question and criticise the decisions of judges, who exercise on behalf of the people powers we are unable to exercise for ourselves. Provided I do not say anything that is false and injurious about any judge, or indulge in what lawyers call 'mere vulgar abuse', I claim to be free to comment on our judges, jointly and individually, and on their decisions.

Understanding Judges

We can gain insight into the personalities of judges by reading their judgments, because every text, even a judgment, tells a careful reader quite a lot about the writer. Some readers may be surprised at the notion that the personality of the judge comes through a judgment. A judgment is supposed to combine an impartial summary of the evidence with a colourless statement of the law, and to record a decision based on combining those two things. Right? Well, that is the theory. But I recall reading four judgments in the same case, one in the High Court and the others by three Supreme Court judges, on appeal.

It was a case involving separated parents who each wanted their child to live with them. ('Custody' is the ambiguous and rather repellent word lawyers use.) The wife was living with another man whose income came from property speculation. (As you will guess, this was some years ago.) The husband was living alone.

The judge in the High Court who made the first decision had had an outstanding career as a barrister before he became a judge, based on exceptional intelligence, a strong personality, self-discipline, preparing meticulously and working very hard. If you read between the lines of his judgment, it is clear that he felt an aversion to the notion that the wife's new partner made money without working for it, by outsmarting other people. The idea repelled this honourable, hard-working, upright man and he awarded 'custody' to the child's father.

On appeal to the Supreme Court, one of the three judges took the view that he should not interfere with a decision by his colleague in the High Court, who had seen the parties. (Appeals to the Supreme Court are based on documents and a transcript of oral evidence, and Supreme Court judges do not normally get to see litigants or witnesses.) Implicit in what he said was, 'if my colleague in the High Court, whom I admire enormously, thinks the child will be better off with his father, I am not going to interfere'. Another Supreme Court Judge delivered a lyrical and quite emotional praise of motherhood – 'who will soothe his night fears?' and so on – and anyone with even an elementary grounding in psychology would have seen his judgment as an expression of his own emotions, traceable back to his childhood. The third Supreme Court judge, who was certainly one of the finest Ireland has been lucky enough to have, took the sensible view that a child would probably be better cared for in a household where a full-time parent, his mother, lived than in one where his father would be out at work most of the day. These two, forming a majority, reversed the High Court decision and decided the child should be reared primarily by his mother.

The point is that each of the four intended to deliver a judgment such as described above – a summary of the facts, a colourless statement of the law and an impartial decision based on putting the two together – but what at least two of them wrote gave an attentive reader an insight into their attitudes and personalities. What is true of a case like that one, where the issues have an immediate emotional impact on the judges, is also true, though more subtly, on more neutral topics. If you were to lock yourself in a room with the Law Reports, focus on one senior judge and read all the judgments he had delivered, even if you knew nothing about the legal issues, you would emerge with a sense of his personality. And if you were an advocate preparing to argue a case before that judge, you would make sure that you had a good understanding of his personality and his foibles before you opened your mouth in front of him. That is one of the less obvious duties of any advocate. (We will return to this topic later.)

Judges in the 'Superior Courts' – the High and Supreme Courts – are vulnerable to an additional pressure, the pressure of collegiality. A lawyer who is appointed to be a judge may take up the job with ideals and convictions, but if he starts in the High Court – as is more common than a direct appointment from being a practitioner to the Supreme Court – he will have to take directions from the Supreme Court, because High Court judges are bound by decisions of the Supreme Court. Judges are also likely to be influenced by their colleagues, to some extent on legal issues, but to an even greater extent towards adopting the prevailing ethos. There is a natural tendency for any new member of a group to defer to his seniors, and most Superior Court judges work in the same building. Becoming a judge of a 'Superior Court' may be the start of a process by which a lawyer loses individuality. And of course the judges of the Supreme Court work together, because they form small groups to hear appeals.

Probably few citizens would recognise the names of most Superior Court judges, and only a handful would be able to list even half of them. (There are, after all, more than forty.) As with any group of that size, some are excellent, others admirable, and some, inevitably, mediocre, but we have generally assumed that they are worthy of our trust and respect. Unfortunately, some things that have happened in recent times have raised legitimate doubts about how far that assumption is justified.

1. 'The Sheedy Affair'

Mr. Philip Sheedy, an architect, was serving a prison sentence imposed in the Circuit Court for dangerous driving causing death when a judge of the Supreme Court, with no valid interest in the case, asked the Dublin County Registrar, the official responsible for listing cases for hearing in the Circuit Court, to re-list Mr. Sheedy's, as though he had filed an appeal – which he had not. If there was a valid reason for the case to come back to court, it should have come before the judge who had imposed the sentence, but it was listed before another Circuit judge. In November 1998, on the basis of what seems to have been a non-existent psychiatric report, and without giving the prosecution a chance of being heard, that second judge ordered Mr. Sheedy's release. Later, by chance, the family of the woman he had killed discovered that he was at liberty, and publicity followed. The then Chief Justice interviewed the people involved, and his report, in April 1999, concluded that the conduct of both the Supreme Court judge and the Circuit Court judge who had ordered his release had damaged the administration of justice. Once the public knew how the order for Mr. Sheedy's release had come about, there was no doubt that the Circuit Court judge would have to leave the Bench, but the Supreme Court judge at first said he would not resign, because he had 'done nothing wrong'. Admittedly, his involvement in the scandal – and scandal is the right word – was less central than his colleague's, but his insistence that his interference with the process of another court was 'nothing wrong' surprised most lawyers and probably disturbed as many as it surprised.

Both judges resigned in April 1999, and shortly afterwards were awarded retrospective pensions. These facts, worrying enough in themselves, were made more so by the fact that Mr. Sheedy had connections with the Fianna Fáil party, as had both judges before they were promoted. They had been appointed to the Bench by a Fianna Fáil government and it was a Fianna Fáil administration that awarded their retrospective pensions. Later, making the picture look even worse, a Fianna Fáil Minister for Finance proposed to nominate the former Supreme Court judge to be a director of the European Investment Bank, though public protest led to this proposal being dropped.

It was only by chance that a relative of the woman Mr. Sheedy had killed discovered that he had been freed without completing his sentence. The Chief Justice's investigation was quite thorough, but it was preliminary, not comprehensive, and it did not become clear whether Mr. Sheedy's release was an isolated incident or the court process had been circumvented in other cases. The judges' resignations meant that no comprehensive investigation took place, leaving unanswered questions.

2. Judge Brian Curtin

The second example concerned a Circuit Court judge who 'came to the attention of the Gardaí' after an investigation into a child pornography ring. The Gardaí seized his computer, its contents were examined, and the judge was charged with possessing child pornographic images. He avoided prosecution, as anyone is entitled to do, by relying on a technical defence relating to the warrant under which his computer had been seized. Such a warrant specifies that if it is not acted on within a specified time, it will cease to be valid. At the time the authorities seized Judge Curtin's computer the time allowed by the warrant had expired. This meant that technically the Gardaí had infringed the judge's legal rights in taking his computer, and since the taking of the computer was illegal, evidence of what they found on it became inadmissible. The proposed trial did not go ahead, so the suspicion that a serving judge was a collector of child pornography was neither proved nor disproved. To most people, that suspicion made it impossible for him to continue to serve as a judge. However, he did not resign, but spun out the process for his removal by a series of legal challenges until he could retire on health grounds and draw a pension. As well as paying for his pension, taxpayers had to pay the lawyers who worked for him to bring about this profoundly unsatisfactory result.

3. Kenny v. Trinity College and Another

A man called James Kenny issued a summons against Trinity College Dublin claiming that the college, in collaboration with its architects, had misled the Court in earlier proceedings. Trinity applied to have his claim dismissed without a full hearing. They failed in the High Court, but in 2003 three Supreme Court judges made the order they sought, dismissing Mr. Kenny's claim. About four years later, Mr. Kenny applied to set aside that decision. He had meanwhile discovered that one of the three judges who had dismissed his claim was a brother of one of the partners in the firm of architects that he accused of collaborating with Trinity, and he claimed that this invalidated the court's decision. There was a new hearing by three different Supreme Court judges who decided that the earlier decision, to dismiss Mr. Kenny's complaint, must be set aside.

Judge Fennelly, who delivered the decision on this new hearing, did not say that the architect's brother had knowingly decided a case whose outcome might affect his brother. He hardly could have, without hearing evidence from his colleague. Nor did Mr. Kenny make that claim. That is, he did not claim what is technically called 'subjective bias', which would mean accusing the judge of consciously using his position as a judge to benefit his brother. What Mr. Kenny alleged was what is called 'objective bias'. The test for 'objective bias' that Judge Fennelly and his colleagues applied was 'whether a reasonable person in the circumstances would have a reasonable apprehension that the applicants would not have a fair hearing from an impartial judge on the issues'. That test may overuse the word 'reasonable', but its meaning is clear. Judge Fennelly and his colleagues unanimously decided that the earlier Supreme Court hearing failed that test, and that the decision that came from it must be set aside.

Such a decision seems to reflect on the judge whose decision was set aside, but it would be wrong to question his role in the case without first looking carefully into the facts, so far as we can. In his favour are the following words, taken from Judge Fennelly's decision:

> The present case involves an allegation of objective bias. The appellant [that is, Mr. Kenny] has made it clear that he makes no allegation whatever of subjective bias. On the contrary, he made it clear at the hearing that he accepted that the learned judge would have recused himself, if he had been alerted to the situation.

Those words seem to indicate that the judge decided the case without realising that his brother's firm was involved, which would mean his conduct was not open to criticism. But if so, surely Judge Fennelly would have said so. And presumably his decision would have been different, because if it had been clear that the judge could not have identified the firm of architects, Mr. Kenny would have had no grounds for seeking to overturn his decision. Moreover, Judge Fennelly's judgment contains the following two statements:

> The application to strike out was grounded on two affidavits. One was sworn by Mr Tom Merriman, acting project officer of the Respondent. The other was sworn by Ms

George Boyle, an architect in the firm of Murray O'Laoire, Architects, Fumbally Court, Dublin 8. Ms Boyle described herself as acting Project Architect engaged by the Respondent for the development.

The appellant swore an affidavit, in which he contested that of Ms Boyle at great length. He accused her of seeking to justify the actions of the Respondent in misleading the Court and of herself making misleading choice of words, and of being disingenuous, naïve, self-serving and scarcely credible.

From these quotations, it seems that the firm of architects involved in the case was identified in the papers the first three judges had considered. Indeed, if we read the judgment in its entirety, that interpretation is strengthened. The nature of the claim is also significant. Mr. Kenny claimed that the Defendants, Trinity College, had deliberately misled the High Court and the local authority. He did not join the architects as co-Defendants in his claim, but did accuse them of co-operating with their clients in what he claimed was deceptive conduct. If that accusation had been right, and had been shown in court to be right, it would have done enormous damage to the business prospects of the firm.

From Judge Fennelly's judgment we understand that his colleague had participated in a decision when he should have known the outcome might affect his brother's firm. The 'reasonable apprehension' of bias that led Judge Fennelly to set aside his colleague's earlier decision still exists, and attaches to a serving judge.

4. The Judge and the Breathalyser

In August 2009, a Circuit Court judge was driving in the West of Ireland when a Garda asked him to take a breathalyser test. He refused. He was prosecuted for that refusal, and in July 2012 (nearly three years later!) he pleaded guilty, was convicted, and was fined. He was not imprisoned, though the offence does potentially carry a prison sentence. He continues to serve as a judge.

Now it would be foolish to say that if a judge is convicted of any offence, he should resign his office. A judge, like the rest of us, may park his car carelessly, or be later than he should in returning to drive it away, or have a car with a defective rear brake-light. If such offences called for resignation, we would not have any judges. But refusing a lawful request from a Garda to take a breathalyser test is in a different category. Such a request may be made only if the Garda suspects the driver has been drinking or taking drugs, and is a danger to the public. Refusing to take the test suggests that the suspicion was justified. After being convicted of such an offence, how can the judge plausibly try a drunk-driving charge? And yet, as I say, he continues to serve as a judge.

How Should We View These Events?

The judges involved in Mr. Sheedy's premature release resigned in 1999. The judge whose computer had been seized retired in 2006. *Kenny v. TCD* was first heard in 2003, and that decision was set aside in 2007. The judge refused the breathalyser test in 2009. So, they are roughly contemporaneous. Should we view each of them as an isolated incident, a reminder that even judges are not perfect? Or are they like peaks breaking through clouds, indicating the existence of a formidable range of mountains, out of our sight but all connected? Are they examples of occasional errors, unavoidable in any human institution, which do not happen often enough to worry us? Or should they lead us to fear that judicial standards have slipped? Are they typical of how some judges behave? Are they unusual only because they have come to light? Have other judges behaved badly without our knowing it, and continued to judge the rest of us? We do not know. But three things seem clear.

First, in their cumulative effect these incidents cause reasonably well-informed citizens to wonder whether standards among Irish judges are as they should be.

Secondly, it is important that the citizens be reassured about judicial standards.

Thirdly, a simple statement from the judiciary that all is well will not give us reliable reassurance.

It also is going to be difficult to reassure us while the judge who refused the breathalyser test continues to serve, and the judge whose decision was set aside by his colleagues does not offer any explanation of how he came to hear the case.

System for Appointing Judges

Let us look now at how judges are appointed. The first piece of good news is that most judges are people of good character and abilities. The second is that nobody can be appointed a judge of any court unless he has qualified as a lawyer and worked as one for some years, so that all judges are both educated and experienced in the law. However, that is pretty well the last piece of good news you will read here about the appointment of judges.

The Constitution provides that they are appointed by the President on the recommendation of the Government, which means in effect by the Government. There is a Judicial Appointments Advisory Board, whose function is to present the Government with a list of up to seven lawyers who are willing to become judges, and whom the Board regards as suitable. But under the Constitution the decision lies with the Government, and it may appoint someone not recommended by the Board. If it does, that fact will be disclosed, but this does not vest substantial power over judicial appointments in the Board.

Appointment by the Government is a constitutional oddity. The Comptroller and Auditor General is nominated by the Dáil, not by the Government alone, which gives TDs an opportunity to express their views on whether a nominee is suitable. Comptroller and Auditor General is an important office, but not more important than a judge, and it seems strange that a nomination for that post must come before the Dáil but the Dáil is not involved in the appointment of judges. That the

Government, meeting in secret, nominates judges whose function is to administer the law in public, and presents the serving judges, the citizens and the legislators who represent them with a *fait accompli*, is not good news in a country where cronyism is rife. The Dáil is, obviously, a much larger body than the Government, and as well as reducing the risk of cronyism in appointments and casting the net wider, involving the larger body would improve the chances that if there are good reasons not to appoint someone, they would emerge before the appointment is made.

But to me it is even stranger that judges have no say in deciding who is to become their colleague, and have to accept the nominee of the Government. In the same way as practising lawyers may be the people best placed to assess judges and form a view on which of them perform well and which do not, judges are in a very good position to observe lawyers who practise in front of them and to make informed guesses about which of them would be likely to make a good judge, and which seem unpromising candidates. But under the Irish Constitution they are not even consulted.

The system produced a strange result in the fairly recent past, if gossip among lawyers is to be trusted. A coalition government was in office, and it is said that the political parties that formed it agreed that as vacancies in the higher courts occurred, they would take it in turns to nominate a lawyer to fill them. When there was a vacancy and it was one party's 'turn', there was no supporter they wanted to nominate, so they named a barrister simply because his father and the father of the then leader of that party had been friendly. As it happened, he turned out to be a good judge, was promoted, and deserved to be. The grudging comment of a former colleague was that he had 'turned out better than expected'. But what a way to appoint someone to an important office!

That was an example of a bad system producing an acceptable result, but Irish governments do not have a good record in appointing judges. There is a convention in England that when a judgeship becomes vacant, it is offered to the Attorney

General of the day. That convention has been followed in Ireland since 1922. It has not worked well. About half the lawyers who have been appointed Attorney General since the foundation of the State went on to become judges of the High Court or Supreme Court, and I estimate at least half of them would be classified by most practitioners as poor judges.

There is another reason to criticise the convention of offering an appointment to the serving Attorney General. Every Attorney General to date has been a practising lawyer up to the time of his appointment. (Indeed, every Attorney General has been a barrister.) The Attorney General may well be the only person sitting at the Cabinet table who knows the people who form the pool of available lawyers, and can assess which of them has the potential to be a good judge. His advice on who should be appointed would be valuable. It seems unwise to put him in a position where he might be tempted to nominate himself in preference to a better candidate, and where his independent, informed advice might not be available.

What Sort of People Should Be Appointed Judges?

This leads to the question: what sort of people would we like to see appointed as judges? Surprisingly, perhaps, expertise in the law is not high on my list. In any trial, it is the duty of the lawyers on both sides to research and expound the law, and to respond to arguments from their counterparts. Someone who is well grounded in the concepts that underlie the law and understands how it operates should be able to apply the law cogently, even in a field of law where he is not expert.

Personal qualities are more important than legal knowledge. A good judge will be calm, not volatile, thoughtful rather than merely clever, a good listener, not impetuous in making up his mind, and profound in his intelligence. He will have a steady moral compass, formed by experience, not by study only, and it will inform all his work. Among other things, it will lead him to treat with courtesy and consideration all human beings who appear before him, including Defendants in criminal cases, and people who have been convicted of crimes. He will have due respect for the Oireachtas as the sole constitutional lawmaker, and the people's directly elected representatives. He will carry a sense of vocation, and understand that when he became a judge he answered a call to serve his fellow-citizens, and that if for any reason he comes to realise he can no longer do so well, his duty to them may include resigning. Finally, he will recognise the psychological pressures that he will come under from the comparative isolation that goes with his job and the insidious flattery of advocates who appear before him (see below). He will maintain self-awareness and monitor his own performance critically. (The above is an accurate though obviously incomplete description of the late Judge Seamus Henchy, whose name you will come across later in this book.)

Experience as an advocate will not much help a future judge to develop those qualities. His training and experience will have taught him to assess the strength of the arguments on each side, in order to negotiate settlements, and of course that will be useful to him on the Bench. An advocate learns to memorise the facts in a case in which he is involved, like someone cramming for exams, and forget them as soon as it is over. He masters and memorises the relevant law, with a view to retaining it, which of course will stand to him if he becomes a judge. He learns to listen. But he listens to his own clients in order to use what they say to construct a legally valid case, not to understand their personalities. And while he listens carefully to the other side's case, it is only so that he can produce effective counter-arguments, not in order to understand the issues from another point of view. So his listening skills will probably not have been developed in a way that will be of much value to him as a judge.

Working as an advocate will not have helped a newly appointed judge to acquire and develop the wisdom and understanding that we would wish a judge to show. A successful barrister is often a clever chap, ingenious and flexible, but clever chaps, ingenious advisers and flexible lawyers seldom make good judges. 'Brilliance' is a quality that one or two barristers in every generation may show, but it is the reverse of the qualities described above that we would wish a judge to bring to his work. 'Brilliant' advocates who became judges have, in my view, almost always been poor ones.

How Judges Operate

Let us look next at what happens when a judge is appointed. The first thing he must do is abandon the clients he has been serving, many of whom may be depending on him. He gets no preliminary training in being a judge and very little time to make the mental adjustment from being a lawyer who serves clients to being one whose calling is to serve the law, the community and justice. When next he comes into a courtroom, perhaps the day after his appointment, instead of facing the judge and looking up at him, he is now the judge and looks down, literally if not metaphorically, on his former colleagues, and certainly, in both senses of the phrase, talks down to them.

A lawyer friend, now a distinguished judge, once described to me sitting in on a hearing in a London court, and watching the barristers play the presiding judge 'like a fish'. Our new appointee changes overnight from being a fisherman to being a fish. His former colleagues will try to do exactly what he would have been trying to do a few days before – to influence him in their client's favour. They will study and exploit his tastes and foibles. If he hates Wagner, they will not mention *Lohengrin*. If he is known to enjoy Trollope they will put effort into apparently casual references to Barsetshire and comparing their client to Doctor Thorne, and the other party to Augustus Melmotte. If he makes a mildly funny remark, they will double over in helpless mirth. If they think of a wittier riposte, they will stifle it, because he may not like to have his joke capped. Whatever his foibles and prejudices may be, his daily work is likely to confirm him in them, since they are greeted so rapturously by the lawyers who appear before him.

An Example: Lord Denning

As it happens, the English judge whose court my friend visited was the late Lord Denning, a judge who prided himself on his rugged common sense, his use of simple English, short sentences (see below), and willingness to set aside legal principle in order to do justice, as he saw it. He was also a judge who became more eccentric and erratic with the passage of time until he became almost a parody of himself. Here, for example, are the opening words of his decision in *Lloyds Bank v. Bundy*:

> *Broadchalke is one of the most pleasing villages in England. Old Herbert Bundy, the defendant, was a farmer there. His home was at Yew Tree Farm. It went back for 300 years. His family had been there for generations. It was his only asset. But he did a very foolish thing. He mortgaged it to the bank. Up to the very hilt. Not to borrow money for himself, but for the sake of his son. Now the bank have come down on him. They have foreclosed. They want to get him out of Yew Tree Farm and to sell it. They have brought this action against him for possession. Going out means ruin for him.*

Nobody who was in court and heard those words can have doubted that Lord Denning had made up his mind that Old Herbert Bundy would not be disturbed in his ancestral home. I quote his words not to denigrate Lord Denning, whom I admired, although warily, but because they illustrate two important points. One is how being a judge for too long can turn even a sensible person into a caricature of himself. Lord Denning was Master of the Rolls, a senior position in the English judicial system when he delivered that judgment, in 1974. I suspect a few years previously a prudent self-censoring mechanism would have warned him not to use such language from the Bench but, by 1974, that mechanism had ceased to function.

The other point about Lord Denning's words is that they illustrate something mentioned earlier: that what we write, even if it is only in the words we choose to express our meaning, tells any observant reader a lot about what kind of person we are.

Nobody can write and hide his personality. If we try, the fact that we have chosen non-committal, colourless language is in itself revealing. The notion that a decision by a judge is the result of an abstract intellectual process, and that it says nothing about the author's unspoken, perhaps even unconscious, prejudices and assumptions is simply that – a notion. The above quotation is simply a more than usually vivid example of judicial self-portraiture. The Law Reports, including the Irish Reports, are full of others. We get a picture of Lord Denning's 'world view' from the opening paragraph of his judgment in the Bundy case.

We can learn another lesson. We can be certain that the advocate who appeared for 'Old Herbert Bundy' had brought his fishing rod to court, and hooked and played the judge, and it seems he did so with some success.

It is worth looking more closely at the opening sentences of his judgment. It may be that Broadchalke is one of the most pleasing villages in England, but, like 'the flowers that bloom in the spring, tra-la', it has nothing to do with the case. Moreover, whether Broadchalke is pleasing or not is certainly not a question a judge is required to decide. It is entirely a matter of opinion, and the judge had no business expressing any opinion on the pleasantness of one village, let alone whether it was more pleasant than others. Perhaps we should not make too much of this, but the opening sentence has no place in a court decision.

That the family of 'Old Herbert Bundy' had lived in Yew Tree Farm for generations was a fact, and to that extent it was something on which a judge could make a finding, provided there was evidence to support it. But, again, it had nothing to do with the case, and by introducing it the judge was openly displaying his prejudices. One is left with little doubt that at some level, of which he may not have been conscious, he has sympathy and respect for some people (the word 'yeoman' comes to mind) and less for others. He will be contented if a clever advocate gives him an excuse to allow Old Herbert Bundy to stay on at Yew Tree Farm in the pleasing village of Broadchalke. He will not care too much if the bankers that lent money to Bundy Junior because Old Herbert guaranteed the loan are at a loss. People who 'make money faster, in the air of dark-roomed towns' are not equal in his eyes to people who have farmed in Broadchalke for generations.

Anyone reading the opening words of Lord Denning's judgment may either laugh at their sheer absurdity or become indignant as he recognises that at an unconscious level in Lord Denning's mind, a Bundy of Yew Tree Farm in Broadchalke is worthy of attention that may be withheld from bankers who rely on the promises of long-established farmers.

By the way, I hope you enjoyed the names: 'Old Herbert Bundy', 'Broadchalke' – the final 'e' is a nice touch, suggesting 'olde Herbert Bundy' – and 'Yew Tree Farm'. I assure you I did not make them up.

Some readers will recall that it was Lord Denning who concluded that it would be better that Irish people wrongly convicted of crime should remain in prison than that an 'appalling vista' of English police corruption and judicial incompetence be exposed. They may wonder if that matter would have been decided differently if one of the people rail-roaded into prison had a name like 'Bundy' or if his family had farmed in a pleasing English village for generations.

Coming back to our archetypal Irish judge, unless he was appointed quite recently, he has become accustomed to being addressed as 'my Lord' and 'your Lordship', as if he was still – as his predecessors had been, for many years – a representative of a quasi-divine anointed monarch. (Strange language, surely, in a country whose Constitution describes it as a 'sovereign independent democratic state' and prohibits it from conferring titles of nobility.) This mode of expression is now much less used than it used to be (though it still 'slips out' of the mouths of some advocates) but there is little sign that the attitudes that made it seem almost normal have changed. For the rest of his working life, every time he comes into the courtroom or leaves it, everyone will have to stand up, as will anybody who wants to speak to him. Nobody will interrupt him or contradict him, let alone tell him to shut up and stop talking nonsense. If he is a High

Court or Supreme Court judge, he will appear in the corridors of the Four Courts preceded by his own personal tipstaff, who will walk ahead of him and clear other people out of his path.

The language advocates, mostly barristers, will use in talking to him (or about him: for example, he will always be referred to as 'learned') is so fulsome that it is embarrassing to quote it. Obsequiousness is normal. Phrases like 'with respect', 'with very great respect' or even 'with the greatest respect' flow from advocates' mouths as though they formed part of normal communication. It is hard to imagine that even the most servile employee would talk to his boss in such a way, or that an employer with any self-respect would tolerate such sycophancy.

All this may be pleasant for a judge, but it is psychologically dangerous. Nobody's mental health is improved by an exclusive diet of flattery. Even the Pope is reminded that the glory of the world passes in a moment.

Permanent Appointment to the Bench

In addition to this unvarying diet of flattery and apparent admiration, which will continue for as long as he continues to serve as a judge, and which might turn even a well-balanced head, our newly appointed judge will be aware of two other unusual aspects of his job description: It is almost impossible to fire him, and he is very unlikely to leave the job until he has reached retirement age. For practical purposes he is stuck in his position even if he comes to loathe it. And we are stuck with him.

Let us look first at why we are stuck with him and then why he is stuck with us. The Constitution makes it very hard to get rid of a serving judge. It must first be shown that he has misbehaved and only then, if a majority of both Dáil and Seanad vote to remove him, can he be dismissed. A removal process has been started twice in the ninety years or so that Ireland has been independent, but has never been brought to a conclusion. It is not hard to see why it is made so difficult. It is important to us that judges are independent of the government, and if the government could remove them at will we might not be able to trust them to show independence. So the rules that say they cannot be removed because they annoy the government of the day are there to protect us, not them.

Why is he stuck with his job? There are two reasons, one that applies only to former barristers and the other to all judges. Barristers have a rule that a former judge who wants to return to being a barrister is limited to appearing only in courts on a higher level than the one where he sat as a judge. The District Court is the lowest level, and a District Court Judge who retired would be entitled to practise in the Circuit, High and Supreme Courts, and in theory might have a prospect of making a living. However, in the real world, very few successful barristers accept appointment to the District Court, and a barrister who had made so little impact that he accepted a District Court judgeship would be unlikely to make a successful comeback as an advocate in the higher courts. A former High or Supreme Court judge would have no chance at all of making a living.

People are not appointed judges in their first youth, but only after some years, when they are likely to have dependants, so a former barrister serving as a Circuit Court judge who wanted to leave the Bench and start again to try to make a living for himself at the Bar would take a huge risk. As a barrister, he could appear only in the High Court and Supreme Court, a serious limitation on his ability to support himself. He could practise as a solicitor after leaving the Bench, even if he had previously been a barrister, but again it is going to be very hard for him to build a practice, attract clients and serve them effectively, because during the time he was a judge he will have lost contact with the day-to-day skills and know-how a practising lawyer needs in order to make a living. He will also have lost contact with the people from whom a practising lawyer hopes to get work, and will have to start building his practice from zero. He might perhaps get a salaried job in a solicitor's firm, but it would be hard for him to find a firm willing to take him on, and the pay wouldn't be good. He is neither qualified nor trained for any other job, except maybe some specialised job in the State service, which is unlikely to come his way.

So, in the real world, once a judge has been appointed, he is not going to leave and we cannot get rid of him unless he is guilty of major misconduct that has alienated a majority of both the Dáil and the Seanad.

In summary:

- Judges are chosen in secrecy and behind closed doors, giving rise to suspicions of cronyism.

- Their appointment is based on a guess or hope that they will be good judges, although their capacity for it has not been tested.

- There is no probation to see if they are going to be good judges.

- We do not give them any training before they start work and only very inadequate in-service training afterwards.

- Their role isolates them and exposes them to psychological pressure, and they get no help in coping with it.

- We cannot get rid of them if they turn out badly.

- They are unlikely to leave, however much they may come to hate being judges.

These are the people who will adjudicate disputes between citizens, preside over criminal trials, and act as interpreters and guardians of our constitutional rights.

It is amazing that so important an office is treated so casually, and hard to imagine any responsible employer recruiting even a junior employee on such a haphazard basis. That Ireland has had, and still seem to have, so many good judges and comparatively few bad ones must be a tribute to the personal quality of lawyers who have risen to the top of their profession. But such a random system of appointment cries out for reform.

Chapter 4

Reforming the Judicial System

This chapter offers suggestions for reform by a former lawyer who left law practice some years ago, long enough to have modified his thinking and assumptions, to make them less those of a lawyer and more those of a citizen.

Probably the single most important reform would be to reduce the levels of remuneration among practising lawyers so as to encourage practitioners to aspire to become judges. We will look at that issue in Chapter 6, and will not go into it here, except to suggest that although Ireland has not treated our judges meanly in comparison to many other countries, they are not over-paid for the services they are called on to perform.

Next, the system of appointing judges by the government without consulting the Dáil should change. (That would require an amendment to the Constitution.) We would also need a code of conduct at the interface between the government and the Dáil in order to protect the reputations of possible nominees. There should probably be informal consultation, presumably with representatives of the major parties within the Dáil, before a nomination was formally proposed. Otherwise a lawyer's reputation might be damaged by his being publicly opposed in the Dáil chamber, where an unscrupulous or irresponsible politician, protected by legal privilege, could do enormous damage to his standing.

Like many of the other suggestions that appear in this chapter, it would require machinery to make it work, but this chapter will focus on principles only, not machinery. If principles are agreed, machinery can be devised to give effect to them. This book would become intolerably long if it debated what machinery for change would work best.

No less importantly, the judiciary as a body should be consulted. Indeed, they should probably have the right to veto any nominee. It would seem wrong to force on them a colleague most of them find unacceptable.

Moreover, in spite of worries expressed earlier, the quality of our Superior Court judges is probably a good deal better than we deserve under our system for appointing them. Their assessment of lawyers who have appeared before them should be of great value in selecting good judges. To give them exclusive power to nominate their colleagues and successors would risk creating a self-perpetuating elite. But to exclude them altogether from any say in who is to join them seems unwise, as well as discourteous. Their views should probably be ascertained through a Judicial Council, a body we will discuss later in this chapter.

Next, when there is a vacancy and a new judge has to be selected, there should be consultation with practising lawyers, people who know the candidates and can assess whether they are likely to be good judges – though an assessment (or, in truth, a guess) is all it can be. Again, this should probably take place through the bodies representing each branch of the legal profession, the Bar Council representing barristers, and the Law Society representing solicitors. If either, or the Judicial Council, advised strongly against a given nominee, the nomination should probably be dropped.

A lawyer who is about to become a judge should complete whatever work he may have in hand for current clients. Some work at an early stage could be passed on to other lawyers without letting the client down, but a client whose case is coming to a hearing and who depends on the lawyer he has chosen to represent him should not be abandoned.

Training for Judges

Anybody who is going to become a judge should have gone through training before he goes on the Bench – as he would have to if he were appointed in the UK. (In many continental European countries, judges are trained and educated separately from students who want to become client-serving lawyers, and are not appointed from the ranks of practitioners. Their training is part of their education.) Training should include a large component of role-play. That is, in an invented scenario the trainee assumes the role he aspires to perform in reality, and other participants, also acting in role, put him under pressure. Training need not be confined to people who have been appointed to act as judges. Any practising lawyer would benefit from being involved in a training that gives him a different perspective on his work, and training is best done in groups, not one-to-one. Moreover, group training, combined with continuous mutual assessment by trainers and trainees, should help to identify good future judges. Lawyers who participate have the opportunity to assess each other. If a lawyer in the course of training acts in a way that suggests to his trainers and co-trainees that he is likely to be a good judge, that should be noted for when the time next comes to make an appointment. Conversely, if his performance in role-play suggests to most people who watch him that he would not perform well as a judge, then that might lead to a decision not to recommend him.

Volunteering for in-service training for judges should not be seen as notice that the volunteer has his eye on appointment. If solicitors were to think, 'I see Joe X has signed up for the judging course. Obviously, he's thinking of leaving his practice and going on the Bench, so I'd better not send him any more work,' that would damage Joe X's livelihood. The danger of that happening might discourage people from signing up for a training course. A solution might be to widen the circle of people taking in-service lawyer training, so that no practitioner would stand out. Training should be a continuous process, for all lawyers, including judges. Indeed, the participation of serving judges should greatly improve the training, as well as helping them to recognise their own weaknesses and become better judges. For some, role-play in which they returned to being advocates and experienced again the misery of appearing in front of a bloody-minded judge could be salutary. Barristers and solicitors are required to spend a minimum number of hours every year in continuing education and training, and judges should be under the same obligation – as they are on the other side of the Irish Sea. There is no obvious reason why hours spent in the sort of training described above, including role-play, should not be counted as part of a continuing education programme, for judges, barristers and solicitors. All should benefit.

In theory, training is available for Irish judges, but it is inadequate and extraordinarily ill-funded. It does not include the kind of role-play described above, which might help judges to do their work better.

Assessment of Judges

There should also be continuous assessment of judges. Initially, perhaps, judges might be appointed on, say, one year's probation, and their appointment should not be confirmed if their work is generally disapproved of by practitioners who have observed them in court. This may seem unrealistic, because it would be unattractive for any practitioner to accept a provisional appointment knowing that if at the end of the year he is not confirmed, he will have lost his client base and will have to start again to re-establish his career. But that problem should not be insurmountable. In Britain there are part-time judges, known as 'Recorders', who sit as judges for part of the year, and work for clients for the rest of the year. They are carefully selected, under a much more rigorous process than any Irish judge faces, and the system seems to work well – for the Recorders, the litigants whose claims they decide, and their clients when they resume their 'normal' role as client-serving lawyers. It is hard to see why it should not work equally well on this side of the Irish Sea.

In Chapter 6, a ceiling on lawyers' incomes is proposed. With such a ceiling, a lawyer who had worked hard for, say, eight months, or whose income for the current year was swollen by belated payment of fees earned in previous years, and who saw that his income for the full year was likely to be perilously close to the ceiling, might be happy to spend a few months as a temporary judge. It would give him a rest from the pressures of his practice. Moreover, showing willingness to take time off from his law practice could be a subtle form of advertising – a means of letting prospective clients know how successful he had been. Both barristers and solicitors might do this, though it might be harder for the latter.

Judges should be assessed at regular intervals, probably every few years. Assessment should involve health-checks, including psychological ones to see how they are coping with the stresses of the job.

Judges should be entitled to take sabbaticals at intervals, and if they do not do so voluntarily, they should be required to take them, in order to experience a change of scene.

Mobility

In their interests and ours, it should be made easy for judges to leave the Bench voluntarily, though not, of course, for the government of the day to remove them. Any restrictions on their right to return to their former work should be abolished. Someone who gives up being a judge should be seen as a likely appointee for most state jobs requiring legal expertise, including Attorney General.

The Attorney General of the day should not be eligible for appointment to any judicial job that becomes vacant while he is in office. His role should be to liaise with the professional bodies that are best able to assess the quality of possible appointees, report to the cabinet and offer his own assessment, before the Minister for Justice proposes a nomination to the Dáil. The community of lawyers in Ireland is not very big and the Attorney General is likely to know any lawyer who might be considered for appointment to the Bench, by reputation if not personally. He should be able to advise whether a potential nominee has the qualities we seek in a judge.

Getting rid of a judge compulsorily should not be made easier, when he has completed whatever probationary period is laid down, but it should be possible for a group of judges authorised by the Judicial Council to say something like the following to a poorly performing colleague:

> *Joe, it seems you are not making a good fist of being a judge. That is the view we are hearing from 85 per cent of the lawyers who have appeared in your court in the last six months. Here are their criticisms, if you want to see them, obviously edited so that you won't be able to identify your critics. We assume that if the general view of your performance is so negative, you can't be enjoying the job. So, what would you like to do? If you'd like to try to improve your performance, and regain the esteem of practising lawyers, there is training available, as you know, and we and your other colleagues will support you. Alternatively, there is a vacancy in the Office of the Parliamentary Draftsman, and we think you would fill it admirably. The salary is less than a judge is paid, but with the pension rights you've accrued on the Bench the drop in income wouldn't be huge. Please think about this and tell us what you'd like to do. We want to be helpful, not to criticise you.*

Receiving such a message would not be pleasant, nor would delivering it, but if the people who said it and the person it was said to recognised that their shared duty was to serve their fellow-citizens by providing an effective legal system, the hearer would recognise that it was the duty of the speaker to deliver the unpalatable message, and his own duty to accept it, and to act on it.

But if it is to be delivered with the authority of a Judicial Council, we should think carefully about its composition. The present proposal is for a Council consisting only of judges, chaired by the Chief Justice. As this book argues, there are grounds for public disquiet about how our courts are staffed and run. A Judicial Council may help to satisfy citizens that our courts are well administered and justice is done by judges in whom we should have confidence, but a Council composed only of judges will not be effective in allaying any worry citizens may now feel. Worried citizens will not be convinced if a Judicial Council consisting only of judges tells them judges are doing a great job.

Laypeople, excluding TDs, Senators and Ministers, should hold an influential position on any such Council, and maybe even a dominant one. Another group that might be invited to contribute is former Superior Court judges who have retired on age grounds but are still physically fit and mentally alert.

Election to the Positions of Chief Justice and President of the High Court

At present, the Chief Justice and the President of the High Court are nominated by the government. Surely, they would command more respect among their colleagues, and be better able to do their respective jobs, if they were elected by their peers. This should also end a pattern by which well-qualified people have been passed over for those positions in favour of others, whose party affiliations have been 'right', though their abilities were less impressive.

At first sight it might seem that High Court judges should elect their President, and Supreme Court judges the Chief Justice, but there may be no good reason why the electorate for both elections should not consist of all judges of the High and Supreme Courts. The vote should be by secret ballot, canvassing should not be allowed, and the person elected should hold office for a fixed term.

Among other benefits of electing these office-holders, there must be times when the judiciary needs to be in contact with the Executive, for example on staffing levels, or on maintaining and refurbishing court buildings. The Chief Justice and President of the High Court seem to be the people who should represent the senior judiciary in dialogue with the Executive. They would be more credible in representing their fellow-judges if they had been elected by them, rather than appointed by the people they have to talk to and perhaps negotiate with.

These are one person's ideas about how the appointment and regulation of judges could be improved. Other ideas should be sought, examined and implemented if they seem constructive. We need to widen our thinking, not restrict it.

Before we move on to look at other components of the legal process, namely lawyers other than judges, let us look at a few other issues.

Judges' Relationships with Other Lawyers

Of forty-five judges of the Superior Courts in 2011, two, both of them High Court judges, worked as solicitors before they became judges. All eight Supreme Court judges and thirty-five out of thirty-seven in the High Court are former barristers. Of those forty-three former barristers, every one continues to be a member of the barristers' body, the Honorable Society of King's Inns. Indeed, every barrister who becomes a High Court or Supreme Court judge is automatically made a 'Bencher' of King's Inns, a sort of inner circle member, if he is not one already.

Let us think first about how that affects solicitors competing with barristers as advocates, as the Competition Authority proposes (see Chapter 7). In the High Court, a solicitor who appears as an advocate on a given day will probably face a judge who is a former barrister. If he appears in the Supreme Court, it is certain that all the judges will be former barristers. Given that few solicitors have 'invaded' what has traditionally been seen as the preserve of the Bar, appearing in court to argue on behalf of clients, examine witnesses and so forth, it is likely that our solicitor-advocate will find himself opposing a barrister as well as appearing before a former one. The judge is also a continuing member, and a senior one, of King's Inns.

That Society is not only a regulatory body. Judges, practising barristers and Bar students are expected to dine together at intervals, so that students may learn from listening to the 'shop talk' that goes on around them. (Dining in an inn while judges and advocates travelled around the country 'on circuit' in days long gone is the origin of the Society and was an early way for aspirant lawyers to learn their trade. It represents a tradition that barristers have maintained, though its value in the twenty-first century must be doubtful.) A solicitor working as an advocate thus has to compete with someone who is not only a member of the same club as the judge, from which the solicitor is excluded, but of the same dining club.

Let us think about what advocacy in the courts means. It involves persuading a judge to give your client what he wants, and to deny the other advocate's client what he wants. In almost every case that comes before a judge, there are solid arguments on both sides; otherwise the case would not have come to court. Advocacy has two aspects. One is to persuade the judge to feel inclined to decide the issue in favour of your client, and the other is to give him valid reasons to do so. An advocate tries to give the judge a reason to want to find in his client's favour, and also presents him with rational arguments to justify doing so. Advocacy starts at gut level, not brain level. Think of Lord Denning and Old Herbert Bundy. Give some credit to the old farmer's advocate for seeing how to get his Lordship to want to decide the case in his client's favour.

Of course, a competent advocate does not treat these two activities, appealing to emotion and appealing to reason, as agenda items to be dealt with in sequence, one after the other. The goal of keeping the judge on your side continues throughout the process, as does the attempt to feed him valid legal reasons for staying there.

If one of the two advocates is a fellow club member of the judge, that may give him an initial advantage. Clearly, that is unfair. If solicitor-advocates start off with a handicap in arguing against barristers, because the barristers are members of the same dining club as the judge, then the solicitors are likely to be less successful. That will not be fair to their clients. Over time, comparative success levels will become apparent. If people see that solicitors are less successful as advocates than are barristers, clients will not be happy to be represented by solicitors alone, and the Competition Authority's hope of encouraging solicitor-advocates to compete with barristers will be frustrated.

Even if none of this actually happens, it is plainly a possibility. It infringes the principle that 'justice must not only be done but must be seen to be done', and should be eliminated.

There is another problem. The fact that after going on the Bench, judges continue to be members of King's Inns is liable to affect how they perform their role of adjudicating between lawyers and the public. This may happen in either or both of two ways: on the level of service the public should be entitled to expect from barristers, and on how much they should pay for it. In Chapter 2 we saw how judges created rules to protect fellow-lawyers who handle litigation incompetently from being sued by disgruntled clients.

Nor have judges been active in controlling the increasing cost to citizens of seeking justice. Having a foot in the advocates' camp may partly explain that. Understandably, they are not keen to slash their dining companions' incomes. But surely there should be some control over the cost of litigation, and a balance between the interests of citizens who have recourse to law and those of lawyers who serve them. If so, and if exercising such control and holding that balance are among the functions of judges, it seems unwise for them to continue to be members of a lawyers' club. By continuing as members of the Inns, judges give us, the people they exist to serve and who pay their salaries, a message that in any dispute between us and the barristers, judges will not hold an impartial balance, because they are aligned, professionally and socially, with the other side.

'Nolumus Mutari'

The motto of King's Inns, the barristers' organisation, is *Nolumus Mutari*, meaning literally 'we are reluctant to change', but in reality, 'we resist change'. King's Inns and the lawyers who constitute the Bar have been fairly consistent in following that motto. Promoting barristers to be Benchers of King's Inns as soon as they become judges is a tradition. In the eyes of people whose motto is *Nolumus Mutari* that is a good reason not to change it.

Barristers have presented themselves over the years as guardians of citizens' rights, pointing out that in 1792 Thomas Erskine defended Tom Paine, at some personal sacrifice. To be fair, there is truth in this self-portrait, even if it does flatter the sitter. But the people lawyers exist to serve, and make their living (and in some cases much more than a living, as we will see) by serving, may reasonably be disconcerted to realise that on the question of how that service is delivered and paid for, one branch of the profession has adopted a motto that embraces the status quo, without seeming to take into account the needs of their clients.

There has been little change since 1922 in how Irish law is administered, and the spirit of *Nolumus Mutari* is probably one of the reasons. If lawyers had co-operated in introducing the changes that were needed, gradually and incrementally, we would probably now have a better legal services, delivered by a healthier legal community. *Nolumus Mutari* has also created a danger that when change that has been too long postponed does come, it will be more radical than it should be, and will have unintended consequences.

Incidentally, the motto of the solicitors' body is *Veritas Vincet*, meaning 'let truth prevail', which seems a more respectable motto for a body of lawyers than 'we resist change'.

Expansion of Courts

Let us look at how the Superior Courts have grown over the past sixty years or so. There were seven High Court judges in the mid-1950s and, as noted above, there were thirty-seven in 2011. The number has multiplied by more than five over less than sixty years. The increase in numbers suggests that the impact of the judiciary on the lives of our citizens in 2013 is greater than it was sixty years ago. (See also comments on the Competition Authority Report, in Chapter 7, where we look at the increase in the amounts spent on legal services between 1992 and 2003.)

The Government proposes to ask us to vote in a referendum to change the Constitution so as to create a new Court of Appeal, between the High Court (including the Central Criminal Court) and the Supreme Court. It would deal with most appeals, leaving the Supreme Court to consider constitutional issues and appeals involving an important point of law. The rationale for this proposal is that the Supreme Court cannot handle the volume of appeals it currently receives.

The Court was increased some years ago from five judges to eight, in order that it could roughly double its throughput by constituting two courts, one of three judges and one of five, that could sit simultaneously. And yet, on the same day as the Minister announced his plan to promote a referendum, we read that seven judges of the Supreme Court were to assemble to hear an appeal. This did not seem to be an efficient use of the Court's resources, at a time when we were being told it could not clear its backlog. Should taxpayers, who would have to support this new tier of judges, be asked to accept that substantial additional cost unless it has been shown that attempts have been made to improve the present system, that they were not successful, and that creating a new layer of judges is the only solution? In times of austerity, all public service bodies must accept the obligation to make their services more efficient and less expensive, and there is no obvious reason why this should not apply to the courts, as to all other bodies funded by the Exchequer.

Reform of the Process of Appeals to the Supreme Court

Parallel with reforming the process of bringing a complaint to a hearing in the High Court, as described in the next chapter, I suggest that the process of dealing with appeals from the High Court to the Supreme Court could be made simpler and speedier, in a way that need not affect the quality of the Court's work.

High Court decisions are appealed for a variety of reasons. Sometimes, the Appellant (the party appealing) believes the High Court judgement is wrong, and is supported in that view by his lawyers. Some appeals are lodged mainly with a view to postponing the day when the Appellant is going to have to comply with the High Court decision. Some are tactical, filed in order to try to negotiate a settlement. ('An appeal will take years, so even if you think your client will win, he'd be better off to take less and get it now.') In the next chapter, I propose that it should be considered unethical for a lawyer, whose duties include serving the legal system, to help his clients to frustrate justice by exploiting the system's tendency to delay. If that argument is accepted, it applies to appeals as well as to hearings at first instance, and it should eliminate appeals on these last two grounds. The number of appeals filed in the Supreme Court should diminish, though we can only guess at the size of the drop. (It might be necessary to penalise lawyers who abused the system by filing unmeritorious appeals, though after one or two had suffered an appropriate penalty, such abuse would probably cease.)

But if lawyers do not accept a changed view of their duties to the community, or if they are slow to do so (and *Nolumus Mutari* suggests they are unlikely to be quick), it is surely time for the Supreme Court to ensure that appeals are not being lodged in a way that is inconsistent with justice. The judges should consider whether some parties who are unsuccessful in the High Court are lodging appeals with little merit or prospect of success in order to postpone the day when they will have to comply with the decision of the High Court. If they acknowledge that is happening, they should consider whether that practice constitutes an abuse of process and a denial of justice to the winner in the High Court, bearing in mind the maxim that justice delayed is justice denied. An affirmative answer would lead unavoidably to two further questions. Is the Supreme Court going to acquiesce in that practice continuing? If not, how is the Court going to stop it?

Currently, all appeals, however motivated, are dealt with in the same way. The Appellant prepares a Notice of Appeal which he lodges in the Supreme Court Office and sends to the other party (the Respondent). Like a Statement of Claim, discussed earlier, this notice is drafted with a view to protecting the Appellant's lawyers from being thrown out of Court on the 'not pleaded' ground. It covers all possible grounds of appeal, realistic or not, and may not give a clear picture of what grounds the Appellant genuinely relies on. The Appellant must then lodge in the Supreme Court Office five copies of a complete transcript of the evidence given in the High Court, plus all documents produced in the High Court hearing, even though 90 per cent or more of them will be irrelevant. When judges are available, they will hear the appeal. The hearing will consist of oral argument, based on the notice of appeal, supplemented by written submissions which the parties are required to file in advance. The Appellant's lawyers speak first, usually at length. When they have finished, the judges may ask the Respondent's lawyers to reply, or may then dismiss the appeal. If they do call on the Respondent's lawyers to argue, when they have finished the Appellant's lawyers have a right to respond. The judges usually 'reserve' their decision, and may ask the two teams of lawyers to file written summaries of their arguments. The judges then go away and write judgments, sometimes separately, and sometimes one or more of them say they agree with a colleague, without writing independently. Advocates and judges then reassemble, probably months later, and the judge or judges usually read their judgments aloud, a process that may take hours.

Clearly, this takes up a lot of time, and costs a lot of money. Surely a better process for appeals could be put in place. Here is one suggestion.

Instead of producing a long meaningless Notice, the Appellant's lawyers file a simple statement that he appeals the decision. Within a specified time (which might be extended in the interests of justice in suitable cases) they file a written statement identifying where and how they claim the High Court decision was wrong, supported by extracts from the oral evidence, and from the documents produced in the High Court hearing. They are not required to file a complete transcript, as at present, but lawyers representing an Appellant must certify that in their opinion their client has *bona fide* grounds of appeal, and are liable to sanctions if they do so irresponsibly. They are also required to certify that the documents and extracts they are filing represent all the evidence produced in the original hearing on the point at issue. This is to ensure appeal judges do not have to waste their time on legal arguments if the factual evidence on which they depend has been refuted by other evidence.

The Chief Justice examines this statement of grounds, with a view to answering one question only: does this case call for a five-judge court or will three be sufficient? (The number hearing an appeal is always odd, to avoid a split decision.) Some recent appeals have been heard by seven Supreme Court judges. I suggest that so long as there are 'arrears' of appeals waiting to be decided – that is, so long as there are people waiting to get justice from the court – the practice of nominating a seven-judge court should be abandoned. If she (the current Chief Justice is a woman) decides a three-judge court should decide the appeal, she nominates two judges to deal with it in the first instance. Two judges would be a majority in a three-judge court, so if two agree, there is no need to involve a third. Similarly, if she considers the appeal should be decided by a five-judge court, she nominates three judges in the first instance.

The nominated Supreme Court judges examine the Statement of Grounds to see if the appeal has merit. If they think it may have, they may seek clarification from the Appellant, without involving the Respondent at that stage. If they consider *prima facie* grounds for an appeal have been established, they invite the Respondent's lawyers to reply, again in writing. If the appeal is rejected without the Respondent being called on, it is probably sufficient to record that the Supreme Court affirms the High Court's decision, without delivering a written judgment – as the Abbé Sieyès said, '*La mort, sans phrases.*'

If the judges entertain the appeal, and the Respondent files written counter-arguments, the judges give the Appellant's lawyers a chance to reply and then decide if they need to hear oral argument. Obviously, if they are in agreement, they do not need to. If they do not agree, they ask the Chief Justice to appoint another judge or judges, and the decision will be made by the majority.

Any oral argument takes the form of the judges questioning the advocates for each party on their written submissions. Neither party is allowed to introduce new material not contained in their written submissions.

The Judges of the Supreme Court should also ask themselves four further questions:

1. Is it necessary for each judge to write a separate judgment, or would a single judgment suffice in most 'routine' cases?

2. Might it not be sufficient in many cases to say only, 'I agree with the decision of the High Court'?

3. Could the average judgment be made shorter?

4. Is it acceptable in the twenty-first century that some judges read lengthy judgments aloud while all their colleagues and the parties' lawyers sit in court? Could not the text of the judgments can be circulated electronically, not only to the parties and their lawyers but to anyone interested?

The above suggested change in how the Supreme Court does its job should make it more efficient, without affecting the quality of decision-making, or infringing the principle that the courts do justice in public. Indeed, if the text of lawyers' submissions, as well as the judges' decisions, appear on the court's website, the process is available to more members of the public than at present.

Doubtless, other reforms could be tried, and might work better. If none produced a timely appeals process, it might then be right to bring into existence a new Court of Appeal. But should public money be spent on creating more courts and more judges until the public can see that such questions have been asked and answered?

The Government has impliedly given an affirmative answer to that question, relying on a 'Report of a Working Group on a Court of Appeal', published in May 2009 – which is now, surprisingly, out of print. The Report identifies the problem in the Supreme Court that in each year more appeals are lodged than are decided by the Court or withdrawn, so that the volume of arrears increases from year to year. It also analyses the constitutional implications of bringing a new Court of Appeal into existence and demonstrates convincingly that if a new Court is needed, amending the Constitution along the lines it proposes is the best way to create one.

It is less convincing in trying to demonstrate that a new Court is needed. This is probably because it presents a conclusion that 'more capacity is needed at the appellate level' as if it proved itself. The Report does not consider what other ways there may be of solving the problem and eliminate them by showing that they would not work. You will not find in it a suggestion, such as you have read above, that a more efficient system of dealing with appeals might increase productivity in the Supreme Court, without affecting quality. Nor does it consider whether litigants who have lost in the High Court are lodging unmeritorious appeals in order to postpone complying with the High Court's decision. Naturally, since it does not consider that possibility, it does not address whether any such appeals are an abuse of process, which the Supreme Court should not permit. The Report assumes that there is only one way to address arrears in the Supreme Court and that is to appoint more judges, who will operate in the traditional way. One is reminded of Lampedusa's *The Leopard*, where Don Fabrizio says things will have to change in order that they remain the same. Which comes close to *Nolumus Mutari*.

Judges and the Community

Judges spend their working day listening and talking to lawyers, most of whom, being barristers, are former colleagues. Probably the closest friends of many judges are professional colleagues, people they have studied with, worked with, shared their failures and successes with, known, liked and relied on, and have in turn been known, liked and relied on by those same friends. That is unavoidable and healthy, even if my criticism of judges continuing in membership of King's Inns is valid. But it creates a danger that the circle in which law is administered may become inward-looking. Some pronouncements by judges over the years about how other people live have seemed, in Max Beerbohm's phrase, 'based less on study than on conjecture'. Judges have little opportunity of getting to understand how the rest of us live, because the accepted view is that they should be somewhat detached. A judge now retired once told me that when he was appointed a judge of the High Court he asked the then President of the Court what limits he should set on his social life, now that he was a judge. 'For example, should I go into a pub?' The cautious reply was, 'It's a matter for you. Personally, I wouldn't.'

There are arguments in favour of judges distancing themselves from how the rest of us live our lives, in order to maintain impartiality, and be seen to be impartial. Even if they are not completely convincing, if it suits judges not to be in touch with the realities of most people's lives, it would seem unreasonable to require them to mix with the rest of us. But equally it would be wise of them to recognise their comparative isolation, and not pretend to have a finger on the pulse of the community. They do not, and they should not. It is not their job. In a democracy, the people whose role it is to know what the bulk of citizens feel and want are our elected representatives. Judges who claim to represent the will of the community, as still occasionally happens, mistake their role, and do not serve us well.

A Role for Laypeople?

The role of laypeople in the administration of law has greatly diminished in recent decades. In the mid-1950s, most litigation in the High Court, including claims for compensation for personal injuries, were heard before a judge and jury. Nowadays, juries are involved only in defamation claims in the High Court and prosecutions for major crimes, where the Constitution entitles a Defendant to a jury trial. Juries can be unpredictable and even silly – as the award of €10,000,000 to a somnambulist who took a libel action demonstrates – but there is merit in not excluding the common sense of the citizens of the country from the process of doing justice. They sometimes made decisions that produced justice, where the law as applied by judges would not have.

For example, there was in those far-off days a rule, devised by judges, called the 'doctrine of common employment'. (It has long since been abolished, by a Statute passed by our elected legislature – another source of lay common sense.) It said that if a worker was injured through negligence by a 'fellow-worker in common employment with him', he was not entitled to be compensated by his employer. The concept of 'vicarious liability', by which an employer is responsible for his employee's misdeeds, did not apply if the person injured was working for the same employer. If an employee of the main contractor on a building site carelessly dropped slates from the roof, one hit a chance passer-by, another hit the architect, the third hit an employee of an electrical sub-contractor, and the fourth hit another employee of the main contractor, the first three victims could claim compensation, but the fourth would be refused, because he and the man who dropped the slates were working on the same site for the same boss. This was nonsense, but it was the law, as judges firmly told juries. And juries, with remarkable consistency, ignored that instruction, because they could see that it was nonsense.

In a recent case, a lady had fallen and injured herself because she had not noticed that there was a hole in the roadway where she was walking. She sued the local authority for compensation. The case went to a hearing and the judge held that the condition of the roadway was the only cause of the accident, and there had been no 'contributory negligence' on the part of the Plaintiff. However, he decided that the roadway was in a bad condition because the authority had failed to maintain it, and went on to apply a rule that says a local authority is liable for 'misfeasance', but not for 'non-feasance'. If the local authority had fixed the roadway and made a mess of it, that would have been 'misfeasance' – doing something, but doing it badly. But instead of trying to fix it the authority had ignored it, even though it was dangerous, which meant their failure was classified as 'non-feasance' – the absence of activity. Since a local authority is not liable for non-feasance, the lady lost her claim.

It is unlikely a jury would have made such a decision, because, even if legally correct, it was contrary to common sense. Someone who falls into a hole in the road hasn't been watching where she's walking, and it seems unrealistic to say there was no negligence on her part. So is the distinction between 'misfeasance' and 'non-feasance', if it means a local authority cannot be blamed for doing nothing, instead of trying to fix a stretch of roadway that was dangerous.

The distinction the judge made in that case between 'misfeasance' and 'non-feasance' was a correct application of the law, but since the law is silly, the decision brings it into disrepute. The same applies to the decision that someone who doesn't look where she is going has no responsibility – not even a little bit – if she trips and falls. And a jury allowed to apply common sense would surely have rejected such nonsense. If so, more use of juries would be good for our justice system, and help to increase respect for it.

In the days when juries played a major role in our courts, they were cooped up together in a box, not shown documents except an occasional photo or map that they were allowed to see provided they immediately handed it back, not allowed to make notes or have transcripts of evidence, not allowed to ask questions, and finally were sent away to answer specific questions formulated by the judge without consulting them. This was an absurd way of involving laypeople in the business of doing justice. (It presumably derived from times when most jurymen couldn't read, and had not changed – a fine example of *Nolumus Mutari!*)

It is difficult to see how non-lawyers should be brought back into the legal process. And there may sometimes be good reasons for excluding the public. For example, people may react emotionally against certain crimes and those people who commit them in a way that in retrospect seems disproportionate. 'Righteous indignation' may sell newspapers, but it can lead to injustice if not restrained. There is often public outrage at judges who have imposed sentences (often on sex offenders) that were thought to be too light. But the sentencing of convicted criminals needs to be in the dispassionate hands of judges, not decided by inflamed – and not always well-informed – citizens.

Still, the common sense of people who are not lawyers, and who are representative of the community in a way that lawyers cannot be, should not be kept out of the courtroom, and a way needs to be found for involving non-lawyers in the judicial process to make it more straightforward, less arcane, and more expressive of the democratic nature of the state. This is a topic on which the government of the day might consult the Law Reform Commission. The principle seems right, but the practicalities are daunting.

Judges' Pay

A referendum allowing the government to reduce judges' pay was passed in 2011. The wording may have been questionable, but the principle that when the pay of all public servants is to be reduced judges should not be exempt is clearly right, as a huge majority agreed.

Unlike other public servants, judges do not rise through the ranks, with ever-increasing salaries, but are appointed from among practitioners. There needs to be some rough parity between the incomes of judges and the maximum income a successful practising lawyer may earn, and lawyers' incomes are discussed in Chapter 6. If judges are not paid adequately, competent lawyers will not aspire to become judges. The government will be acting foolishly if it reduces the salaries of judges without also reducing the incomes of practising lawyers. Indeed, we may regret it in years to come if we wind up with mediocre judges, appointed not on merit but because nobody fit for the job would take it at the salary offered. And remember, it is very difficult to get rid of incompetent judges.

Finally on this topic, it has been suggested that judges' pay should be set by some independent body, so that judges would be seen to be independent of the other branches of government.

This seems unrealistic. It is the function of the government to see that access to justice is available to all citizens, and this includes ensuring that courthouses are staffed with competent judges. Citizens will blame the government if there are no judges, or only incompetent ones. If we give them that responsibility, they must also have the means to discharge it. How can they recruit good judges – or fairly be blamed for not recruiting them – if they cannot fix the pay and conditions that go with the job?

The Commercial Court

Since 2004, there has been a separate division of the High Court to handle commercial litigation. There is general agreement that it works well and has justified its existence. It is available only for business disputes exceeding one million euro. Claims for personal injuries and family disputes are excluded. An action that has been admitted to the Commercial Court will be processed much more rapidly than other actions, and the judges who administer the Commercial Court participate actively in moving litigation through the system.

That is good news, for Plaintiffs whose claim is handled by the Commercial Court, perhaps more than for Defendants. But what about the rest of us? We wait in a queue for a hearing. So long as all litigants stood in the same queue, the service may have been inadequate, but at least it was fair. It ceases to seem fair when people standing in that queue see other litigants drive past them in Rolls-Royces.

As well as seeming unfair, is it unconstitutional? Article 40.1 of the Constitution says: 'All citizens shall, as human persons, be held equal before the law.' With a Commercial Court in place, one citizen commences litigation in the High Court, his claim qualifies for admission to the Commercial Court, and he therefore receives the treatment available to people engaged in commercial litigation, while another whose claim does not qualify for the Commercial Court has to go through a much less streamlined process and wait much longer for a hearing. Are they held equal before the law? The establishment of the

Commercial Court has led to a situation where there is a two-tier system for administering justice. The public might discuss whether this is fair. And should not lawyers debate whether it is constitutional?

If it is not, the answer should be to give all litigants the kind of treatment that only 'commercial litigants' currently enjoy, not to downgrade the services of the Commercial Court.

Medical Negligence

Has the law relating to medical negligence swung too far in favour of Plaintiffs, and against doctors and hospitals? Claims where children have been injured in the course of their birth are a striking example. Parents bringing up a badly damaged child face enormous difficulties and we give them very little of the help that their situation requires, and that decent human feeling should willingly supply. But is suing the doctor a satisfactory solution? In some cases, the answer will be yes. A doctor who fails to deliver the standard of care his patients are entitled to expect should be answerable to them. But doctors, like the rest of us, blunder innocently, and innocent errors are much more common than intentional 'badness' or serious incompetence.

A maternity hospital that is not busy and does not handle a substantial volume of work will not serve its patients well, because the people who staff it will not develop the expertise their patients need them to bring to their difficult and demanding work. (I do not describe such a hospital as a 'Centre of Excellence', because I think that phrase and its companion 'Fair Deal' are slogans dreamt up by the Department of Health in an attempt to mislead the public, not accurate descriptions.) So, women about to give birth act wisely if they choose a busy hospital with well-trained, experienced staff. But in a busy hospital, however well run, things can go wrong. Vigilance can reduce the incidence of error, but can never eliminate it.

There is something incongruous about a High Court trial of an action against an obstetrician, a midwife or a maternity hospital. The litigation proceeds slowly, over days, at a pace set by the judge and lawyers. *Andante* would be a kind description. At the end of the hearing, the judge will often 'reserve his decision', that is, postpone it and take his time about writing it. This contrasts dramatically with what happened in the hospital, maybe years before, in the events the judge is trying to understand. The process of giving birth does not always start when it was expected to, but once it does, it continues. No doctor, nurse or midwife can delay it or take time to ponder how to respond, let alone 'reserve a decision'. Inevitably, some of the decisions they take under pressure will be good ones, some will be less than perfect, and some may have tragic consequences. That is the nature of their work. Childbirth is natural, but it is not risk-free.

It is understandable that a judge does not want to leave a brain-damaged child in the care of parents who cannot cope because they lack the resources. But a finding in favour of a Plaintiff is a finding against Defendants, and a finding of professional negligence against a medical professional stigmatises him. There are situations where that is as it should be, but there are also many conscientious and skilled medical people who have been unfairly found to have wronged their patients.

A distinguished US judge once said that a Defendant in a criminal trial is entitled to a fair trial, not a perfect one. Similarly, patients of any medical professional, whether in a maternity hospital or elsewhere, are entitled to a competent professional service from people trained to the level they claim, and with the competence that they ought to have acquired. They are not entitled to a perfect service, and to impose on the medical profession an obligation to provide a perfect service is unfair, to doctors and their patients.

I suggest that if a judge finds a medical practitioner to have been negligent, he should automatically notify that person's professional body of his finding so that they can consider whether to remove that person from their register, to safeguard other patients. If the evidence does not lead the judge to doubt the professional's fitness to practise, he should, at the very least, hesitate before bringing in a finding of negligence. The same principle should apply to a hospital. A finding of negligence should normally constitute a recommendation to the Health Information and Quality Authority that the hospital be considered for closure.

But before we could justify amending the legal standard of what constitutes medical negligence in that way, we would have to have put in place effective systems, adequately financed, to support people who are wholly or partly disabled through medical mishap, and their families.

'Right-thinking People'

Finally, here is a phrase to beware of: 'all right-thinking people will agree...' You will see it only in judgments. Lord Denning used a very similar phrase – 'every sensible person in the land would say...' – when he ended, for a time, attempts by prisoners of Irish origin to get justice. As he said, rightly, their claim that they had been unjustly convicted as a result of police misconduct and judicial incompetence opened an 'appalling vista' of institutional injustice, but he went dramatically wrong when he ignored the maxim *'Fiat justitia ruat caelum'* – 'let justice be done though the heavens fall'. Beware of any pronouncement in which you see a reference to 'right-thinking people', or equivalent. It is an attempt to conceal the lack of any justification for the conclusion that follows it, and to exercise a not very subtle psychological pressure on us not to question that conclusion. (If we do, we identify ourselves as 'wrong-thinking' and may be ignored.)

They can also be interpreted – but not justified – in a different way, as an indication that the judge is about to express what he takes to be the views of 'the man in the street'. If so, it means he is about to do something for which he is not qualified, and for which many people, some of whom may be sensible, or right-thinking, or both, think the nature of his job disqualifies him.

Chapter 5

Proposals for Reform at Practitioner Level

This chapter offers some suggestions about how to reform the practice of law in Ireland. It is based on a view that over a period of years the legal profession has lost its way, has become detached from its essence, and that the people who run our legal system, both practitioners and judges, need to recover their focus on what they ought to do and how they ought to do it.

Both organisations of lawyers in Ireland, barristers and solicitors, have evolved elaborate written codes of practice, setting out in detail what members of each are allowed to do, what they should not do and what they must not do. These codes say what they consider is acceptable and what is not for practitioners vis-à-vis their clients, their colleagues and the courts. They do not necessarily represent how the citizens of Ireland might think lawyers should act and should not act, in exchange for the monopoly they enjoy.

As discussed in Chapter 1, the monopoly lawyers enjoy, of being the only people allowed to represent clients in court and perform a wide range of other legal work for payment, was conferred on them in the public interest, not so that they could exploit it to make themselves rich. That view underlies everything that follows.

If we consider that the system of Pleadings described in Chapter 1 has existed for hundreds of years, from a time when communication was difficult and slow, it is not hard to see that *Nolumus Mutari* has influenced the practice of law. Lawyers have accepted modern communications to the extent that documents can now be exchanged electronically, but not to the extent of considering whether it is still sensible that those documents must follow a formula that was evolved in former times, to meet different conditions. They may tell you that it would be foolish to abandon a system that has worked well for hundreds of years. But has it worked well? Is it not, as Chapter 1 of this book argues, too slow and too expensive? Does it not operate in a way that denies access to justice to a substantial group of citizens?

The system may work well for those who operate it, and the Competition Authority's statistics about lawyers' incomes suggest that it does, as we will see in Chapter 7. But the legal system exists for those who seek justice, not for those who make their living by serving it. And if there is a conflict between potential 'consumers' of justice and those whose job is to supply what they need, consumers should prevail. We need a rethinking among lawyers about their role in the community. And we need a reformed legal process, ideally one set up in collaboration between lawyers and the rest of the community.

Few people will dispute that a culture of greed infected Ireland in recent decades. Few will dispute, either, that it infected lawyers, like others. However, there is a core of idealism among lawyers, too, and it would be cynical to assume that they will not embark on re-examination of their role in society without compulsion.

As a starting point, I propose that lawyers should consider the following questions:

• Given that lawyers enjoy a monopoly over the supply of legal services, does that impose on them duties or obligations that other citizens do not have?

• If so, to whom are those duties owed?

- Do lawyers as a group have different sets of duties to different sets of people?

- If so, what are their duties to each set?

To these questions, I suggest the following replies. Lawyers are morally obliged, both as individuals and as a group, to any client who may seek their services to ensure so far as they can that those services are made as good as they can be. 'Good' includes as cheap as they can reasonably be made, consistent with meeting the clients' needs. That is, lawyers as a group have a moral duty to the rest of us to ensure that the courts deliver justice as inexpensively and as quickly as is consistent with doing justice; that the transfer of property is made as cheap and as rapid as it can be consistent with its being legally effective; and that all other legal services are delivered adequately, meaning that they meet the reasonable demands of citizens, including a valid preference for a speedy service and to avoid having to pay more than they need.

Thus, lawyers have a duty not only to the individual client, but also to the community within which they live and work, and to all the members of that community – users and prospective users of legal services – to ensure so far as they can that legal services are as cheap and as fast as they can realistically be made. If the two lawyer bodies were to accept such obligations, lawyers would enjoy greater public confidence and respect than they do now. They would be trusted and respected because they would deserve trust and respect. (And there would be fewer anti-lawyer jokes.)

Some lawyers may feel that these recommendations go beyond what is reasonable. But surely it is not for lawyers to decide unilaterally what responsibilities they should accept in exchange for the monopoly the community has given them. At a minimum, there should be dialogue. And if there is disagreement, we, who through our organs of government gave lawyers their monopoly, should have the casting vote.

Litigation Lawyers' Obligations

If lawyers accept the above concept, it seems to follow that lawyers who engage in litigation should accept additional responsibilities:

- To their clients, to help them to settle their disputes as quickly and cheaply as possible, assuming settlement is their first choice, as it usually is. If settlement is not possible, they should make the process of litigation as speedy and inexpensive as it can be.

- To judges who will try disputes in which they are engaged, to give them a comprehensive written summary of the issues, so that they can perform their function of doing justice, efficiently and at minimum cost. That includes not wasting their time on irrelevancies or issues that do not require their attention.

Of course, the primary duty to help litigants through the process cheaply and quickly falls on the lawyers representing each client, but I argue that each lawyer has a secondary duty to the client of the other, based on the fact that the other's client is a member of the community from which the lawyer has received his monopoly. A lawyer who delays or complicates litigation, or needlessly increases its cost, is in breach of his duty to citizens and others, irrespective of whether his own client or someone else will pay the bill.

If this proposition is accepted, it will require rethinking among lawyers. For example, it is generally assumed that if a Defendant instructs a lawyer to delay the legal process, the lawyer is not merely entitled to comply but is bound to. But if someone seeks justice, he should not be denied it, nor should it be delayed. This is a concept that has been part of English law as far back as the Magna Carta, in 1215. I contend that someone whose calling is to help the community through the process of asserting their rights in law and in justice perverts that calling if he conspires with his own client to frustrate another's quest for justice. It follows that a lawyer is ethically obliged not to engage in delaying tactics, and should decline instructions to do so.

It should be the first duty of lawyers on both sides of a dispute to try to negotiate a settlement. If they fail, they ought to consider mediation, and consider which of the two types of mediation described in Chapter 2 is likely best to meet their clients' needs. Lawyers will need to ensure they are adequately informed in this area, as they should on any topic where clients may look to them for advice. Advice is part of what lawyers sell, so they are bound to ensure it is of what they call 'merchantable quality'.

The second duty, to bring the complaint to a hearing quickly and cheaply, falls on lawyers representing both the Plaintiff and the Defendant. How is it best discharged? The traditional method is through Pleadings, as described in Chapter 1. But is that what clients want? Does it help judges? Surely a better approach would be for lawyers on both sides in litigation to agree and to record, *in a single document*:

- The uncontested facts

- Facts requiring formal proof, but not seriously in dispute

- Whatever facts are in genuine dispute, and the different versions of them

- The issues to be decided by the judge

- The names of prospective witnesses and a list of relevant documents

- The legal principles each party claims should be applied.

Probably, most cases could be summarised in not more than two pages. Very complex litigation might require more, but that is exactly the kind of litigation where the parties and the judge would benefit most from having the issues summarised succinctly, instead of in an indigestible mass of Pleadings.

There might be an incidental benefit. Since the lawyers on each side would have to collaborate in preparing the document, instead of firing Pleadings at each other, they would be nudged towards dialogue, and perhaps settlement.

Two other propositions follow from this one, as corollaries:

1. Matters not seriously in dispute but requiring formal proof should be disposed of before the court hearing. Lawyers who insist on wasting a judge's time by demanding formal proof of such matters in court should be penalised. There should be an exception if the lawyers can show that their intransigence was because of peremptory instructions from their client, given after receiving adequate written advice on the consequences. If the lawyers were exempted from liability, of course it should fall on their client.

2. If the lawyers cannot agree the wording of the summary for the judge, each of them might present his own version, but unreasonable failure on either side to agree should attract penalties, as in 1 above. Either party would be entitled to apply to a judge to arbitrate on a failure to agree, if it seemed separate versions would make the judge's task harder. Again, there should be similar protection from penalties in favour of a lawyer who can show that he acted on his client's peremptory instructions, but the sanctions would then fall on the client.

The purpose of all this, of course, is not to penalise either litigants or lawyers, but to protect clients. Citizens who are involved in litigation should not have to pay more than is needed in order for them to get justice, and anyone unnecessarily inflating the cost to them of pursuing justice should foot the bill.

A system by which lawyers present such a summary document to the trial judge, instead of the traditional Pleadings, would require an amendment to the Rules of Court. Since they are prepared and amended by lawyers and changes can be speedily ratified by the Minister for Justice, this need not take long or cause problems, if lawyers are willing to co-operate.

Disposing of Non-contentious Issues before a Hearing

What lawyers call the 'onus of proof' lies on a Plaintiff in civil proceedings, and he will lose his case if he fails to prove it 'on balance of probability'. A Defendant is entitled to 'put the Plaintiff on proof' of all issues, that is, to require him to produce formal evidence of every aspect of his case, and to ask the judge to dismiss his claim if he fails on any issue. This should not change, though, again, a Defendant who puts a Plaintiff to unnecessary expense or wastes a judge's time on issues that are not genuinely in dispute should pay the additional expenses incurred. If the lawyers are to blame, they should pay, not their clients. For example, a Plaintiff's lawyer might write to the Defendant's along the following lines:

> *Dr. Peter Jones, who treated our client when he was brought to hospital after the accident, is now working in Somalia. We propose his written report (copy enclosed) should be admitted as evidence at the hearing without his being required to return to Ireland to give oral evidence of what he has stated in the enclosed report.*

If the Defendant's lawyers said no, the Plaintiff should have the right to ask a judge to rule on his proposal. Alternatively, if the Plaintiff can afford it, and Dr. Jones is willing, the Plaintiff could fly him back from Somalia for the hearing. Either way, the same principle should apply. If someone unreasonably puts another to expense, justice requires that the person who has acted unreasonably should pay the cost incurred. This should be so irrespective of whether he is a litigant or a lawyer, and irrespective of the outcome of the litigation.

Applying this principle should have one very useful result. It should bring to an end a practice in litigation by which lawyers obstruct each other, and each other's clients, knowing that they will not have to face any unpleasant consequences.

'Not Pleaded'

As noted in Chapter 1, a claim may be dismissed if the facts that emerge in evidence are significantly different from what the Plaintiff's lawyers set out in the Statement of Claim. It will be harder for a Defendant to advance that proposition if the document presented to the judge is the work of both sides. But whatever the machinery and practical problems may be, the same principles apply. I think they are as follows:

- If the facts as they emerge show that the Plaintiff has no valid complaint, his claim should be dismissed.

- If that does not apply:
    * a Plaintiff should not be deprived of justice because of an error in recording his claim
    * a Defendant should not be prejudiced by having to respond on the spot to a claim of which he did not have fair notice
    * people, including lawyers as well as litigants, should accept responsibility for their errors
    * a judge's function is to do justice.

Let us see how that might work in practice. Take the litigation described in Chapter 1, where a company sued its former auditors, and their 'audit papers' would be crucial in deciding the issue of whether the auditors had done their work negligently. You may remember that the current system of Pleadings made that case almost unmanageable.

Under a reformed system, the first step, as at present, would be for the solicitors representing the company to write to the auditors setting out their client's complaint – or, rather, their suspicion, since they would not have seen the crucial audit papers and therefore could not formulate their complaint. Then, unless the auditors admitted negligence, the next step, as now, would be for the company's solicitors to issue a High Court summons, and the solicitors representing the auditors would 'appear', that is, go on record as solicitors for the Defendants.

Nothing new, so far, but the next step would be novel. The solicitors for the Plaintiff (the company) would write to the solicitors for the Defendant (the auditors) seeking access to the auditors' working papers, so that they could start drafting the summary document to be placed before the trial judge. If the auditors gave them access, the company's lawyers would examine the audit papers. At that point, each party would have the same information and the same opportunity to assess it. If the papers disclosed no grounds for complaint against the auditors, and the company acknowledged that this was so, they would presumably discontinue their court proceedings, pay any expense the auditors had incurred, which would probably not be large at that stage, and the matter would end. If the parties could not agree on whether the auditors had been negligent or not, or on the extent of the company's losses, their lawyers would start negotiating a settlement. If negotiation failed, they might invite a mediator or conciliator to help them, and if all efforts to settle failed, they would agree their statement of the issues and go to trial on them. The judge would read that statement before the hearing started.

The company's advocate might not think it was necessary to make an 'opening statement', but if he did, it would probably not be very long. If he started on a long oration, the judge might interrupt him to ask if he proposed to say anything that was not included in the agreed statement of the issues. Such a question would be both useful and pointed. If the company's advocate said he was going to talk about matters that were not contained in the agreed statement, the judge could then ask why that material had been omitted. If he said he was not going to add anything, the next question – probably not asked, because it would not be necessary – would be why was he wasting the judge's time going over material the judge had already read?

If the auditors refused access to their working papers, the company's lawyers would apply for an order directing the auditors to allow inspection of them.

How would the judge decide that request? Traditionally, judges have been reluctant to allow Plaintiffs to engage in what they call 'fishing expeditions' to find grounds for pursuing an action. But that approach may not be sustainable to the extent that it may be inconsistent with a legal maxim, *ubi jus ibi remedium*, which means that in a society where law and justice prevail, there must be a remedy for injustice. Allowing someone who may be a wrongdoer to escape responsibility by withholding evidence of his wrongdoing infringes that principle. A further argument in a case such as this is that the company has paid the auditors for their work and is now asking the people it employed to account for how they did the job.

If a judge ordered the auditors to give the company and its lawyers access to their working papers, he should also order that whoever was responsible for the auditors' initial refusal of access should reimburse the Plaintiff company what it had cost them to enforce what the judge had decided was their legal right.

Under such a system, the litigation described in Chapter 1 would either have been disposed of without a court hearing or would have been brought into court reasonably briskly and without unnecessary documentation, instead of being irretrievably bogged down in a mass of paper.

Finally, one thing that emerges from the list of lawyers' duties proposed in this chapter is that the interests of lawyers in earning a living, and keeping files active in order to do so, is often in conflict with their client's wish to have a dispute disposed of as quickly and as cheaply as possible. Inherent in what has been said earlier in this chapter is that lawyers have two additional duties. They should always be conscious of that conflict of interest. And they should always resolve it in their client's favour.

In the next chapter we will look more closely at lawyers' fees.

Chapter 6

Lawyers' Fees

A barrister called Kevin Liston, who died a few years ago, had a long career, and eventually became the longest-serving member of his profession, and was automatically 'leader' in any case in which he appeared. Being 'leader' meant that he decided the level of fees, for himself and for his colleagues. He was exceptionally able, and also remarkably modest. I was told that younger 'Seniors', while respecting Kevin's exceptional ability, and being delighted to work with him, were always a little disappointed to be 'led' by him, because as well as being old-fashioned in his standards he was, in their view, old-fashioned in the level of fees he sought. They thought they were worth more than he felt he and they should be paid. For his part, he was content to have a comfortable lifestyle, did not aspire to become wealthy, and seems not to have wanted his income to rise to the level he could have commanded if he had been willing to charge what the market might have borne. His example influences what follows.

As mentioned earlier, after a case has been decided in court, the loser will usually be ordered to pay the winner's legal bills. The winner's lawyers must produce their bill, and here is another example of how tradition operates against the interests of clients – and clients, let me remind you, are you and me. You might think that if a lawyer has quoted to his client an hourly rate of so many euro for himself, a lower rate for assistants, and lower again for a trainee working on the case, establishing the total would be matter of recording time accurately, followed by simple arithmetic. Not so. There is a traditional style for preparing solicitors' bills for what is archaically called 'taxation' by a court official. Busy lawyers do not have either the time or the expertise to prepare such bills, and they invariably contract the work out to another professional, who used to be called a 'Costs Drawer' but now styles himself a 'Legal Costs Accountant'. He is another person who makes a living from the legal process, and who is eventually, though indirectly, paid by the community. His work is currently indispensable, but in a better-ordered system he would be redundant. He prepares a bill in the archaic (or 'traditional') style and presents it to the court official to be assessed. If the claim was heard in the Circuit Court (which is ranked between the District Court at the bottom of the scale, with power to order only comparatively small awards, and the High Court, which has unlimited jurisdiction), a County Registrar will assess their bill, but if it is in the High Court, a Taxing Master will.

You would assume that if a bill is examined by a County Registrar or Taxing Master that would prevent over-charging. And you would be partly right, but only partly. When barristers' fees are included in a bill, their 'brief fee' for appearing in court and the daily 'refreshers' (paid for each day after the first) are usually the biggest items. And each of these officials, whether County Registrar or Taxing Master, is accustomed to applying a rule that they should not question the level of those fees. The theory is that if a responsible solicitor, looking after his client's interests, negotiated and agreed that level of charge on behalf of his client, it would be wrong to renegotiate that agreement. There are examples of Taxing Masters departing from this rule in some cases, perhaps where the level of charge was exceptional, but it still stands as the general rule.

Like many of the concepts we have looked at, this is plausible, but does not stand up to examination. In the first place, it has no relevance in the 'no foal, no fee' cases we talked about earlier, where lawyers take on a claim on behalf of a client who cannot afford to pay them, knowing that, if they win, the other side will pay them and, if they lose, they will not be paid. A solicitor in such a case has no reason to protect his client from over-paying the barrister, because both know the client will never be called on to pay. Moreover, in 'no foal, no fee' cases both solicitor and barrister are unlikely to undercharge for their work. Unlike a claim where they represent a well-off client and know they will be paid whatever the outcome, they are taking a gamble. Like any gambler, they may feel entitled to a bigger prize if they win than they would accept from a safe investment.

But even in cases where the client is solvent and the lawyers do not take on the risk of working on a 'no foal, no fee' basis, solicitors have a number of incentives not to engage in hard bargaining about the level of a barrister's charge. First and most significant is the solicitor's interest in his own income. If a barrister's fee is modest, that suggests the case did not call for heavy work or carry great responsibility, and implies the solicitor's charge should be modest, too. And, of course, vice versa. But there are other reasons why solicitors and barristers do not engage in hard bargaining about fees.

They work together. Barristers expect a flow of work from a solicitor with whom they have established a good relationship – and this of course may act as an incentive to charge his clients modestly. Similarly, solicitors come to rely on barristers they are accustomed to working with. Such a relationship between solicitor and barrister, as described in the next chapter, involves give and take on both sides. A solicitor who sends plenty of work to a barrister will feel justified in asking him to take on a job that may be under-rewarded or even unpaid, because he has offered the barrister much well-paid work, and knows the barrister values their relationship and how it contributes to his income. Against that, in another situation, representing a different client, a solicitor may feel he should not haggle over a fee proposed by the same barrister. So, if one party has lost his case in court and an award of costs has been made against him, the comfortable relationship between the solicitor and barrister on the other side may mean that he will find himself paying the winner's lawyers more than is justified. The assumption that a fee agreed between those two lawyers was negotiated at arm's length in the interests of their client, and therefore should not be reopened, does not reflect reality.

Judges usually make an order that the losing side should pay the winner's expenses incurred at all stages of the proceedings, without enquiring whether that order represents justice. For example, during the early stages of the process leading up to the trial, the parties may have come into court on a preliminary issue, such as whether the Plaintiff's replies to the Defendant's Request for Particulars are adequate. If such a preliminary issue had come before a judge and he decided it, one way or the other, he probably ordered that the costs incurred on that issue should be 'reserved'. That is, he did not decide who should pay them, but left that decision to be decided at the full hearing. Almost invariably, 'reserved costs' are ordered to be part of the 'costs of the cause', which means they are to be paid by the loser. That hardly seems fair, if on the preliminary issue the ultimate loser was in the right and the winner in the wrong.

Of course, it can be argued that if the loser had not contested a claim which he ultimately lost, but had settled it at the outset, the costs on the preliminary issue would not have been incurred. Nevertheless, it seems doubtful that either justice or the public interest in controlling the cost of litigation is served when the loser has to pay extra because the lawyers on the ultimately successful side earlier took an unjustified position.

That pattern may have another result, which it would be hard to measure. If lawyers know that their client has an excellent prospect of emerging as the winner, they may be tempted to 'chance their arm' on preliminary issues. If, instead, lawyers knew that taking an unjustified position in a preliminary skirmish would cost their client, or themselves, money, irrespective of the eventual result, there might be fewer such skirmishes.

And, while lawyers' fees have been rising to the point where Kevin Liston seems like a relic of times long past, judges have done little to resist. Lawyers come under the jurisdiction of the courts. Judges formally admit new lawyers to the profession.

They also decide whether a lawyer who has misbehaved should be disqualified. So why have they not been active in protecting the interests of the public, by keeping lawyers' charges within reasonable limits? In Chapter 4 we saw how judges who are former barristers continue to be members of the barristers' 'club'. Another, related, reason for judicial inertia on fees may be illustrated by a story told by the late Judge Kingsmill Moore. He was stopped in his car by a Garda for some parking offence, and told he would be prosecuted. The Garda asked his name, was told it was 'Kingsmill Moore', and then asked his profession. On hearing 'Judge of the Supreme Court' the Garda solemnly tore the page out of his notebook, explaining, 'Dog doesn't eat dog'.

Charging, and Overcharging

The proposition that lawyers have a moral duty not to charge excessively for their services does not seem open to serious objection. Surely, then, it should apply irrespective of who is going to have to pay. The identity of the person mulcted is beside the point. To overcharge is to behave less than honestly towards the person who has to pay. It is also an abuse by the lawyer of the monopoly the community has awarded to him and his colleagues. If so, overcharging should be regarded as professional misconduct, creating an obligation to make restitution to the overcharged person, whether it is the lawyer's client or someone else who wound up paying.

But what does 'overcharging' mean? The view current among lawyers is that if the client agrees to pay the fee the lawyer proposes, nobody else is entitled to question it. That most clients have no idea of what represents a fair charge, and that the bargaining positions of lawyer and client are unbalanced, are irrelevant. The client has agreed the fee, and that is the end of the matter. The same applies even if the client hasn't personally agreed a barrister's fee, if his solicitor has agreed it on his behalf. Clearly, that view is inconsistent with any serious attempt to limit lawyers' charges or curb the cost of litigation.

Let us look at how lawyers charge for their services, and try to identify when a charge becomes an overcharge, and, of more practical relevance, how we can know if that line has been crossed. The simple approach, as of the judge who said of pornography, 'I can't define it but I know it when I see it', does not work. To take an hourly rate of charge and say no lawyer should exceed it would seem simple, but it would also be impractical. Barristers are 'sole traders', and do not need much in the way of premises to work from or staff to support them in their work. A solicitor has to do a great deal of mundane work that barristers avoid. He also has to take responsibility for money belonging to clients, and is rightly required to maintain a fairly sophisticated accounting system. Unlike a barrister, a solicitor cannot operate on his own. He needs an office and an organisation, in order to serve his clients. And, of course, he has to pay for them.

In years gone by, a well-managed solicitors' firm would expect that at least two-thirds of its income would go on overheads, with a balance of perhaps 30-33 per cent available for the owner or owners. The mammoth law firms that now dominate that branch of the profession may perhaps benefit from economies of scale, and be able to distribute among their partners more than one-third of gross fee income. But whatever the percentages may be, disposable income for any lawyer in any year is the amount by which his total income exceeds his expenses, and for solicitors those expenses are much higher than they are for barristers. They must generate more income to produce an equivalent level of reward. An hourly rate that rewarded adequately a barrister with low overheads would probably leave a solicitor trading at a loss. Conversely, a rate universally applied that would leave a well-managed solicitors' practice with a reasonable income for its partners or owner would probably grossly overpay a barrister.

Perhaps the best way to decide whether a lawyer is overcharging or charging fairly is not to look at the amount paid to him by each client but at the amount left in his hands at the end of the year, after paying his expenses. If we adopt that approach, then a lawyer whose income from his work substantially and consistently exceeds an agreed level is probably (*prima facie*, as lawyers say) overcharging his clients.

What should that level be? As we will see in the next chapter, a Competition Authority report showed that in 2002 the average annual income for all lawyers was €164,000, and for Senior Counsel it was €330,000. Lawyers, of course, will argue that market forces should dictate the level of legal fees, and this also seems to be the assumption of the Competition Authority. That has been to lawyers' advantage, because they, the suppliers of legal services, have had much more influence on fee levels than consumers, who pay them. We all, lawyers as well as clients, should acknowledge that this approach has not worked for clients, and that it should be abandoned.

But how? As described earlier, the citizens of this country have decided, though their representatives, that they should be advised and represented on legal matters by people who have been trained to the work and have been tested and found to be competent, and that people who have not been through a fairly rigorous process of training and testing should not be allowed to practise law. We took that decision in our own interests, because we want to be advised and represented by competent people. In giving a monopoly over that kind of work to adequately trained people, we recognise that they expect to make a living by serving us. Indeed, given that what they do is not simple, and that in order to become qualified to do it they have to go through a long and expensive education and post-qualification training, we do not grudge them a decent standard of living, well above the average industrial wage. We also recognise that solicitors act as trustees of their clients' money, and we acknowledge that people who do so should be decently paid, for numerous valid reasons.

But conferring a monopoly on lawyers does not mean we intended that a significant number of them should use it to become very wealthy, paid much more than we pay judges, or that it should be a financial sacrifice, not a benefit and an honour, for a practitioner to become a judge. Nor did we intend that in attaining such incomes lawyers would put justice beyond the pockets of middle-class people, as described in Chapter 1.

In trying to work out a formula for halting the ever-upward progress of lawyers' incomes, I was helped by one of history's great figures, Benjamin Franklin. James Madison's semi-official record of the Debates in the Federal Convention of 1787, from which the US Constitution evolved, includes this account of a characteristic contribution by Franklin (I have not modernised the spelling, which I think is pretty clear):

> *Docr. Franklin observed that two modes of chusing the Judges had been mentioned, to wit, by the Legislature and by the Executive. He wished such other modes to be suggested as might occur to other gentlemen; it being a point of great moment. He would mention one which he had understood was practiced in Scotland. He then in a brief and entertaining manner related a Scotch mode, in which the nomination proceeded from the Lawyers, who always selected the ablest of the profession in order to get rid of him, and share his practice among themselves. It was here he said the interest of the electors to make the best choice, which should always be made the case if possible.*

The approach to choosing judges that Franklin described would be impossible in Ireland in the twenty-first century. Too many well-qualified lawyers, like the barrister mentioned in the next chapter, would decline to become judges because they 'couldn't afford it'. But what Franklin' said gives us a benchmark for deciding a reasonable level for lawyers' income. Lawyers should aspire to become judges, not refuse the job because it does not pay enough. Judges should be paid at a rate that makes the position reasonably attractive, and recognises the importance of their work and the responsibility a judge carries. No lawyer should be paid so much that accepting a Superior Court judge's salary would represent a sacrifice for him.

I think it would be unreasonable to say the incomes of practising lawyers should never exceed that of judges, because a judge has a secure, pensioned job until he retires, and practising lawyers do not. It seems fair that there should be some element of extra pay for lack of security. But if a lawyer's income consistently and substantially exceeds that of a High Court judge, I propose it should *prima facie* be a reasonable inference that he has achieved that level of income by overcharging his clients.

We need to give a precise meaning to those words 'consistently' and 'substantially'. I propose the inference should apply if a lawyer in any year is paid more than one and a half times a High Court judge's income, or if his average income over a period of, say, three years exceeds that of a High Court judge by, say, one-third. I suggest those ratios mainly to illustrate the concept, recognising that they may be too high, or too low.

I used above the expressions *'prima facie'*, and 'reasonable inference'. They mean that if a practising lawyer's income exceeds the agreed level, he appears to have over-charged. He has the right to show other reasons for his income, and demonstrate that over-charging is not the cause. But when the level of his income has been established, the onus of showing that he has not been overcharging falls on him.

Could it happen that in a given year a lawyer's income was extremely high in comparison with a judge's, without over-charging being the reason? I think so. Lawyers are not always paid promptly, particularly where 'costs' have to be 'taxed' as described earlier. A big fee earned in a long drawn-out case in one year, but not paid until the following year, could cause a bulge in income in the year when it was paid.

It can also happen in the life of a lawyer that he suddenly becomes much sought-after, for example if he has been involved in a high-profile case and won a conspicuous success. If work from new sources comes flooding in, he may not have the courage to refuse it. Most lawyers go through a phase in their working lives of worrying about whether the next client or the next case is going to materialise, and are reluctant to refuse any work that comes their way. Sudden success might lead to a lawyer being swamped with work before he has learnt that to say no may be right and wise and doesn't necessarily involve professional suicide. A lawyer who can show that during a given year he worked very long hours and can produce records of the fees he charged and show that they were not excessive, should readily rebut the presumption of overcharging.

If lawyers' incomes are to be compared with judges', both must be looked at on the same basis, that is, before tax, and after reasonable pension contributions. Of course, the comparison should not take into account any schemes either may have adopted to reduce their tax bills. But such incomes, though adequate for anyone to live on in comfort, would not be at the level that would lead many people to think of tax avoidance. Lawyers would have to file a record of their incomes annually, presumably with their respective professional bodies. Since we all file tax returns, that does not seem an excessive burden.

A system like this should not be difficult to operate. A lawyer can estimate at the beginning of the year what his overheads are likely to be for the following twelve months. He knows how many hours' work he can put in during those months without endangering his health, or depriving himself of a life outside work. It does not require a difficult calculation to show approximately how much he needs to charge for each of those hours in order to cover his overheads and earn a reasonable income. He should also be able to assess how much unremunerative or under-remunerated work he will have to do. He will certainly have a pretty clear picture of the ratio of well-paid to underpaid work by the time his income has reached the level at which the question becomes relevant to him. He should then be able to calculate how much he can honestly charge his clients. He can also assess whether a higher rate would leave him open to being accused of overcharging, an accusation that implies a lack of honesty.

Fixing a maximum income for lawyers should lead to standard rates emerging over time, as lawyers make the sort of calculation described above. Rates will presumably be at different levels for barristers and solicitors. Once experience has shown what rates of hourly charge provide acceptable incomes (acceptable, that is, to the people who pay their lawyers, as well as to the recipients), rates should become reasonably standard among lawyers. We could then say that a lawyer is *prima facie* guilty of overcharging if:

1. His income exceeds the established ratio of a High Court judge's income, or

2. He charges a client at a rate that significantly exceeds what has emerged as standard.

Standard hourly rates should go a long way to discouraging lawyers from trying to circumvent 'maximum income' rules, but the rules should be worded to provide that any attempt to conceal income while appearing to operate within the limit would be regarded as dishonest, and punished severely.

People who see their barrister in court, winning their case for them by his skilful advocacy (or losing it, in spite of his skill) may resent having to pay their humdrum boring solicitor more per hour for sitting in court saying nothing, while the barrister triumphs, or bravely and skilfully goes down to defeat. But the skill of the advocate is useless if the preparatory work has not been done, that work requires an organisation, and the organisation will not exist or will not operate effectively unless clients pay for it.

It hardly seems necessary to say that the calculation of income would assume a minimum number of hours worked. A lawyer who found he wasn't sufficiently in demand to be kept busy would not be entitled to raise his rate of charge to compensate.

Another advantage to clients in such a system would be that lawyers should give them a faster service, because they would be less likely to hold on to work they are not doing. Under the current system, many lawyers take on work that they cannot do immediately, justifying it in the following way. 'Client 1's problem is urgent and I must deal with it today. Client 2's problem isn't urgent, so I can agree today to represent him and tackle it next week, when I'll be under less pressure, and his interests won't suffer from a week's delay. Client 3's problem is difficult. I'll need time to think about it and do some research.

But so would any other lawyer he might consult, so it's OK for me to take it on but not to tackle it at once. So that's what I'll do, because each of these will develop into an interesting and well-remunerated piece of work, and I don't want to pass any of them up.'

But what tends to happen is that before a successful lawyer has got round to client 2's problem, or client 3's, he becomes involved with the urgent problems of clients 4, 5 and 6, who have appeared subsequently. Clients 2 and 3 keep being moved down the list. Their lawyer begins to feel guilty about how he is neglecting them. Feelings of guilt and shame when he thinks of them and how he is failing them make it harder for him, with each day, to pick up their files.

It is unlikely there is a lawyer in Ireland who has been even moderately successful who does not have on his conscience a client he has failed in this way. I was lucky enough to work in a firm where the problem was recognised, and someone else would take over work that one of us had effectively become unable to do. But there are still some clients whose names I cringe to remember. I would hope that a system that caps lawyers' incomes and fees would make it less likely that lawyers and, more importantly, their clients, would get into the sort of mess caused by lawyers clinging on to work that they do not have time to do. If so, that will be good for lawyers as well as for their clients.

Standardising rates of charge, for barristers and solicitors, should have an additional advantage for them, as well as for their clients. Lawyers should have a good idea at the beginning of each year of how many hours they need to work in order to enjoy a decent income, and not to risk their incomes increasing to a level where they are open to an accusation of overcharging. This should make their lives easier.

Adjudication

If it seems a lawyer may have been overcharging clients, but he denies it, who is to say whether he has? As in any other dispute, the parties should first explore settlement, including at least considering mediation or conciliation. (But a settlement should never be concluded on a basis that allows a lawyer to hold on to the fruits of overcharging, because that would be unjust to the clients who have overpaid him.) The issue has the appearance of a trial, with the accused lawyer as Defendant, so it should presumably be decided by a judge, if outside adjudication is needed. Another, more compelling, reason for a judge adjudicating is that if overcharging is agreed to be professional misconduct, penalties should attach to it, including the lawyer being required to make restitution to the people whose money he has taken. This, clearly, could seriously damage his reputation. So the arguments favour judicial decision-making.

Dealing with such matters will be disagreeable for judges. They are all former practising lawyers, whether barristers or solicitors, and they will be called upon to administer rules that will probably first be resisted and then, assuming they have become binding, resented by their former colleagues. As current judges retire and new ones take their place, the difficulty will tend to increase, not diminish, because the new appointees may see themselves as former 'victims' of rules they are now required to enforce. A few things seem clear.

First, a judge should not adjudicate on a complaint about a lawyer he knows personally. Secondly, so long as ex-barrister judges maintain their membership of King's Inns, they are bound not to adjudicate on a complaint about a barrister, who must be a fellow-member. (This is a further argument, if one were needed, in favour of judges breaking that link when they are appointed.) Thirdly, decisions by a judge against the lawyer concerned should include a written judgment, recording his findings of fact and explaining the reasons for his decision. Fourthly, to secure public confidence in the system there should be some monitoring of decisions, to ensure that the judges are upholding the principle of protecting clients against being overcharged, and not leaning in favour of their former colleagues, whether by exonerating them, imposing very light penalties or not requiring them to make restitution.

An earlier draft of this book proposed that these claims should be dealt with in private, so that a lawyer who was accused of overcharging but exonerated should not suffer damage to his reputation. In the process of revising, I thought about it further and became convinced that a lawyer who has defended himself successfully is unlikely to be injured by an accusation that he was able to rebut, and that the public interest in such matters being dealt with openly, and reported in the media, overrides any interest in keeping such matters private.

Consequences of Proposed Reform

Undoubtedly, if the reforms suggested above, of limiting the incomes of lawyers and simplifying the procedure to be followed before a trial takes place, are adopted, there will be less work for lawyers as well as less income, and some people now gainfully employed in the practice of the law may have to look for a different career. Would it seem harsh to them to introduce reforms immediately? Better to bring them in gradually, over a period of time, or to stagger them? At first sight, that seems attractive. But if we view it from the point of view not of the lawyers but of their clients, it looks different. It would involve saying that for a limited time the public should continue to go through an excessively slow and expensive process to get justice, and should continue to overpay their lawyers.

So, although it may cause difficulty for some lawyers, if we agree that the public interest has priority over the interests of lawyers who serve the public, and that our present system is unfair to the public, reform should be introduced without delay. Lawyers who currently enjoy excessive incomes at our expense are unlikely to experience real hardship, but even if some did, it is not our duty to protect them. As the work is simplified, the number of lawyers needed to do it should diminish and some lawyers may have to seek other careers. Lawyers have valuable skills, are trained to be mentally alert and to respond to reverses. If any find they need to redeploy, the process should be easier for them than for many other redundant workers.

Other Responsibilities of Practitioners

I think practising lawyers should accept that two other, related, responsibilities 'go with the territory'. The nature of their work means that they are more likely than the rest of us to identify weaknesses in the law. A lawyer who specialises in criminal defence work may spot a defect in the wording of a section of an Act or a Rule of Court that enables his client to escape being convicted. One who specialises in taxation law may find a loophole in the tax code that enables his client to wriggle out of paying tax that would otherwise be due. It has been assumed that a lawyer who finds such a loophole is entitled to exploit it indefinitely, and to advance his reputation by doing so. I think that is wrong. A lawyer owes a duty to the community of which he is a member to contribute towards eliminating defects in its legal code. Of course, his first duty is to his client, and he should exploit the loophole to save his client from prison or taxes as the case may be, but having done so he should report it, so that the law can be improved by closing the loophole – unless, of course, the way he exploited it will have brought it to the attention of the relevant authorities.

Lawyers should have a similar duty in relation to the quality and performance of judges. Lawyers have opportunities that the rest of us do not to see whether a judge is doing his job as he should. If he is not, lawyers have a duty not to ignore or hide that fact. If there is a system for keeping an eye on judges to see how they are performing, as suggested in Chapter 5, lawyers should accept a duty to notify those in charge of it if a judge's conduct causes reasonable concern.

Some lawyers may find the idea of 'sneaking' distasteful, but think of it as 'whistle-blowing' and it becomes a duty. And, of course a weakness, like an ailment, may be cured if it is identified and treated early enough, but if it is left undiagnosed for too long it may become incurable. By drawing attention to a problem at an early stage, the 'sneaking' lawyer might be doing the judge a favour. But even if not, he would serve the interests of his fellow-lawyers and the community.

False Witness

One last point about the cost of litigation. In my experience, perjury is rife in Irish courts and it is very hard to prosecute. There is a tendency in Ireland to see perjury as merely exaggeration, or mild self-serving amnesia, rather than what it is, deliberately lying under oath. I propose that if either party in litigation produces evidence a judge rejects as knowingly untrue – not merely mistaken – he should lose any right to recover costs from the other side, even if he is the winner, and should usually be ordered to pay the other party's legal bills, too. If such a rule was introduced and if it discouraged false evidence, the administration of justice would be enormously helped.

Chapter 7

Previous Attempts at Reform

In this chapter, we look at two recent proposals to improve the provision of legal services. Both were embarked on with excellent intentions, but neither seems likely to produce good results. The first is the report of the Competition Authority, published in 2006. The second is the Legal Services Regulation Bill, introduced by the Minister for Justice and Equality in Autumn 2011.

The Competition Authority Report

In December 2006 the Competition Authority published a report entitled 'Competition in Professional Services: Solicitors and Barristers'. It describes many of the arcane rules and conventions that have evolved over hundreds of years, mostly for the benefit of lawyers rather than their clients, and it is impossible to read it without being reminded of the line in Shaw's *The Doctor's Dilemma*: 'All professions are conspiracies against the laity.' Unfortunately, it also reminds us of the brilliant comic scene that includes that famous line, where each of the assembled medical experts insists that his speciality provides the only cure for all known ailments, irrespective of the patient's symptoms. One says, 'Stimulate the phagocytes!' and another 'Blood Poison! Remove the nuciform sac!', and so on. Like Shaw's doctors, the Competition Authority offers what it takes to be the only solution to the failures it identifies in the provision of legal services: 'Open the system to competition!'

The text suggests that its authors have not worked as lawyers. Much of their criticism is valid, but I wonder if they understand the reasons for some of the practices they condemn, and I doubt that their proposed solutions would be effective.

Information about Lawyers' Incomes

But first, let us look at one of the report's big successes, which is that it provides more information than we had before about the cost of legal services and the incomes of lawyers in Ireland in the twenty-first century. Its figures are taken from the years before Ireland's financial collapse, but even so they are revealing. While lawyers' incomes have fallen since 2006, law is still one of the more protected professions.

One firm of Dublin solicitors publishes information about its gross income, but to explore it would be confusing. As explained earlier, solicitors have to run offices, pay rent, staff and so forth, so the gross income a given firm or partner in it generates is not a reliable guide to partners' take-home pay.

The first, and most dramatic, statistic in the Competition Authority's report is that the amount spent in Ireland on legal services in 1992 was about €320 million and that by 2003 it had risen to about €1 billion, a staggering figure for so small a country and a multiplier of three over 12 years.

We learn that the average annual income for all lawyers in 2002 was €164,000. For solicitors who were sole practitioners or partners it was €210,000, for Junior barristers €121,000, and for Senior Counsel €330,000. (All figures are rounded to the nearest thousand.)

We also learn that the average income in each category is higher than the mean. That is significant. The average is the figure obtained by adding up all incomes and dividing that total by the number of earners. The mean is the midway figure. The number of earners who earn less than the mean is equal to the number who earn more. For example, if the total payroll of a factory is €500,000 and it employs ten people, then their average income is €50,000. We then calculate the mean, the figure for income that is higher than the five lowest-paid workers get and lower than the five highest-paid. Let's say we find that figure is €20,000. That tells us that the cost of paying the five lowest-paid workers does not exceed €100,000, since there are five of them and none is paid more than €20,000. Therefore, since the total payroll is €500,000, the balance, €400,000 or more, must be shared between the five highest paid, so that their average income is at least €80,000. If we repeated the calculation, ignoring the five lowest-paid and doing it only for the top five, and found again among those five that the average was higher than the mean, that would indicate one or two very well-paid people at the top.

So, if we find the average exceeds the mean, we know that the gap between the highest-paid and the lowest is quite big, and we can make a reasonable guess that the people at the top of the scale are a lot better paid than the average figure suggests. And that is the pattern we see in all the categories the Competition Authority report gives us. For example, average income for Senior Counsel at €330,000 tells us that some are paid more. The fact that the mean is €252,000 suggests that those who earn more than the average probably earn quite a lot more. The report confirms this by saying, 'Fewer than 25 per cent of Senior Counsel earn under €100,000, with the top 10 per cent earning more than €500,000 per year.'

Of course, the word 'earning' is ambiguous. If we draw a distinction between 'earned income' and 'unearned' or 'passive' income – money someone gets without having to work for it, like rents or dividends from investments – lawyers' incomes are in the 'earned' category. But we also say, 'You've earned that', meaning that the reward is just. The word 'earned' suggests not merely that the income is a reward for work done, but that it is a fair reward. I use the word 'earned' to mean 'paid for work done', and nothing more. I do not imply that the income has been fairly earned.

A comment by a Senior Counsel some years ago gives anecdotal support to the Competition Authority's assessment of lawyer income. We were discussing the then current crop of High Court judges and I asked him would he think of joining them. 'Couldn't afford it' was his reply. A High Court judge was then paid not much short of €250,000 per year. This barrister had a lifestyle that could not be supported on that income.

Now, even if we did not look at those figures with feelings of anger, probably partly motivated by envy, we should remember that the figure of €1 billion – that is, one thousand million euro – paid to lawyers (in 2003 but it is unlikely to have shrunk greatly since) comes from three main sources. First is the government, which pays a lot of money, collected from taxpayers, to lawyers. Next are businesses, many of which are struggling, and on which we depend for our economic recovery. The last group includes the rest of us, ordinary citizens also struggling to survive. If the cost of lawyers could be reduced, all of us, except the lawyers, would benefit.

Commission's Proposals

And that, of course, is what the Competition Authority wants to bring about. It proposes three main methods of achieving that result. First is to eliminate a number of the restrictive practices that lawyers have built up over the years. There is room for haggling around the edges of that concept – something lawyers are rather good at – but not much room for disagreement with the principle. It is hard to assess how much would be saved by doing away with these practices, but however little difference eliminating them may make, they may be good for lawyers but are bad for clients, and should end. Indeed, many of them already have, and we can ignore them.

The second proposal is to promote lawyer advertising. The third is to foster competition between lawyers on rates of charge. The purpose of each is to put lawyers under pressure to reduce their fees and, accordingly, to reduce the amount of money transferred out of the general community into the legal community. Let us look at these two in turn, taking advertising first.

Advertising

The theory is that if advertising by lawyers tells prospective clients what services each can provide, then they can make a more informed choice. The solicitors' profession abandoned its traditional ban on advertising some years ago, and the Competition Authority wants barristers to be free to advertise too. Let us look at how it has worked for solicitors and, more importantly, for their clients.

Most solicitors who had campaigned against the ban on advertising began to advertise as soon as it was revoked. Soon, others who had held back from that form of self-promotion felt that if they didn't join in they would lose business. So, most firms of solicitors nowadays spend money on advertising. Naturally, they include that money in the financial estimates they prepare at the beginning of each year.

Having estimated how much it is going to cost to run their firm for the forthcoming year, including the provision for advertising, the next step is to work out how much per hour they need to collect from their clients in order to meet their expenses and leave an acceptable income at the end of the year. Advertising probably isn't a major component in most solicitors' expenses, but it is one component. Adding it to their overheads means that their rate of charge increases.

Whether there is benefit for clients is doubtful. Advertising is economically justified when its effect is to increase public knowledge of the goods or services available, and to entice people to look for them and pay for them. So, advertising the latest film may draw into the cinema people who might otherwise have stayed at home. Advertising a new ice cream may lead people to spend money on it, particularly in hot weather. But people consult a lawyer only because they have to. They have to make a will, or buy or sell a house, or claim compensation from a motorist who has run over them. Advertising by lawyers is unlikely to increase the volume of work people will bring to the lawyers in their community where they work. An advertisement by an individual lawyer may result in work coming his way instead of to another, but that affects only the distribution of work between lawyers. And, as noted, advertising increases the amount their clients will have to pay, since it is an addition to the lawyers' overheads.

It could have a negative effect in another, more subtle, way. Traditionally, lawyers build their business by word of mouth. A lawyer who works hard and competently for his client and charges a reasonable fee hopes the client will return to him when he next needs legal services. The client may also speak well of his lawyer to his friends, so that when they need a lawyer they may choose one who has earned their friend's confidence. This benefits clients and the community in which they and their lawyers live, as well as the legal profession, because it rewards lawyers who are hard-working, skilful, conscientious and fair in their charges. It may even encourage lawyers who are none of those things to improve their performance if they see what they think of as 'their' clients switching to others.

Advertising doesn't prevent the process of building a reputation and a practice by earning them, but it dilutes it. If a lawyer can attract new clients by splashing out on advertising, why should he waste his life slogging away for his existing clients, and charging them modestly? And if he is confident that by clever advertising he can attract new clients to replace current ones who leave him because they think he is too expensive, why shouldn't he charge as much for his services as he can get?

It is surely not fanciful to suggest that a lawyer who has built a reputation over years by deserving the trust and respect of his clients is likely to be a more reliable adviser than one whose reputation comes from an advertising campaign? In fact, of the two ways a lawyer can go about building a reputation and practice, one seems to be honest and the other less so. Not that advertising has to be false, but someone who says to prospective clients, 'consult me, because I'm better than the others' seems, as a minimum, to 'beg the question' – that is, to assume something that it is up to him to demonstrate, not merely assert.

Disclosing Rate of Charges

The report's third approach is to require lawyers to be open about their charges, which certainly seems sensible. It is almost impossible for lawyers to say in advance how much time they are going to have to put into a given piece of work, so, instead of saying how much the job will cost, they often tell the client the basis on which they propose to charge him. (Money payable by the 'other side' to a victorious litigant's legal team, under 'taxation' as described earlier, is a separate matter, discussed later in this chapter.) The charge is usually so much per hour, with an estimate of how many hours they expect to have to devote to the problem. This does not sound ideal for the client, but may be better than it seems. If your lawyer agrees at the outset to handle a transaction for a fixed amount, he will be tempted to overestimate the number of hours it will take, and if he does, you may wind up over-paying. If he underestimates, and finds he is working for you at a loss because the job is taking more hours than he allotted to it, he may be tempted to skimp on it, and again you may be the loser.

Publishing rates of charge sounds good, and essentially is, but there is a disadvantage, too. If clients have ready access to the rates lawyers charge, lawyers have equally ready access to the rates their competitors are charging. A solicitor in a not very well known firm who knows the top brass, partners in the leading firms, are charging €500 per hour may decide to undercut them. But he will hope to pitch his charge at maybe €450, or at worst €400, and is unlikely to go below €350 – which, he can point out to any client who queries it, is a discount of 30% on what he would have to pay one of the 'big guns'. He will keep his charge at about that level unless he finds another colleague is charging less and attracting clients away from him. But he knows that is not likely, because his colleagues know as well as he does what the top brass are charging, and recognise it would be silly to undercut them by more than they have to.

Lawyers work in a close-knit community, know a lot about their colleagues, and even exchange confidences. So the advantage to clients of knowing how much their lawyer will charge them, or what rate he will apply in calculating his charge, may be outweighed by the fact that other lawyers have access to the same information and can fix their prices accordingly.

To a professional group whose members want to maximise their incomes, there is a lot of attraction in a system under which everybody knows what everybody else is charging. Provided nobody breaks the circle, they can all set a price that offers them a generous profit, and they cannot be accused of price-fixing.

If you doubt this, think about supermarkets. Milk may be cheaper in one this week, and pork chops in another, but we do not save much by circulating from one to another. They all know what the others are charging, they are up-front about their own prices, and they all seem to be happy with their profits. And, like lawyers, they are secretive about them.

A Drawback to a System of Charging Based on Time Taken

Incidentally, for lawyers to charge based on the time they devote to your work is probably the best system, but it does have a disadvantage, as the following story illustrates. Some years ago, two commercial entities wanted to merge their businesses, but there was a technical problem that seriously threatened the merger. Both entities consulted their lawyers, and a third lawyer was also involved, for reasons we need not go into. The lawyers met to try to find a way around the problem, initially with no success. But after a while one of them came up with an imaginative solution. The others examined it, all agreed it would work and it was adopted successfully. Now, each of those lawyers had put about the same amount of time into their clients' problem, and if they all charged at so much per hour, their fees would have been roughly equal. There would be no extra reward for the lawyer who had solved the problem. This suggests an hourly rate may not reward ingenuity, and therefore may fail to encourage problem-solving lawyers. If it leads to lawyers not being inventive in the service of their clients, the clients will suffer.

Furthermore, a lawyer who specialises in a particular area of law may be able to complete a transaction in fewer hours than a less experienced colleague might need. If so, it may be in clients' interests to be served by fast-working lawyers rather than slower-paced ones, provided speed is not allowed to diminish quality. If hourly rates work the other way, by encouraging lawyers whose clients do not keep them busy to dawdle over the work in the hope of chalking up 'billable hours', again, their clients will lose out.

It is of course a good idea for lawyers to be required to let clients know what their services will cost, and solicitors are now rightly obliged to give that information. But the assumption that removing restrictions on advertising and requiring lawyers to disclose the level of their fees will lead to a reduction in the cost of legal services seems to me unrealistic.

Before moving on to the Legal Services Regulation Bill, I should come back to my comment that the report's authors may not have fully understood how the system operates. Two examples illustrate this.

The Report's Criticism of the Title 'Senior Counsel' being Confined to Barristers

The Report argues that it is anti-competitive that only barristers, not solicitors, may become 'Senior Counsel'. At first sight, and if we accept their assumption that it is a title that promises superior skill, that seems valid. But if we look at what actually happens when a Junior becomes a Senior ('taking silk' as it is called), the argument is less convincing. Here is how it works.

The first few years of most Junior barristers' working lives usually bring very little work or reward, and there is a high dropout rate, but let us look at a Junior who persists and begins to get work and earn an income. The work he gets will be what solicitors send him. The Competition Authority suggests that clients should have direct access to barristers, but, even if this happens, it will not much change the pattern for a long time, particularly for an unknown barrister. He will still depend on solicitors for most of his work and income and will have to do whatever work they send him. Most of it will consist of drafting, that is, producing words on paper. He will have to draft Pleadings, Affidavits, 'Notices of Motion' and a myriad of other documents, mainly those described in Chapter 1 – unless, of course, that system is abandoned. He will get some experience of oral advocacy, but mostly in relatively minor matters in the lower courts, because for an important issue in the higher courts a 'Senior' will probably be briefed and will do most, if not all, of the talking in court.

In order to gain the confidence of solicitors and build his reputation, the barrister will obviously have to produce competent work. If it is more than merely competent, so much the better for his clients and his prospects, but a minimum level of competence is essential. A solicitor whose client's case is thrown out of court because of flaws in the Junior's drafting is unlikely to offer him more work. Almost more importantly, his work must come back quickly. Solicitors accept that if they ask a busy Senior Counsel for an opinion on a difficult point of law they may have to wait for it, but they will not – indeed cannot – accept delay in the sort of court applications where they rely on a Junior. So an aspiring Junior barrister has to show a fast turn-round of papers sent to him. In his early days this may not be hard, since he probably has time on his hands, but as time goes by and he becomes better-known and trusted by more solicitors, the volume of work he is expected to process increases. He is likely to find himself working a long day, and the strain can be considerable. His rising reputation will bring him more opportunities to speak in court, and in more and more weighty matters, but drafting will probably still represent the bulk of his work and income.

Some Junior barristers get to the stage where they want to change not just the emphasis of their work but its nature. They want to move from being a draftsman who sometimes appears in court to being someone who checks and approves ('settles' is the technical term) the drafting work of other barristers, and spends more of his working day in court as an advocate. They decide to 'take silk'.

The Competition Authority rightly notes a difference between 'taking silk' in Ireland and in Britain. In Britain, a request by a barrister to become a Queen's Counsel, the British (approximate) equivalent of our Senior Counsel, is made to a central authority, investigated, including informal consultation with judges, and may be granted or refused. In Ireland, while there is a similar formal application, a request for permission to 'take silk' is seldom if ever refused. This means it is essentially a decision of the barrister alone. Accordingly, the fact that one barrister has 'S.C.' after his name does not imply that he is a more skilful advocate than another who doesn't.

So, 'Senior Counsel' is not a 'quality mark', as the Competition Authority assumes. If it is not, then the argument that solicitor advocates suffer from not being allowed to use it cannot be sustained. (We will come back to this issue later in this chapter, when we consider the Bill.)

You may have noticed the phrase 'oral advocacy' above, and the adjective may have seemed unnecessary. Most of the paperwork the Junior barrister will prepare contains an element of advocacy, too. For example, an affidavit is supposed to be a sworn neutral statement of facts, but any competent lawyer who drafts an affidavit knows that unless it is a purely administrative narrative, it should aim to influence the judge in his client's favour, as well as recording the facts. The message may be fairly simple; for example, 'see how reasonable my side is, and how unreasonable the other side', or quite complicated, depending on the circumstances, but there is usually an element of written advocacy. That is why I describe the spoken word as 'oral advocacy'.

The Suggestion that Junior Barristers Might Thrive Faster if Allowed to Advertise

This appears in paragraph 5.241 at page 115 of the report. It seems to show a lack of understanding of the relationship between solicitors and Junior barristers. Solicitors try to develop a working relationship with barristers they see doing good work, because they want those barristers to work well for their clients, too. Over the working life of a solicitor whose line of work involves retaining barristers, he will probably have this sort of relationship with at least half a dozen Junior barristers. He will look out for a trustworthy, hard-working, accommodating Junior, and will identify him by observation, comment from colleagues and by trying him out, most likely on a matter where if he proves not up to the job, the solicitor can ensure that the client does not suffer. If the solicitor finds the barrister good at his work, hard-working, conscientious, and speedy in his response, a symbiotic relationship may develop between them, each supplying what the other needs – respectively, income and service.

A solicitor who sees advertising by a barrister he doesn't already know and trust will ignore it or, perhaps more likely, assume that a recently 'called' barrister who advertises his services in competition with experienced colleagues is too brash and full of himself to be worth trying out. This suggestion in the Competition Authority's report reminded me of a quotation from Kipling's *The Jungle Book*, the best present I got on my seventh birthday:

> 'There is none like to me!' says the Cub in the pride of his
>   earliest kill;
> But the jungle is large and the Cub he is small. Let him
>   think and be still.

Lawyers have eagle eyes for spotting cubs. The cub whose career the Competition Authority wants to advance by allowing him to advertise his services would do better to save his money.

Finally, the report recommends that a 'Legal Services Commission' should be established, and this recommendation seems to be the genesis of the next proposal we will examine.

The Legal Services Regulation Bill, 2011

Anyone who has reached this point in this book and has agreed with even half of its contents might be disposed to welcome legislation aimed at reforming how legal services are provided. Unfortunately, the storm of criticism that this Bill provoked when it was first published, most of it in my view justified, deprived it of the support the Government and Minister for Justice might have expected, and has coloured reactions to it, even though its most objectionable feature will have been deleted by the time this book is published. The Bill was introduced in 2011, and passed Second Reading in the Dáil in February 2012. This is the stage at which the Dáil debates the principles of a Bill, and the next step in the process is Committee Stage, at which the details are examined, and amendments considered. Minister Shatter announced that he intended to introduce changes to the Bill at Committee Stage, and in July 2013 he delivered a first instalment on his promise, setting out changes he proposes to the first thirty Sections of a Bill that runs to over one hundred.

These changes so alter the effect of the Bill as to render much of the Second Reading debate meaningless, but it seems the Bill in its new form will proceed as though a realistic Second Reading debate had taken place. We will look at the Bill with the Minister's first instalment of amendment, but it is worthwhile to first compare what the Minister originally planned with what he now proposes.

In its original form, the Bill brought all lawyers under the control of a Regulatory Authority which would be a puppet of the Minister for Justice of the day. The Minister would appoint all its members, and could remove them at will. The Authority was to report regularly to him, and many of its powers could be exercised only with his approval. This proposal was vehemently opposed, by Irish lawyers, by some other citizens, and by lawyers from other countries. The reason for this general opposition is perhaps best explained by looking at a piece of legislation decided in 1995, *Brennan v. the Minister for Justice.*

Article 13.6 of the Constitution provides that the President has power to commute punishment imposed in the criminal courts, that is, to pardon people convicted of crimes. An Act of 1951 authorised the Minister for Justice to exercise this power to pardon, on behalf of the President. In the mid-nineties, Máire Geoghegan-Quinn, who was Minister for Justice at the time, developed a practice of cancelling or reducing fines and other penalties imposed by judges. The beneficiaries seem to have been mostly her own constituents or constituents of like-minded TDs who got in touch with her on their behalf. A constitutional prerogative of mercy vested in the President was used to promote political clientelism. A District Judge called Patrick Brennan objected to this practice, and took proceedings against the Minister to bring it to an end. His claim succeeded. As it happened, Máire Geoghegan-Quinn had left office before Judge Brennan's claim was upheld, but if she had still been Minister the decision would certainly have been a major embarrassment for her, and would probably have been seen as a resigning issue, even in Ireland.

Now, imagine how a politician, faced with a legal action that threatened his career, and who had control of the body that regulated lawyers, might be tempted to further abuse his power in order to prevent that action from going ahead – for example, by letting the lawyers on the other side know that the Authority would make their lives more difficult if they advanced in court a case that brought the Minister's conduct into question.

The lawyers, Irish and international, who opposed the Minister's original scheme, under which the new 'Authority' would be his puppet, did so in the interests of the public, not merely in their own interests or their colleagues'. We need lawyers to be independent of political influence because, while judges are there to protect us and give us justice, they, and we, depend on lawyers who are willing to represent us when we suffer injustice, and who are not going to be intimidated. Lawyers are needed if the judicial arm of government is to operate as it should, and to protect citizens from abuse. To create a structure in which politicians may bring pressure to influence how lawyers operate, and whether they will agree to serve clients in 'delicate' situations, puts at risk the ability of independent judges to protect us from political oppression or wrong-doing. Essentially, this is a question of the protection of citizens' rights. We need to be protected from a situation where a future Minister could put pressure on lawyers to discourage them from doing their duty, as Judge Brennan's legal team did. If any reader thinks no Minister for Justice would yield to such temptation, he might like to look at the list of politicians who have held that office since 1922. He might also remind himself of the well-known story of the Garda who caught the Minister for Justice and his cronies drinking illegally after hours, and was asked, 'Do you want a drink or a transfer?'

And of course the structure originally proposed in the Bill, with an 'Authority' in the front line and an all-powerful Minister in the background, would make it easy for a Minister to exert pressure indirectly and without being seen to do so, in a country where a nod and a wink are so effective. During my time as a lawyer, I have seen a solicitor of good reputation who was so intimidated by the idea of confronting a Minister that he let his client down. It was not in our interests to create a structure that makes such a failure more likely, and the lawyers who opposed this plan acted in our interests.

Incidentally, if Judge Brennan had not brought his case to a hearing, it is likely that Minister Geoghegan-Quinn, and in all probability her successors as Ministers for Justice, would have continued to operate what the trial judge in District Judge Brennan's action called a 'parallel system of justice'. It might by now have become 'normal' or even 'traditional' that citizens who broke the law but had the ear of a TD of the appropriate party would receive preferential treatment. We owe Judge Brennan thanks, which I do not think he got.

As I said above, the present Minister has agreed to abandon his original plan by which he and his successors would control the new Authority. But it was surprising and disappointing to many that a Minister who had spent much of his working life as a practising solicitor, as Minister Shatter has, was willing to introduce legislation that would have brought the legal profession under political control. That he did so leads many of us to be suspicious of any amendments he proposes, and, unfortunately, at the time this book goes to the printers we have only an incomplete picture of what he plans. Reading the changes he has disclosed is not encouraging.

Let us start by examining the structure for the Authority that the Minister now proposes. It is to consist of eleven members, of whom seven will be a 'lay person', one each will be nominated by the Bar Council and Kings Inns, and will presumably be barristers, and two will be solicitors. All appointments will be by the Government, who may reject a nomination if they consider the nominee does not have relevant expertise.

Of the seven lay members, one each is to be appointed by three statutory bodies, the Citizens Information Board, the Higher Education Authority and the Competition Authority. The Human Rights Commission (which is currently being merged with the Equality Authority, another statutory body) will nominate one, as will an independent body, the Consumers' Association. The final nominating body is to be the Institute of Legal Costs Accountants. Strangely, under the Bill's definition, a Legal Costs Accountant is to be classified as a 'lay person'.

I find that last provision both strange and worrying. The work of a Legal Costs Accountant (formerly called 'Costs Drawers') is described in Chapter 6, and as I said there, he 'prepares a bill in the archaic style and presents it to the court official to be assessed'. The Minister's decision that Legal Costs Accountants should be included among the nominating bodies for the Legal Services Regulatory Authority seems to be a clear message that it is Government policy that the archaic system for assessing lawyers' charges should remain.

Making the Institute of Legal Costs Accountants a nominating body for the Authority puts in question its ability to carry through a reform agenda, even though 'lay persons' will in theory be in the majority. In a body of eleven people, four will presumably be practising lawyers, two barristers and two solicitors. A fifth, though classified as a 'lay person', will also be a worker within the courts system and one who has a special interest in preventing reforms that might make him and his colleagues redundant. All five will be trained and experienced in advocacy and negotiation. It is likely that the remaining six, the genuinely lay members, will be inclined to defer to any shared opinion they may express, recognising that each of them has an expertise that lay members of the Authority lack. If those five want to block radical reform in the provision of legal services, they will need to persuade only one of the remaining six to support them in order to command a majority. The Minister has recently promised to reflect on a suggestion that the Authority should consist of thirteen members, consisting of eight lay people, four lawyers and one Legal Costs Accountant, instead of eleven as the Bill provides. If he accepts this suggestion, the prospect of the Authority turning out to be a useful body should improve.

But let us look further into what is implied in the Minister's decision to include the Costs Accountants' professional body among the nominating bodies for the new Legal Services Regulatory Authority. It is impossible to imagine any other profession – doctors, engineers, architects – allowing the method of calculating their incomes to become so obscure and difficult that they need to bring into existence a new profession to assess and debate how much they should be allowed to charge. The fact that lawyers use such people, who make no contribution to the process by which justice is done, is a reflection on lawyers and on the system they have evolved and under which they work.

A genuinely reforming Legal Services Regulatory Authority would include on its agenda introducing a system of charges for legal services that clients would understand and that could be implemented readily and without additional expense. One of the criteria such an Authority would be likely to adopt in assessing progress on that reform would be whether the profession of

Legal Costs Accountant had been rendered redundant. If lawyers still need Legal Costs Accountants (and clients have to pay, directly or indirectly, to support them), reform in legal charges cannot be said to have been completed. To include the Institute of Legal Costs Accountants on the list of nominating bodies for the Legal Services Regulatory Authority seems rather like giving the Humanists' Association the right to nominate a member to the Vatican Congregation of the Doctrine of the Faith.

Absence of Fundamental Questioning of the Provision of Legal Services

Let us now look at what the Bill contains. I think that anyone who has read this book to this point, who even half agrees with what it says, will conclude upon examining the Bill that it fails to take the opportunity to make radical changes in how lawyers work for and charge their clients, and the amounts they charge.

The Bill does not propose to simplify the steps taken in order to bring a dispute before the courts, or to address the possibility that lawyers might be made to pay expenses incurred because of their bad decisions. It does not forbid lawyers to assist their clients in delaying or defeating justice.

Nor does it offer any encouragement to clients who would like legal services to become cheaper. Schedule 1 to the Bill lists 'Principles' that should govern lawyers' charges, and they do little more than repeat the rules currently in force, under which some lawyers have become extremely wealthy and many citizens can no longer risk going to court. There is no suggestion of capping or reducing lawyers' incomes.

It ignores the essential inequality of knowledge and bargaining power between a lawyer and a client seeking his services when they come to negotiate the lawyer's charges. Section 90 of the Bill requires a lawyer to 'disclose' the basis on which he will charge. It does not require him to 'negotiate' his charges, or to 'agree' them with his client.

A lot of assumptions, most of them, unfortunately, justified, lie behind that word 'disclose'.

The Bill does not contemplate ending the distinction between 'solicitor and client costs' and 'party and party costs',
something we have not looked at up to now, but should. The
first are the fees and charges a client is bound to pay to his own
lawyers, irrespective of the result. The second are the 'costs' the
loser in litigation may be ordered to pay to the winner's lawyers,
and they are usually much less than 'solicitor and client costs'.
The thinking behind this is that someone who was not the lawyer's client should not be required to pay that lawyer for any
services that were not essential. At first sight this seems reasonable, but does it not assume that it is all right for the lawyer to
charge his own client for unnecessary work?

Surely a more rational principle should govern lawyers'
charges. A lawyer should not be entitled to recover fees or out-
lays incurred in doing unnecessary work, irrespective of who
is going to pay the bill. If a lawyer is in doubt about whether
a given piece of work is going to be needed, and, hence, about
whether he ought to be paid for it, he should write to the client
describing the work involved, its value to the client, and the
likely cost. He should go on to explain why he is not certain the
work is necessary. If, having had that advice, the client authorises the lawyer to do that work, then he is liable to pay for it,
irrespective of whether the outcome of the case will make the
other party liable for his legal expenses.

The fact that he agreed to it, and the correspondence between client and lawyer should be available to the Taxing Master (or 'Legal Costs Adjudicator', as the Bill proposes to re-name
this official) on an assessment of 'party and party costs', when
the Taxing Master has to decide whether the additional charges
should be paid by the other side. The fact that the lawyer's own
client approved the work, knowing that he might have to pay
for it, should be a strong argument that it was necessary – except of course in 'no foal, no fee' cases.

Nor should lawyers be required to charge other people's
clients less for doing the same work than they are entitled to
charge their own clients. (Or, if you look at it the other way
round, they should not be allowed to charge their own clients

more than they may charge others.) If the difference between 'solicitor and client' costs and 'party and party costs' means that it is all right for a lawyer to overcharge his own client, but not another's, or that the loser in litigation should not have to indemnify the 'winner' against what it has cost him to vindicate his position, it should be abolished. And it is hard to see what else it can mean. ('Winner' appears above in quotes because I do not believe anyone unlucky enough to become involved in litigation can really emerge as a winner. The incidental cost is too high, whatever the outcome.)

The Bill provides that adjudication of lawyers' bills should take place in private, and that seems wrong. Lawyers' bills are part of a country's system of justice, and an important part, to lawyers, to the clients who pay them, and to citizens generally. In a healthy democracy, justice is administered in public, not in private, and exceptions to that rule should not be made for any privileged group. (See comments in previous chapter.)

Does the Bill Contain Useful Reforms?

Regrettably, the answer has to be 'not many'. The Bill does not specifically state that lawyers should continue to advertise, but Section 123 gives the Authority power 'with the consent of the Minister' to decide who may advertise, how they may be allowed to do so, and who should be forbidden to advertise. It seems the Bill contemplates that lawyers should continue to spend money on advertising in competition with each other. The effect will presumably be to increase their overheads and charges, with little gain for clients. (See comments earlier in this chapter about the Competition Authority's recommendations.)

It seems to assume a merger will take place between the barrister and solicitor branches of the legal profession, but also appears to envisage that instead of a unified profession we would still have two branches – lawyers (formerly barristers and solicitors) and a new breed of lawyers called 'conveyancers'. Otherwise, its premise seems to be that the legal system will continue to operate as it has up to now.

Solicitors as Senior Counsel

Finally, it addresses the Competition Authority's proposal that solicitors should be allowed to qualify for the title 'Senior Counsel', and creates a ponderously named 'Advisory Committee on the Grant of Patents of Precedence' for that purpose. The plan is that if a lawyer wants to become a 'Senior Counsel' his request will be vetted by a committee consisting of the Chief Justice, the President of the High Court, the Attorney General, the current heads of the two bodies representing lawyers, and a lay member of the Legal Services Regulatory Authority. The committee may consult other people if its members think fit. The 'patent' is to be granted by the Government on the committee's recommendation and designates its recipient 'Senior Counsel'.

This would certainly give some value to the letters 'S.C.' after a lawyer's name. Or, rather, it would do so when all the people who already have that rank without having needed to show they had earned it have died or retired, which is likely to take many years.

However, the Bill requires that someone applying for a 'Patent of Precedence' (that is, to be called 'Senior Counsel') must have shown a capacity for advocacy. A lawyer whose work does not often bring him into court, or who briefs other lawyers to handle court appearances, will not qualify. This would mean that in a firm of solicitors, a lawyer who spends time appearing in court may qualify to put the letters S.C. after his name, while another, whose abilities may be of a higher order but who does different work, may never qualify to become an S.C., and will appear to be 'junior' to his colleague. This may be no more than an anomaly and irritation within a partnership, but much more between competing firms, if the letterhead of one firm includes a lot of 'S.C.'s and another's does not.

Capacity for advocacy is only one of many qualities people seek in their lawyer. Depending on why they need a lawyer, it may not be the most important. It is also much easier to acquire than real wisdom and the ability to give sage advice. With time and perseverance, a person of moderate ability, or even one whose ability is mediocre, can master the skills required to make him a passable advocate. He may never become a really fine one, but he will get by, make a living, and reach the point where it would be difficult to refuse him a 'Patent of Precedence'. For example, it is not difficult to pick up the tricks – they are little more – needed to conduct a cross-examination so as to confuse a witness and make him seem unreliable. Another lawyer, perhaps of greater ability, who dedicates his working life to helping his clients to keep away from court, will never qualify to be called "Senior Counsel'. This seems unfair. If we think about what the word 'counsel' means, it seems silly.

Chapter 8

Some Supreme Court Decisions

In this chapter and the next, we will look at five contemporary decisions of our Supreme Court that have four things in common. First, the issues in each case arose at the interface between the judicial organ of government (the Courts) and the legislative or executive organs (Oireachtas and Government), or both. Secondly, each decision curbed the powers of the Oireachtas, the Government, or both. (*A v. Governor of Arbour Hill* is an exception. In it, the protection of citizens, not the powers of government, was curtailed.) Thirdly, each was a precedent, meaning that it laid down rules or established legal principles that judges in the other courts are bound to follow. Fourthly, none of them was made unanimously by all the judges who heard them. Some were majority decisions, and a minority took a different view. (The Supreme Court always sits with an odd number of judges so that it cannot split 50/50, producing a deadlock.) Where there was no dissenting minority in the Supreme Court, the decision overruled what the High Court judge who first heard it had decided.

In my view, these cases share a fifth characteristic. In each of them I argue that the dissenting minority or the overruled High Court Judge took the correct view of the law, and the majority decision does not represent good law. Given that, as described above, their effect is to curb the powers of other organs of government or to deprive citizens of protections against injustice, that is a cause for concern.

I do not ask you to accept that a majority of our top judges erred five times, simply because I say so. But neither do I think it will be helpful to a reader not trained in legal concepts if I interrupt such flow as this book may have to explain why I say so, presenting technical arguments. So, what I have done is this. In this chapter you will read a summary of the five cases I have chosen, a brief explanation of why I argue the decisions were wrong, and some of their consequences. In the next and final chapter, we will look at their cumulative effect, which I think erodes our democracy. I have transferred all the technical arguments into an Appendix at the end of this book, hoping that most readers will think it worth their while to read it.

We will look at these five cases in what seems to be a logically coherent order, not a strictly chronological one.

C.C. v. Ireland

The initials C.C. identify a teenager who was being prosecuted for having sex with an under-age girl. To protect these young people from being identified by the public, his name does not appear in the Court Reports, and initia! are used instead. C.C. challenged the constitutional validity of the Section under which the Director of Public Prosecutions proposed to prosecute him, and the Supreme Court, overruling a decision of the High Court, decided it was inconsistent with the Constitution, was therefore not part of Irish law, and C.C. could not be prosecuted under it.

The decision is questionable for three main reasons. First, the majority did not apply a legal rule that says that legislation should not be interpreted in a way that renders it unconstitutional, if another interpretation is possible.

Secondly, they took an understandable but short-sighted view about the absence of guilty intention in the mind of a man who has sex with a girl whose age he did not know with certainty. The mental state of such a man is something judges assess in trials of individual Defendants, but I argue that they usurped the role of legislators by laying down universal propositions about the mental state of all men in such situations.

Thirdly, they do not seem to have considered Article 45 of the Constitution, which lays down 'Principles of Social Policy' that the Oireachtas should have in mind in framing legislation. It also provides that the courts may not interfere with legislation aimed at giving effect to one of those principles. One of them is that 'the tender age of children shall not be abused'. None of the judges mentioned Article 45, or considered whether the plain intention of the legislation – to protect young girls from sexual exploitation – took it outside their jurisdiction.

A v. Governor of Arbour Hill Prison

The man identified as 'A' was an adult who had raped a twelve-year-old girl, a friend of one of his own children. (He was not entitled to anonymity, but his name was not disclosed and a letter was used instead, because if his identity became known that might have allowed people to identify his victim.) He had been charged under the same Section as C.C., had pleaded guilty, and at the time of the *C.C* case had almost completed a three-year prison sentence. Within days of the Supreme Court delivering its judgment in the *C.C* case, A applied to be released from prison on the ground that he had been convicted of a crime that did not exist, given that the Court had removed the relevant Section from the Statute Book, and that the removal operated retrospectively. In the High Court, Judge Laffoy decided she had no choice but to accept this argument, which was as convincing legally as it was objectionable morally. But the State appealed to the Supreme Court, which reversed her decision and ordered that A should be returned to prison to serve the balance of his sentence. While the result may have pleased some people, particularly his victim and her family, and it could be argued it produced justice, it seemed to many people, including most lawyers, that it was legally wrong to keep a man in prison for doing something that was not a crime at the time he did it. The reasons the judges advanced for their decision seem unconvincing to most lawyers. Moreover, in reaching it the Supreme Court laid down a general rule whose effect is that a trial in which a judge has made a 'final order' should not be reopened. If there should be a miscarriage of justice in the future, this decision will make it very difficult for its victim to pursue a remedy.

The *'Abbeylara Case'*

A man called John Carty had been shot and killed by police officers near Abbeylara, County Longford. The Oireachtas decided to investigate how this had happened, and a Joint Committee of the Dáil and Seanad was established to investigate and report. Police officers who would face questioning by the Committee applied to the High Court for an order preventing it from going ahead with its enquiry. The case went to the Supreme Court, which decided that the process in the Oireachtas of setting up the Committee had been so incompetently handled that the Committee had no standing. But they did not stop there. They went on to decide, by a three to two majority, that the Oireachtas and Dáil had no power to conduct an enquiry whose report might be critical of anyone who was not a member of the Oireachtas.

That amounted to a ban on any enquiry by the legislature, because any enquiry about such an event as the death of Mr. Carty was bound to try to identify who had shot him, and determine how and why this had happened. An enquiry that was not allowed to make any such finding would be a useless exercise. An enquiry that was not to be meaningless would unavoidably produce a report that might be regarded by some as critical of people involved. The decision meant that the Dáil was prevented in the future from doing something it had done for years: investigating 'urgent matters of public importance'. Given that the function of the Oireachtas is to make laws for the country, and that laws are likely to be better framed if the people making them have relevant facts at their disposal, the *Abbeylara* decision makes it more likely that citizens will suffer from bad laws, passed by ill-informed legislators.

Criticism of the legal grounds for this decision are unavoidably technical. Readers are referred to the Appendix.

McKenna v. An Taoiseach

This case came before the courts as follows. In 1995, the government started the process to amend to the Constitution by deleting the provisions prohibiting divorce and inserting new ones, setting out in what circumstances a divorce might be granted. Of course, that would require a referendum.

But the Government did two other things. It announced that it intended to campaign actively, as the Government, not merely as political parties, for a 'Yes' vote, and sought and was granted Dáil approval to spend public money on its campaign. At that point Patricia McKenna issued her proceedings, seeking an order from the courts prohibiting the government from spending public money on campaigning for one side in the referendum, and prohibiting the Dáil from voting funds for that purpose. At the first hearing, in the High Court, Judge Keane (who later became one of our finest Chief Justices) turned her down, but on appeal the Supreme Court decided, four to one, in her favour. The late Judge Egan agreed with Judge Keane, but the late Chief Justice Hamilton, current Chief Justice Denham, former Judge O'Flaherty and, to my disappointment, Judge Blayney, now retired, upheld her claim, over-ruling their colleagues.

The decision did not affect the outcome of the referendum, which was carried. But it does involve a substantial curtailment by the courts of the Government's ability to govern the country, and the Dáil's to control the supply of funds. A careful reading of the judgments suggests the judges made assumptions about what is involved in a referendum to amend the Constitution, and failed to consider alternative views, which show more respect for the other organs of government.

Damache v. DPP

This is the last case we will look at in this chapter. In my view, of these five decisions it is the most worrying, and we will see why in the next and final chapter. Mr. Damache's home had been searched under a Search Warrant, a mobile phone was seized, and it seems, based on what was found on it, the DPP planned to prosecute Mr. Damache for serious offences. However, he challenged the Section under which the search had taken place. It allowed a Police Superintendent to authorise a search of a house, and did not specify that he must not be connected with the relevant investigation. Reversing a decision of the High Court, the Supreme Court held that the Section was unconstitutional. The judges decided that a police officer could authorise a search of a citizen's home, but the decision to do so must be taken 'judicially', by someone independent of the investigation, and since the Section did not specify such independence, it was unconstitutional. When the Supreme Court declares legislation to be unconstitutional, the Constitution specifies that there will be only one judgment, so that the public will not know whether there was a dissenting view. (This is a provision of our Constitution that I and many other people think we would be better off without, and the Government has said we will have an opportunity to remove it in a referendum shortly.) Accordingly, there was only one judgment, delivered by Chief Justice Denham, and we do not know if all five Supreme Court judges agreed.

Authorising police officers to enter a citizen's home against his will, to conduct a search there and to take away with them his personal belongings, is not a light or routine matter, and it seems strange that the Oireachtas produced a Section that authorised a police officer, even a senior one, to take so serious a step, without either limiting his powers or guiding him on how to exercise them. At a minimum, we would have expected the law to specify the criteria that must be met in order to justify such an invasion of a citizen's home, and to provide that, except perhaps in an emergency, the decision should not be taken by a police officer involved in the relevant enquiry.

The Section the Court rejected was sloppy work, reflecting no credit on the Minister who introduced it or the Dáil that enacted it. The judges' negative reaction to it is understandable, but their decision has major consequences, in addition to that of allowing Mr. Damache to avoid prosecution.

The obstacle the judges faced in striking down the Section was that the Constitution provides that the Oireachtas is the State's sole lawmaker. If the Oireachtas has framed a law, even a bad one, it should stand, unless it is shown to be inconsistent with an identified provision of the Constitution, because it is the work of the only organ of government authorised to make laws.

The decision in *Damache* gets around that obstacle in two ways, both of which seem questionable. First, the judgment quotes with approval the views of former judges and foreign judges about the circumstances in which a house search should be allowed. It goes on to say that the view of the Supreme Court on the question of when and by whom a search warrant should be issued is authoritative, and binds the legislature, that is, the Oireachtas.

Secondly, it introduces a new concept, which it calls 'fundamental norms of the legal order postulated by the Constitution'. Let us focus on that word 'postulated', because it is crucial in understanding how the Damache decision shifts political power. The New Oxford Dictionary gives its meaning as 'suggest or assume the existence, fact, or truth of (something) as a basis for reasoning, discussion or belief'. When this judgment speaks of norms 'postulated by the Constitution' what it says is that Ireland's Constitution is not complete in itself, but assumes the existence of 'legal norms' that must have existed before Ireland adopted the Constitution in 1937. Those norms are not listed in the Constitution, or anywhere else. If the *Damache* decision is correct, it means that identifying those norms is the function of the judges, and particularly the judges of the Supreme Court. It follows that once they have formed an opinion about what the law ought to be, and promoted that opinion into a 'fundamental norm', it overrides the constitutional power of the Oireachtas to make laws. Any law the Oireachtas may pass that is inconsistent with such a 'norm' is invalid.

The judgment starts from the (valid) proposition that the Oireachtas may frame only laws that are consistent with the Constitution, but then extends that proposition to create a new and highly questionable one, that laws passed by the Oireachtas must also conform to 'fundamental norms' which are to be identified and defined by the judges. In simple terms, what that proposition means is that although the Constitution identifies the Oireachtas as the State's sole lawmaker, it is to be limited to making laws that meet the approval of the judges, or, rather, of a majority of the judges sitting in the Supreme Court on a given day.

You do not need to be a lawyer, or to have read the discussion of this decision in the Appendix, to see that this represents a major shift in political power in this State. We will discuss its effect, and the cumulative effect of the other cases described in this chapter, in the next and final chapter of this book.

Chapter 9

The Supreme Court versus the People?

This chapter starts, lawyer-style, with a disclaimer. Public controversy in Ireland often becomes rancorous. We do not limit ourselves to attacking other people's positions; we attack the people who hold them. Lawyers do not do that, at least not in their working lives. They may disagree with each other, often vehemently, but their focus is on the topic, not on the other side, they do not criticise each other, and they maintain amicable personal relationships. This book is critical of the Irish legal system and of some decisions of our judges, and does not try to avoid controversy. This, its last chapter, will not depart from that pattern. But it should not be read as attacking the people who have made the decisions it criticises. I know personally some members of our Supreme Court, and respect and admire them. They are thoughtful, conscientious public servants, who have made a financial sacrifice in agreeing to serve us as judges, and have earned our respect. When I question their decisions, I do not cease to respect them. I certainly do not intend to denigrate any of them.

Nor should we forget that over the years when our Supreme Court has intervened to declare legislation unconstitutional, the effect has almost always been beneficial. The *McGee v AG* case, where the Court removed from the Statute Book laws that prevented a married couple from choosing how to limit their fertility, is one striking example, out of many. The Supreme Court also declared invalid laws that obliged workers to join trade unions, laws and company rules that forbade them to do so, and over the years have removed from our Statute book many provisions that we are better off without. If I am right in arguing that it has erred in the cases discussed in this book, the errors were honest, and the people who made them are wise judges and honorable people, who inherited and continue a tradition that has earned our respect and gratitude. Please read what follows with that in mind.

Further Criticism of the *Damache* Decision

In *Damache*, the Supreme Court 'struck down' legislation not because it was inconsistent with an identified provision of the Constitution, but because the judges decided it was inconsistent with judicial thinking in this and other jurisdictions and with what the judgment calls 'fundamental norms of the legal order postulated by the Constitution'. As the previous chapter and the Appendix argue, these words can only mean 'what judges think the law ought to be'. What the decision in the *Damache* case means is that in approaching how to vindicate or protect a constitutional right, the legislature must comply not only with the provisions of the Constitution but also with the views of judges on what the Constitution ought to say, or rather, what the judges think it implies.

The judges took the view that a citizen's home should be protected from unlawful intrusion, and that this can be done only by requiring the decision to authorise a search to be taken 'judicially', and not by a police officer involved in the relevant investigation. The Appendix seeks to show that the method the judges selected was impractical, but the point here is that the Supreme Court now requires the Oireachtas to legislate along lines that judges approve.

Clearly, that requirement – that the law must be what judges, not legislators, think it should be – must apply consistently. If it applies to one issue, how and by whom a search warrant may be authorised, it must apply equally to all areas of law-making.

That is, judges claim to be entitled to supervise how the legislature frames all legislation, not only legislation in the area of citzens' constitutional rights. It is for them, the judges, to decide whether to approve or veto the efforts of the legislature.

Let me put this another way, because it is probably the most important issue in this book. If judges do not have a general right to impose their views on the legislature, they cannot instruct the legislature on how to protect or vindicate 'personal rights'. That they have done so in the *Damache* case means that they claim to exercise on a specific matter – the issuing of search warrants – a general power to 'correct' how the Oireachtas legislates. If the Oireachtas passes legislation along lines that the judges approve, the judges will probably not interfere with it, but if legislation does not meet with judicial approval, it will be deemed to be unconstitutional, and deleted from the Irish legal code.

In a previous draft of this book, that last sentence ended with the words 'if legislation does not meet with judicial approval it will be declared to be unconstitutional, and deleted from the Irish legal code'. In revising it, I substituted 'deemed' for 'declared' because 'deemed' is accurate and I doubt if 'declared' is. Anything may be 'deemed' to be something, whether it is so or is not. For example, if the Oireachtas was in the process of passing a 'Cattle Act' and came to realise its provisions should also apply to sheep, they could include a Section that said that for the purpose of the Act a sheep should be deemed to be a cow. It could not declare a sheep to be a cow, because it is not one, and such a declaration could not make it one. In the *Damache* case, because legislation dealing with house searches did not follow a pattern that judges approved, they decided it was unconstitutional, though they did not identify a provision of the Constitution that the legislation infringed. 'Deemed' is an accurate word to describe that process. I doubt if my first choice, 'declared', is.

Constitutional Boundaries Breached – or Obliterated

The Constitution draws a boundary between the legislative function and the judicial. The Oireachtas, consisting of public representatives whom the people have elected, makes laws. Judges give effect to those laws, and administer justice in accordance with them. The decision in *Damache* involves the judges crossing that boundary. But I think it does more than cross the boundary: it obliterates it. It establishes the judiciary, not the Oireachtas, as the people who decide what Irish law ought to be and therefore is to be. Article 15.2 of our Constitution provides that the sole power to make laws is vested in the Oireachtas. It is hard to see how judges holding and exercising the powers they have implicitly claimed and exercised in the *Damache* case can be reconciled with Article 15.2. The decision also seems inconsistent with Article 5, which says that Ireland is a sovereign, independent, *democratic* State.

Of course, the judges are the ultimate interpreters of the Constitution, and the Supreme Court is its supreme interpreter. Legally, the Constitution means whatever the judges say it means. But I argue that it is at best unwise for the judiciary to read into the Constitution provisions that it does not actually contain. And I say that when judges do that, and their interpretation interferes with the ability of the other organs of government to function, then both the ability of the government to govern the country and the democratic nature of the State are endangered.

Cumulative Effects of Decisions, Including *Damache*

In four of the five decisions we examined in the preceding chapter of this book, the Supreme Court limited or reduced the powers of the Oireachtas. In *C.C*, it struck down one Section of an Act, not on the basis of what the Constitution says, but on their recollection of what it says. The judges failed to recall Article 45 of the Constitution, which, if words mean what they say, provides that they were not authorised to decide as they did. (One is reminded of John Proctor in Arthur Miller's *The Crucible*, whose memory failed him when he was asked to list the Commandments, and he couldn't bring to his mind the one he had broken.) In *Abbeylara*, the court deprived the Dáil of its

traditional power to conduct enquiries, and in *McKenna* it prohibited the Government from campaigning for an outcome to a
referendum that the Government thought was in the public interest, and the Dáil from exercising its constitutional power to
decide whether to authorise expenditure by the Government. In
Damache, it took a further, giant, step by deciding that judges
may determine how legislation is to be framed, and legislation
that does not comply with their requirements will be deleted
from our legal code.

Consequences of Judgments, from three Perspectives

Let us look at this series of decisions, culminating in *Damache*,
from three points of view: first that of the judges, next how it
impacts on the Oireachtas and finally how it affects us, the people of Ireland.

The view from the Four Courts presumably is that these
cases represent an orderly development of the law, proceeding on traditional lines. Judges decide cases that come before
them, each on its merits. Legal principles emerge from some
of their decisions. They apply those principles in future cases
that come before them, and use them to illuminate judicial decision-making. That is what judges do, and have always done.

The view from the Oireachtas must be less cheerful. The
Dáil (ignoring the Seanad because its powers are so limited) always knew that if it passed laws that offended the Constitution,
those laws might be 'struck down' by the courts. *McKenna* curtailed the Dáil's constitutional power to decide how State funds
should be spent, and *Abbeylara* deprived it of its traditional
power to enquire into urgent matters of public importance.
Those decisions greatly reduced its ability to function effectively, both as a legislature and as the protector of the public purse.
Now, the *Damache* decision requires that its legislation must
not only comply with the Constitution but must also meet with
the approval of judges, applying 'norms', which are largely subjective, and may also be ephemeral. Any legislation that does

not pass that test will be struck down, as though it breached the express words of the Constitution.

Our legislators should be concerned by this pattern, and might well see a parallel between the Dáil and the city of Pisa. Pisa was originally a port, and a major maritime power in the Western Mediterranean. But it was built on a river that carried mud downstream. Change took place over years, starting with its harbour silting up. As time passed, more and more silt was carried downstream and deposited at the mouth of the river. New land came into existence, between the city and the sea. Pisa is now an inland city, and its status as a maritime power is a dim historical memory. Legislators should wonder if they are going to find themselves similarly landlocked by encroaching judicial intrusion – or if indeed they have already been deprived of their power as the State's sole legislative authority.

The *Damache* case tells them they should not pass controversial legislation, because the courts may reject it. They are presumably trying to educate themselves in judicial thinking, so that they will come to understand the judges' views, and produce only Acts that will pass muster with them. If so, judicial thinking will dominate the legislative process, without the judges actually needing overtly to exercise the power they have claimed. A process by which judges dominate the legislature has probably started. If not, so long as *Damache* continues to represent Irish law, it is inevitable.

From the third point of view, that of Irish citizens, there has been a transfer of political power. The power to decide the content of legislation has moved from the Dáil and government of the day, our representatives whom we have elected, expecting them to give effect to our communal will, and knowing that if they do not we can replace them. It is now held by the judges of the Supreme Court, people we did not appoint and cannot easily get rid of.

Moreover, if ultimate political power is vested in the Supreme Court, then Ireland is no longer a democracy. We do not have a word in common use for 'a state governed by its judges'. (There is an obscure word, 'kritarchy', which may now describe us.) The word normally used to describe such a country is 'oligarchy', meaning a country governed by a small, unelected, group of people. This may seem extreme, but I think it is the effect of the *Damache* decision.

An Objection

Should we not welcome the input of judges into our law, and even seek it? Should we not remember *McGee* and the other cases where the judges set aside bad laws, and trust them to continue to ensure we are well governed, by good laws only? We may answer yes, if we are happy to live in an oligarchy. But if we want to go on living in a representative democracy, a country where the source of political power and decision-making consists of the people, not a small elite group, we accept that some legislation passed by the people we elect to represent us will displease some of us. We put up with their errors and blunders in preference to what might be a more polished and sophisticated political order, such as the judges might impose – and 'impose' is an accurate word. We cling to democracy, in spite of its defects, and resist any transfer of political power from our representatives, whom we have elected and we can remove, to people we have not chosen and cannot get rid of.

Administering Unjust Laws?

What, then, do I say a judge should do if he is called upon to enforce a Statute that seems to him to produce injustice? Well, if he can identify a provision of the Constitution and show that the relevant Statute or Section is repugnant to that provision, he is entitled to declare it not to be part of the law of Ireland. Indeed, he may even be bound to do so. That is simple and, to him, satisfactory.

But suppose the Statute or Section cannot be shown to be repugnant to an identified provision of the Constitution? The answer is again simple, though less agreeable to the judge. Constitutionally, he is bound to give effect to laws passed by the

State's only lawmaker, whether he thinks the result is just or not. He is not entitled to override a decision made within its powers by the body authorised by the Constitution to make it, or to prefer his view of what justice requires to the decision of the democratically elected representatives of the people.

If he thinks the result is unjust, and the injustice arises from a drafting error, or a failure to recognise consequences, he may express his views in a written judgment, and forward it to the relevant Minister, hoping he will take note and introduce the necessary amendment. (High Court Judge Hogan has done that.) But the declaration he made on taking office – 'that I will uphold the Constitution and the laws' – seems to require him to give effect to legislation that cannot be shown to be repugnant to an identified provision of the Constitution. Otherwise, 'hard cases' that come before him will produce 'bad law' – as I argue *Damache* and the other cases I examine did.

'Unspecified Personal Rights'

This leads us to look at another concept that judges have evolved to help them with the dilemma described above, where an Act or Section requires them to do something they consider unjust. In a series of cases, they have applied a concept (they would probably call it a 'doctrine') of 'unspecified personal rights'. They say that the Constitution does not list all the personal rights citizens have or should have, and there are other citizens' rights, not mentioned in the Constitution, that should be given constitutional protection. They also say that they, the judges, are the people who should identify those unspecified rights and enforce them.

Judges have relied on that concept to remove from the Statute Book a number of provisions that offended their sense of justice. As mentioned earlier, most of them were provisions we are better off without, so the concept has been seen as a useful means of getting to a desirable destination, and the means has not been much questioned. The *Damache* decision seems to make that concept redundant, but if the Supreme

Court were to retreat from the position they have taken in *Damache* (which I would describe as extreme), the concept of unspecified personal rights remains, and is worth examining. It seems to be based on three propositions:

1. People have rights that the Constitution does not mention.

2. It is for judges to identify those 'unspecified personal rights'.

3. Once they have done so, those rights are to be deemed to be part of the Constitution, so that judges may declare legislation or executive actions that infringe them to be unconstitutional and therefore void.

Of these three propositions, the first is obviously right, and the second at first sight seems unobjectionable, but the third is highly questionable. What it means is that judges assert they have the right to make decisions that amend the Constitution. Admittedly, they can amend it only by adding to it provisions it does not already contain. They may not delete or change any existing provisions. But it is hard to see how such a right can be constitutionally vested in the judicial organ of government.

With that in mind, let us look again at the second proposition above, that judges are the people to identify those 'unspecified personal rights'. If such a power should exist, surely the Oireachtas, our sole lawmaker, should exercise it. Of course, the Oireachtas may not change the Constitution, any more than the judges may. But deciding what rights the people should have in addition to those listed in the Constitution seems to be a function of lawmakers, not judges. Unquestionably, the Oireachtas could pass legislation in the form of a 'Bill of Rights', recognising and listing 'citizen rights' not mentioned in the Constitution, and supplementing rights created under European law. Such a 'Bill of Rights' could declare that personal rights it listed could not be infringed by future legislation (except a 'Bill of Rights Amendment Act'), and authorise the Courts to protect these new personal rights. That would mean that for example, if a section of a future Local Government Act infringed one of the 'statutory rights' brought into existence by the Bill of Rights

Act, the courts would be entitled to declare that section void. That would be within the powers of the Oireachtas, as the State's sole lawmaker.

But judges expanding the provisions of the Constitution? It is hard to see how that can be justified, even if we approve of their intentions. Moreover, it is by no means clear that judges are qualified to decide what personal rights not mentioned in the Constitution should be given constitutional force. Many such 'rights' are social or economic, and judges, whose job is to try to do justice between litigants, have no expertise in identifying or defining them. Their sheltered lives, as described earlier, do not equip them to do so, and may actually disqualify them.

Many of the rights citizens might want to claim relate to the extent to which the state is entitled to interfere in citizens' lives, or is bound to support citizens. Of these, the first is a matter for legislators, elected representatives of the people, not for judges. The second may be seen as an attempt to balance the conflicting wishes and aspirations of those who seek aid from the state and those who fund the state as taxpayers. Again, it is not clear that judges have the relevant expertise. Balancing those conflicting interests is surely the function of elected lawmakers.

And, of course, bestowing rights on people will often produce an expense to be met out of the national purse. For example, when judges decided that people accused of crime who cannot pay for lawyers are entitled to be represented in court, the other organs of government had to introduce and fund a Legal Aid Scheme. That meant reducing the amount available for other causes. Common sense requires that the body that decides how to raise and spend public money should be in charge of defining people's rights, and not be presented with a *fait accompli* by a different organ of government and be told it must find the money to pay for it. If judges identify an 'unspecified personal right' that people should enjoy, and direct the state to provide funds to meet it, that may mean the Exchequer cannot meet obligations to other people that may be no less valid and important. Those citizens will be deprived, because their claim did not come to the attention of the judges, and another did. As a way of governing a country, that leaves too much to chance.

It seems incongruous to look at the power judges have claimed for themselves in the light of their decision in the *Abbeylara* case. In that case, they decided that the Dáil, one organ of government, should no longer be allowed to do something it had done for years, because the Constitution does not specifically authorise it to do it, and (they said) it has no inherent power to do it. But they have decided that they themselves may expand the provisions of the Constitution, something that, equally, the Constitution does not authorise them to do, and which they do not seem to have an inherent power to do. The phrase, 'Don't do as I do; do as I say' comes to mind.

Incidentally, in the *McKenna* case the late Judge Hamilton quoted with approval a statement by the late Judge Walsh that the People are the guardians of the Constitution. I do not know what that means, but it is hard to reconcile with the claim that the judiciary is entitled to amend the Constitution without reference to the people, by reading into it provisions that it does not contain, and giving them constitutional force.

Finally on this topic, the notion of 'unspecified personal rights' looks like a step in a direction that leads to 'fundamental norms of the legal order postulated by the Constitution'. That is, to the judges breaking down the boundary that separates them from lawmakers, and occupying territory where they are trespassers.

Reform?

Should the political situation we are left in as a consequence of the *Damache* decision be changed? One purpose of this book is to persuade its readers to answer that question with an emphatic 'yes!'

But can it be changed? Again, though less emphatically, the answer is yes. It can be changed by the Government and Oireachtas asserting themselves, insisting on their constitutional powers, and reversing judicial intrusion into territory where judges do not belong. However, reform probably cannot be brought about in that way without some element of visible confrontation, which would almost inevitably be bad for the country.

By far the best way of restoring balance between the different organs of government is through the judges acknowledging that they have over-reached themselves, and retreating from their current untenable position. If they were to decide to do that, I do not doubt that they would find a path and a formula that would minimise the risk of damage. Given the respect and admiration expressed earlier in this chapter for the judges of our Supreme Court, and in spite of the doubts that attach to the judiciary as a whole, as described in Chapter 3, it may not be foolishly optimistic to think that they will.

That is why the heading to this chapter ends with a question mark.

Appendix

Additional Commentary on Cases Discussed in Chapter 8

In this Appendix, I explain why I contend the majority decisions in the five cases examined in Chapter 8 represent bad law. Some people who are not lawyers may find it hard going, though I have worked to make it as transparent as I could. I also acknowledge that I am even more liable to error than the judges whose decisions I criticise, and that others, whether lawyers or not, may pick holes in my analysis and refute my conclusions. Nobody, including judges, is infallible, or has a monopoly of wisdom. Choosing a democratic form of government, as the citizens of Ireland have done, is an implicit acknowledgement of that fact.

1. C.C. v. Ireland 2005 and 2006 (two judgments)

C.C. was charged under Section 1 (1) of the Criminal Law Amendment Act 1935, which read as follows:

> *Any person who unlawfully and carnally knows any girl under the age of fifteen years shall be guilty of a felony, and shall be liable on conviction thereof to penal servitude for life or for any term not less than three years or to imprisonment for any term not exceeding two years.*

We will need to compare this with Section 4 (1) of the same Act, as follows. (In the twenty-first century its wording seems strange, even offensive. It is of its time.)

> *Any person who, in circumstances which do not amount to rape, unlawfully and carnally knows or attempts to have unlawful carnal knowledge of any woman or girl who is an idiot, or an imbecile, or is feeble-minded shall, if the circumstances prove that such person knew at the time of such knowledge or attempt that such woman or girl was then an idiot or an imbecile or feeble-minded (as the case may be), be guilty of a misdemeanour and shall be liable on conviction thereof to imprisonment for any term not exceeding two years.'*

Section 1(1) makes it a crime for a man to have sex with a girl under a certain age, and Section 4 makes it a crime for a man to have sex with a mentally defective woman, but only if he knew she was mentally defective. From now on I will refer to these two as 'Section 1' and 'Section 4'.

C.C. admitted he had had sex with a girl, but said he believed she was of age and took proceedings asking the High Court to forbid his prosecution. The High Court refused and C.C.'s lawyers appealed to the Supreme Court, which reversed the High Court and decided Section 1 was invalid because it was inconsistent with the Constitution. The judges broke the argument down to two issues, decided one in July 2005, left the other undecided and said they wanted to a second round of legal argument on it. After that second round, they delivered a second judgment, in May 2006.

The issue in the July 2005 judgment was how to interpret Section 1. Did it mean C.C. was entitled to defend himself against the charge by saying he believed the girl was of age, and therefore had committed no crime? There was no doubt that he would be entitled to claim 'innocent mistake' as a 'plea in mitigation' if he had been found guilty. The question was whether Section 1 allowed someone charged under it to claim that he believed the girl was of age, accordingly did not have a criminal intention and therefore was not guilty of a crime. Could he plead 'innocent mistake' about the girl's age as a defence, entitling him to a 'not guilty' verdict? Or could he plead it only in mitigation of his punishment, after being found guilty?

In the first judgment, in July 2005, a majority of the Supreme Court interpreted Section 1 to mean that it did not allow him to plead 'innocent mistake' as a defence. The second hearing was to decide whether that interpretation meant the Section was unconstitutional. The second decision, in May 2006, answered 'yes' to that question, because the first had meant a citizen could be convicted of a serious offence even though he had an 'innocent mind', and this was inconsistent with constitutional justice.

Unless you read the judgments critically, each decision seems right. It would be unjust to send someone to prison if he didn't intend to do anything wrong. A law that might send an innocent man to prison seems unjust. The Constitution requires our laws to be just. So it seems logical to strike down Section 1. However, if we study each decision we will find serious flaws in both.

The July 2005 Decision

Three Judges, Denham (who is now Chief Justice), Geoghegan (who has since retired) and Fennelly, delivered judgments. Judge Denham interpreted Section 1 as allowing a Defendant to advance a defence that he had made an 'innocent mistake' about the girl's age, believed her to be older then she was, and therefore was not guilty of a crime when he had sex with her. If her view had prevailed, Section 1 would not have been found unconstitutional. Judges Geoghegan and Fennelly held that Section 1 did not allow that defence, and Judges Hardiman and McCracken (who has also since retired) agreed with Judges Geoghegan and Fennelly, but did not write separate judgments. So the majority overruled Judge Denham's view, four against one. Because I agree with Judge Denham's view, I will leave her judgment to one side and focus on the judgments I think were wrong.

Section 1 an Exception to a General Rule?

Judges Geoghegan and Fennelly started out by accepting a general principle that where a Statute says a given act is criminal, it is to be interpreted as allowing someone accused under it to defend himself by showing that he did not know he was committing a crime, that he had no reason to suspect it, and did not intend to do anything illegal. That principle is embodied in a Latin maxim: '*actus non facit reum nisi mens sit rea*', which means, 'an action is not a crime unless it is done with a criminal intention'.

However, the two judges went on to decide that Section 1 was an exception to that principle, for two reasons. The first was that another section of the same Act, Section 4. (quoted above) specifically allowed the defence of innocent mistake, while Section 1 did not. If the Oireachtas provided for such a defence in relation to one offence but not in relation to the other, it was in accordance with established legal principles of interpretation – and apparently with common sense – for the judges to assume that the omission was intentional.

I think Judge Fennelly was mistaken in relying on the legal maxim '*expressio unius exclusio alterius est*', which means 'if a Section of an Act mentions one thing but not another, then its effect is to exclude the thing not mentioned'. That maxim applies only where a single Section of an Act is under scrutiny, not where two different sections are to be compared. '*Casus omissus pro omisso habendus est*' seems to me to be the relevant one. Rather than offer a literal translation of the Latin, I will just say that its effect is, 'if something you might expect to see included in legislation has been omitted, assume the omission is intentional'. But even if the judge quoted the wrong maxim, that does not invalidate his conclusion. If Section 4 specifically allowed a defence of 'innocent mistake' and Section 1 did not, it seemed reasonable to assume that the Oireachtas intended to word them differently, and therefore did not intend to allow someone accused under Section 1 to claim to be innocent on the ground of 'innocent mistake'.

Their second reason was as follows. Section 1 was a replacement of a similar section of a previous Act (of 1885) which prohibited sexual intercourse with a girl or young woman, but laid down a different age limit, and the purpose of Section 1 was to change the age at which a girl could legally consent to sexual intercourse. The 1885 Act specifically allowed a defence of 'innocent mistake', but Section 1 (of the 1935 Act) did not, so the judges said it should be assumed that when the Oireachtas passed Section 1 in 1935, 50 years later, they intended to amend the law by excluding a defence of 'innocent mistake'.

In my view, although each of these lines of reasoning seems plausible, neither stands up to analysis. Let us look at them in sequence.

Comparing Section 1 with Section 4

Generally, it is right to assume that where something is mentioned in one Section of an Act but omitted from another Section, otherwise similar, the omission is intentional. However, the judges did not take into account that there is a difference between the purpose of the two Sections and the situations they address, and that accordingly parallels between them may be misleading. Section 4 made it an offence for a man to have sexual intercourse with 'any woman or girl who is an idiot, or an imbecile, or is feeble-minded', but only if he knew of her mental incapacity. It is directed at a man who knowingly takes advantage of a mentally defective woman. It is not intended to make a criminal of one who had sex with a woman when he had no reason to suspect she suffered from major mental incapacity.

Sexual intercourse with a girl in her mid-teens or younger, whose face and body are those of a young girl, is in a different category. Unless the man knows such a girl's age, he can only guess at it, and must know his guess may be wrong. So, a man who engages in sexual intercourse with a girl whose age he does not know but who clearly is not a fully mature woman should know that he is in dangerous territory, in a way that a man who meets an obviously mature and sexually available woman need not. When the Oireachtas specified that a man who has sexual intercourse with a 'feeble-minded' woman is guilty of a crime only if he knew of her mental incapacity, it aimed to strike a balance between two needs: the need to protect such women from sexual exploitation and the need to protect innocent men from unjust conviction. Drawing conclusions based on the absence of similar provision in legislation that governs an offence where the danger signals are clear and the mental element is not the same ignores the fact that the two sections contemplate different situations. (We will come back to this later, when we look at the May 2006 judgment.)

Comparing the 1885 and 1935 Acts

There is an established rule that when judges interpret legislation, they examine only its wording, on the assumption that the words were chosen to express the intention of the legislature. Judges do not look at Dáil or Seanad reports for guidance on what the legislature intended. In the *C.C.* case Judges Geoghegan and Fennelly observed that rule. Instead, they isolated one out of many of the circumstances surrounding the passing of the Act, a difference between the wording of Section 1 (which did not mention 'innocent mistake') and the legislation it replaced (which did), and decided that the difference indicated an intentional difference in policy. That was an entirely reasonable hypothesis. But a hypothesis is not a conclusion. Perhaps when the Criminal Law Amendment Act was going through the Dáil, a dialogue like this took place:

> A TD: *'I propose to put down an amendment to include in Section 1(1) a proviso, such as appears in the 1885 Act we are proposing to amend, that having carnal knowledge of a young girl is to be a crime only if the accused knew her age.'*

> Minister for Justice: *'I am advised that is not necessary. There is a well-established legal principle to that effect, which the Courts would automatically apply in any prosecution. I'm told it's expressed in a Latin maxim well known*

to lawyers, actus non facit reum nisi mens sit rea. In case your Latin isn't up to it, Deputy, that means, 'an action isn't a crime unless it's done with a criminal intention'. So there's no need to amend the wording, and I suggest the Deputy should withdraw his amendment.'

TD: *Thank you, Minister, for that clarification. In light of it I will not table my amendment.*

The judges seem to have assumed no such dialogue took place. If their assumption is wrong, their interpretation of Section 1 collapses. To look at one set of circumstances, a difference between the wording of the repealed section and its replacement, and to form a hypothesis from those circumstances, is legitimate. But to convert that hypothesis into a conclusion about the legislature's intention, without examining available evidence that might prove or disprove the hypothesis, is inconsistent with logic. Judge Geoghegan says of the difference in wording between Section 1 and the 1885 provision, 'by necessary implication, this must have been deliberate'. Neither 'necessary implication' nor 'must have been' is justified. Logic would allow no more than 'possibly', perhaps even 'probably' and 'may have been'.

I argue that in interpreting a Statute judges should be required to make a choice. They can stick to the traditional approach of looking only at the words of the Section whose meaning is in question. Or they can look at other things in order to understand what the legislators intended. (This is called the 'purposive approach'.) However, if they do decide to take that approach, it seems logical that they must not be selective, and should examine all possible information that might help them to understand the thinking behind the legislation. The first and most obvious is surely the report of what legislators said, because that is the best guide to what they meant.

There are good arguments in favour of examining only the words of a Section to establish its meaning, and that is the traditional approach in Ireland to interpreting Statute law. If there is ambiguity, there are also good arguments in favour of the purposive approach, by which judges stand back from the text and widen their view in order to try to understand the background against which the legislation was passed, and get to the thinking behind the words. But it is not rational to mix the two approaches. If judges want to stand back in order to see the wider picture, logic requires them to look at the entire canvas, not only at one corner of it. Looking at the entire makes Judge Denham's view, that the rule *actus non facit reum nisi mens sit rea* should apply in interpreting Section 1 more convincing than making the Section an exception to the rule.

The May 2006 Judgment

For the second hearing, Chief Justice Murray (as he then was) took the place of Judge Denham. This was a decision on the constitutional validity of legislation, so, as I mentioned earlier, only one judgment was delivered. We know that three of the five judges must have agreed on the conclusion, but have no way of knowing whether all of them did, or, if one or two disagreed, why they did. Judge Hardiman delivered the judgment.

He started by saying that the offence created by Section 1 has to be classified as serious because the name of anyone convicted under it must be entered on the Sex Offenders Register under an Act of 2001, and this might have serious consequences for some people. This was surprising, because the question before the judges was whether a section of an Act passed in 1935 was inconsistent with the Constitution and was therefore repealed in 1937 when the Constitution was adopted. Legislation passed years later cannot be relevant to that question.

It also seems surprising that Judge Hardiman assumed the 2001 Act was constitutional, because it seems to me to be much easier to argue against its validity than against Section 1. It requires a judge to order that the name of anyone convicted of certain offences must be entered on the Sex Offenders Register, which as Judge Hardiman pointed out, can operate as a heavy punishment. The Act does not allow any discretion. Even if the trial judge thinks that, on the facts of the case as they have emerged during the trial, or the character of the Defendant, it would be unjust to enter his name on the Sex Offenders Register, the Act requires him to do so. This looks like an interference by the legislature with a function that is constitutionally vested exclusively in judges: to decide what penalty is right for a given offender. In other words, there is a strong argument that it is an unconstitutional interference by the legislature with the functions of the judiciary. I find it odd that Judge Hardiman did not mention this, but assumed, first, that the 2001 Act was valid and, secondly, that it could affect the interpretation of legislation passed years earlier.

Belief versus Knowledge

But there is a more fundamental objection. The core of the judgment lies in the following words:

> If a person has consensual intercourse with another whom
> he honestly and reasonably believes to be over the relevant
> age, he is not aware that anything unlawful has occurred.
> ... The Section ... wholly removes the mental element and
> expressly criminalises the mentally innocent.

These words fail to analyse adequately an accused man's state of mind at the time of an alleged offence. He may have believed his partner was of age, or he may, theoretically at least, have 'known' she was. But believing and knowing are different things, and cannot coexist in the same mind about the same thing. We either believe something or we know it. If we know something, there is certainty in our mind about it, and no room for doubt, opinion or belief. If we do not have that level of certainty about a factual situation, we may believe it or doubt it, or we may have an open mind. There is a process by which hypothesis may develop into belief, and belief may be converted into certainty. 'Maybe quinine is useful in treating victims of malaria' was originally a hypothesis, which become, after years and experience, 'We think quinine is useful in treating victims of malaria'. That was the opinion stage. Further experimentation then established that quinine is useful in treating victims of malaria, and we no longer say we believe it to be so. We know it as a fact, in the same way as we know two plus two equals four.

A man contemplating (if that's the right word) sexual intercourse with a girl that he knows well, knows how old she is. If he doesn't know her age, can he be said to know her well? If he knows her age and knows the law, he also knows whether having sex with her will be criminal or not.

If he does not know her well enough to know her age, he can ask her, but common sense will tell him that if she wants to have sex with him, she will tell him she is of age, whether it is true or not, so he cannot rely on what she says. If he is of an age to be physically capable of having sex, he knows that a teen-aged girl does not look like a mature woman. At most, he may believe she is over the relevant age, but his belief can only be a matter of degree. It may rise to high probability in his mind if her story seems plausible and she gives an adult impression, but it can never reach certainty. He must know that if he has sexual intercourse with a youthful stranger, there is a possibility that he will commit a crime. If a man knows there is some risk that what he wants to do may be a crime and decides to take that risk, it is hard to justify describing him as 'mentally innocent'.

Let me illustrate this by way of an analogy. In a civil action between a Plaintiff and a Defendant where the facts are disputed, the Plaintiff is required to prove his case on the 'balance of probability'; that is, he is entitled to win if he shows that his account is more likely to be true than the Defendant's. A judge or jury deciding such a case may recognise that they cannot be certain which story is true, but may decide which of two conflicting stories to believe. If someone is prosecuted in the criminal courts, he may not be convicted of a crime unless his guilt is proved 'beyond reasonable doubt', which is a much higher standard than 'balance of probability', close to certainty, even if it may not quite get there. If a man has sex with a youthful stranger he cannot say that he had no suspicion that he might be committing a crime, unless he can show that he was satisfied – meaning beyond reasonable doubt – that she was of age.

Saying that he believed it on balance of probability would be an admission that his mind was not wholly innocent.

I have tried to imagine a scenario in which a man could be satisfied beyond reasonable doubt that his sexual partner was of full age, if in fact she was not. It is not hard to invent one that might pass muster in the kind of fiction that requires readers to suspend disbelief, but I have so far failed to devise one that could happen in real life. Unless a plausible scenario can be devised, the 'mentally innocent' man that Judge Hardiman seeks to protect in his judgment does not exist.

Let us imagine a different situation. A man is arrested and charged with burglary, and tells the Gardaí, 'I was walking home, minding my own business, when I saw a man trying to break into a house. I asked him what he was doing, he told me he owned the house and had accidentally locked himself out, so I decided to help him to break in. That's what I was doing when the squad car arrived.' We can't rule out with absolute certainty the possibility that he was mentally innocent, but it hardly justifies rewriting the law on burglary. And we would be surprised if a jury acquitted him.

The judgment's failure to distinguish between these two mental states, of believing and of knowing, is a major weakness in its reasoning. But it can be criticised on other grounds. The judge does not establish that a man who has sex with a girl whose age he does not know is 'mentally innocent': he assumes it. At first sight, that assumption may seem acceptable. But what do the words 'mentally innocent' mean? Clearly, we cannot interpret them in a theological or moral sense, because this is a legal question, not a theological or moral one. It seems to me that we can understand those words best if we say that a man is mentally innocent if he is not conscious of acting contrary to the mores or ethos of the society in which the action takes place, or, to put it in simpler terms, if he is not doing something of which members of that society might disapprove.

But how is that to be established? Attitudes change. Fifty years ago, any sexual activity between consenting adult males was criminal, but now gay partnerships are legally valid and generally accepted, and gay marriage is an imminent prospect. Less than fifty years ago, someone who bought anything for more than it was worth was considered a fool who had only himself to blame. Nowadays, someone who engages in 'insider trading' is required to hand over his profits, which are regarded as ill-gotten.

The best guidance on what the People think on such an issue must surely come from those we have elected to represent us – TDs in Dáil Eireann. Judges may have views on such issues, and may apply them in cases they have to decide, in the absence of guidance from the Dáil, in the same way as they may identify and apply legal rules in order to do justice in situations where there is no relevant Statute Law. But they are not entitled to prefer their view on such an issue to that of the Dáil, legislating as the dominant house of the Oirechtas, if the Dáil has expressed a view. By passing the Act, including Section 1, the Oirechtas seems to have expressed a view that the activity it declared to be criminal could not be performed with an 'innocent mind'. The fact that the legislation still stood, years later, indicates that the People's view on that issue, reflected by our public representatives, had not changed. If so, when the judges substituted their view on that topic for that of the People's elected representatives, they exceeded their authority.

Presumption of Constitutionality

The sequence in which the issues were decided seems to have affected the outcome. As I have described, the judges first interpreted Section 1 and a majority decided that it did not allow a Defendant to plead 'innocent mistake'. They then adjourned, and after hearing further argument they decided that the Constitution did not allow the Oireachtas to criminalise someone whose mind was 'innocent', and that since they had decided that was the effect of Section 1, it had to be unconstitutional.

Because they approached these as separate questions and took them in that order, they failed to take into account a principle in the interpretation of legislation called the 'Presumption of

Constitutionality'. That principle says that if legislation passed after 1937 is ambiguous, with two (or more) possible interpretations, and if one of them would put the legislation in conflict with the Constitution, then the judges are required to reject that interpretation, because they are bound to assume that the Oireachtas did not intend to pass unconstitutional legislation. Now, of course, we are considering Sections of an Act of 1935, which was passed before the Constitution was adopted, so it might seem that the Presumption of Constitutionality does not apply. But a later Act, passed after 1937, amended another section of the 1935 Act. That amendment had the effect of re-enacting the 1935 Act as amended, thus converting it into post-1937 legislation for the purpose of the principle of the Presumption of Constitutionality. That meant that the Court was bound to choose an interpretation of Section 1 that would not render it unconstitutional, in preference to one that did.

None of the judgments in this case, either the three in July 2005 or the single judgment in May 2006, mentions the Presumption of Constitutionality. In fairness to Judges Geoghegan and Fennelly, and to the judges who agreed with them in July 2005, it did not seem to arise on the issue they were considering at the time. But it is an established rule in the interpretation of statutes, and the judges in this case struck down legislation without mentioning it or, apparently, considering it.

What would have been the result if they had taken those two questions in reverse order? The first question would then have been: does the Constitution allow the Oireachtas to pass a law under which a citizen may be sent to prison for making an innocent mistake? They would have said no to that question. They would next have looked at how to interpret Section 1. There were two possible interpretations. One, that it allowed the defence of 'innocent mistake', would mean that it was within the Constitution. The other, that it did not, would make it unconstitutional. If they had chosen between these two, with the consequences clear before them, the Presumption of Constitutionality would have constituted a strong argument for the view that Section 1 should be interpreted as allowing the defence of 'innocent mistake'. That is, for Judge Denham's view. Indeed, it is hard to see how Judges Fennelly and Geoghegan could have interpreted Section 1 as they did if they had applied the Presumption of Constitutionality.

Section 1 was struck down without consideration of this principle because the judges separated the issues and chose to view them in a particular sequence. It may have seemed to them the obvious order, but does not seem to have been the right one, since it led to their ignoring a rule of interpretation that pointed to a different outcome.

Article 45

I come now to what I think is the most serious flaw in the decision, which infects both judgments: the failure of the judges to consider Article 45 of the Constitution. That Article lists 'principles of social policy' that should guide the Oireachtas in making laws. (Some of them now seem rather old-fashioned, and any revision of the Constitution should probably reconsider them, but meanwhile they stand.) Article 45 provides:

> *The application of those principles in the making of laws shall be the care of the Oireachtas exclusively, and shall not be cognisable by any Court under any of the provisions of this Constitution.*

This means that the courts may not 'strike down' legislation on the ground that it is inconsistent with the Constitution if that legislation is intended to give effect to one of the principles listed in Article 45. One of those principles is:

> *... the tender age of children shall not be abused ...*

Clearly, the purpose of Section 1 was to protect female children from being initiated into sexual activity at an age the Oireachtas considered premature, and that purpose, and the attachment of criminal sanctions, indicates that the Oireachtas regarded such conduct as abusive of the girl involved. On the plain meaning of the words, therefore, Section 1 seems to be an 'endeavour ... to ensure ... that the tender age of children shall not be abused'. If so, Article 45 means that the courts had no jurisdiction to interfere with it.

Before examining Article 45 to see if that is really its effect, we should ask why it is not mentioned in any of the judgments. Even if it was not going to determine the outcome of the case, it is obviously relevant, and should have been considered. There is only one possible explanation, astonishing though it may seem: both the legal team for the state and all the six Supreme Court judges who heard the appeal at different stages overlooked it.

Of course, Section 1 was enacted before 1937, when the Constitution came into force, and it might be argued that Article 45 does not apply, accordingly. But, as mentioned above, a later amendment to the 1935 Act operated to re-enact the entire Act, as amended, converting it into post-1937 legislation. In any event, it is by no means clear that Article 45 applies only to post-1937 legislation.

Would the Result Have Been Different if the Judges Had Considered Article 45?

The best answer is that we cannot know for certain how they would have decided. If the provisions of Article 45 had been contained in a Statute, not in the Constitution, the Supreme Court might well have applied standard rules about how to interpret Statutes, which would have meant that the Article did not apply. These rules include two that are identified by their Latin names, the *'ejusdem generis* ('of the same kind') rule and the *'noscitur a sociis* ('we are known by the company we keep') rule. Although they have different names, they have much the same effect, which is that in interpreting a Statute, we must consider words in their context. For example, if a Section of an Act refers to 'underground cables, wires, sewers, drains and pipes' we should not read it to include a Kapp & Peterson that happens to have been lost and buried.

The reference to protecting children from abuse occurs in Article 45.4.2, which reads:

The State shall endeavour to ensure that the strength and health of workers, men and women, and the tender age of children shall not be abused and that citizens shall not be forced by economic necessity to enter avocations unsuited to their sex, age or strength.

If we were to apply the rules described above, we might conclude that Article 45.4.2 applies only to what might be called economic abuse. But the Supreme Court has laid down, not once but many times, that it is not right to interpret the Constitution pedantically, as if it were a Statute of the Oireachtas. It is a 'living document', to be read 'broadly, not restrictively', without applying the 'rules of construction' that govern the interpretation of Statute Law. 'Plain words are to be given their plain meaning'. If we give the 'plain words' quoted above their 'plain meaning', it seems clear that Section 1 was an attempt by the Oireachtas 'to ensure that the tender age of children shall not be abused'. Since that is an Article 45 principle, the Section is outside the remit of the courts.

Could it be argued that the Article does not apply because a girl of sixteen is no longer a child? I think not. It is for the Oireachtas, not the courts, to define childhood and to say who is a child and who is not. Furthermore, if the purpose of Section 1 is to protect girls younger than sixteen from sexual abuse, the fact that it also applied to older girls, who might be classified as young women rather than children, would not bring it outside the provisions of Article 45.

It could be argued that since the effect of Article 45 is to create an exception to the general rule that the Courts may declare legislation unconstitutional, it should be construed narrowly, so as to keep that exception to a minimum. But that argument cannot stand against the reply that the primary purpose of the Article is stated to be to guide the legislature on how to prepare legislation, not to create a class of legislation immune from judicial interference. To construe it narrowly would be inconsistent with that purpose.

Did the people who drafted the 1937 Constitution intend Article 45 to be construed so as to exclude legislation such as Section 1 from judicial examination? Probably not. But the Supreme Court has made clear that that is the wrong question. According to the Court, the Constitution is a 'living document', to be interpreted in the light of current views and mores, not those of 1937. Given what we now know about how children have suffered sexual abuse in this State, and how it has affected them, to interpret Article 45 as meaning that protecting children from economic abuse was a constitutional principle but protecting them from sexual abuse was not would be unacceptable to most Irish citizens.

To me, that last argument is decisive, and my answer to the question: would the result in the *C.C.* case have been different if the Supreme Court had considered Article 45, is that it should have been. I concede there are arguments the other way. But there is no room for argument about the fact that the judges should have considered Article 45 before declaring Section 1 unconstitutional, and it appears from the judgments that they overlooked it.

C.C.'s Consequences for Other Legislation

As well as *C.C.* being in my view a bad decision, it has another worrying legacy. At some stage, the Supreme Court is going to have to address the question that it overlooked in *C.C.* and that, strange though it seems, has never been comprehensively addressed: how far does Article 45 go in denying the courts authority to interfere with legislation? When that time comes, the Supreme Court is going to be inhibited in its decision-making by the embarrassment of having previously decided issues without considering the Article. If it rules that Article 45 is a bar to judicial interference with other legislation similar to Section 1, it will face the embarrassment of having to acknowledge that its decision in *C.C.* was wrong. If it rules the other way, many people will believe that its decision is motivated by the judges wanting to avoid that embarrassment.

Astonishing?

I used the word 'astonishing' above to describe the failure of all six Supreme Court judges who heard the *C.C.* case to consider Article 45, and I think that word is justified. But this is not the first time the Court has struck down legislation without considering whether Article 45 protected it from their interference. There was for many years in Ireland a legislative code that controlled the rents landlords were allowed to charge on residential lettings, contained in a series of Acts called the Rent Restrictions Acts. The Supreme Court decided in 1982 in a case called *Blake v. Attorney General* that the Rent Restrictions Acts were inconsistent with the Constitution, and no longer formed part of the law of Ireland. None of the judgments mentioned Article 45.2.2, which reads:

> *The State shall endeavour to secure that private enterprise shall be so conducted as to ensure reasonable efficiency in the production and distribution of goods and as to protect the public against unjust exploitation.*

The Rent Restrictions Acts seem to have been an 'endeavour to ... protect the public against unjust exploitation' by landlords (conducting a private enterprise) at a time when many people could not buy a home, rented property was scarce, and the legislature took the view that tenants should be protected from rapacious landlords. If so, there was a strong argument that they were not 'cognisable by any Court'. But, as I say, the Supreme Court deleted the Rent Restrictions Acts from the Statute Book. Article 45 was mentioned, but not analysed in any thoughtful way in that decision.

2. *A v. Governor of Arbour Hill*

Reading the criticism of this decision will require some mental gymnastics. I argued above that the Supreme Court's decision in *C.C.* was wrong. But even if it was wrong, it had the effect of deleting Section 1 of the Criminal Law (Amendment) Act 1935 from the Irish legal code. The decision we examine here follows from that deletion. You will have to approach what follows on the basis that Section 1 has been deleted and is no longer part of the law of Ireland, even if you have been convinced that the decision to delete it was wrong.

Some years before C.C. was arrested, A, a middle-aged man, raped a 12-year-old girl, a friend of his daughter. He was prosecuted under the same Section 1, pleaded guilty and in 2004 received a sentence of three years. At the time of the *C.C.* decision, he had served most of his sentence, and was due to be released shortly.

Within a few days of the Supreme Court's decision in *C.C.*, A started proceedings to be released from prison, on the ground that he was detained for committing a crime that the *C.C.* case had decided did not exist. Lawyers representing the State contested his application, but on 30 May 2006 High Court Judge Laffoy granted it. The State's lawyers asked her to postpone A's release in order to give them time to appeal, but she refused. Having decided A was a citizen in unlawful custody, she held that she was bound to order his immediate release, and had no jurisdiction to postpone freeing him.

The State's lawyers appealed her decision to the Supreme Court, which responded in two ways that I for one found surprising. (I understand some practising lawyers do not share my surprise.) First, it allowed the appeal to jump the queue of appeals that were waiting their turn. It was heard on 2 June 2006, three days after Judge Laffoy's decision. Allowing the appeal to jump the queue would have seemed right if it had been an appeal by A against an order refusing to release him, because a citizen who claims to be unlawfully in prison should have his application for release heard quickly – a classic illustration of the legal maxim that 'justice delayed is justice denied'. But A was at liberty, and reasons for urgency were not obvious. Certainly, his victim and her family were distressed by the prospect of his appearing in the neighbourhood where they lived, before they expected him. But that was going to happen in a few months anyway, and their reaction did not seem to justify the appeal against his release jumping the queue.

The second surprise was that the five Supreme Court judges who heard the appeal announced their decision immediately after hearing the appeal, reversed Judge Laffoy's decision, and ordered that A should immediately return to prison. When judges 'reserve' their judgments, it is usually so as to give themselves time to think about the issues. Like any human being facing a decision, a judge may start off thinking he will go one way, but, on thinking more deeply about it, may decide first thoughts were not best. By announcing their decision at once, the judges cut off any opportunity for second thoughts. They said they would deliver judgments explaining the reasons for their decision later, and did so about six weeks afterwards, on 10 July 2006.

An immediate decision with reasons to follow was an indication that the judges would be unanimous, and they were. This, combined with their not allowing themselves any possibility of second thoughts, might give the impression that the issue was a simple one on which there was little room for a contrary opinion, and that Judge Laffoy, who had decided the issue differently, was wrong. In fact, she had based her decision on existing law. The Supreme Court's decision made important changes in the law.

This section will look at the law as Judge Laffoy applied it, how the Supreme Court changed it, the grounds they gave for their decision, and some reasons why the decision should worry us.

The Law before the Supreme Court Judgment in 'Mr A's Case'

The following are the legal principles in force when Judge Laffoy made her decision. Since I will be referring to them again, I will number them and use Roman numerals.

I. When a Statute or a Section of a Statute passed before 1937 is found to be inconsistent with the Constitution, this means it was automatically repealed in 1937 when the Constitution was adopted.

It ceased to be law from that date, not from the later date when a judge decides it is unconstitutional.

II. As a general rule, anything done under the authority of an unconstitutional statute or section is void. However, as an exception to that general rule, the courts have authority to validate void actions that are impossible or almost impossible to undo.

III. 'The finality of proceedings both at the level of trial and possibly more particularly at the level of ultimate appeal is of fundamental importance to the certainty of the administration of the law, and should not lightly be breached'.

Principle I comes from the Constitution itself. Principle II comes from the late Judge Henchy, a former Supreme Court judge, and probably the finest jurist Ireland has produced since 1922, and his colleague Judge Griffin, and was a practical solution to a problem that faced them. They had decided that a provision of the tax code was unconstitutional, and were then faced with a practical question: should the Revenue be required to refund the small additional amounts they had added to some tax bills in reliance on the void Section? The administrative burden of tracing all overcharges and sending out cheques would have been huge, and the amounts were tiny. The judges decided not to direct the Revenue to make the refunds. Judge Griffin used the attractive analogy that 'an egg, once scrambled, couldn't be unscrambled'. Judge Henchy used a less homely one, of a statue that had been completed, had become a finished work of art, and ceased to be merely a lump of stone that belonged in its quarry.

Principle III is a quotation from a judgment of the late Judge Hamilton, a former Chief Justice.

Applying Principle I, Judge Laffoy held that A's continuing detention was illegal. If Section 1, under which he was charged and pleaded guilty, had been repealed in 1937 and did not exist when he was prosecuted (even though both prosecution and defence believed it did) then his actions could not have been in breach of it. He should not be in prison for doing something that was not a crime at the time he did it, even though we might think it should have been.

How the Supreme Court's Decision in the *A Case* Changed the Law

I can best summarise the changes in the law brought about by the A case by quoting three passages from the judgment of the then Chief Justice, Judge Murray. His is the longest judgment of the five, three out of four of the other judges expressly agreed with it, and the fourth follows much the same line of reasoning, so if we look carefully at what he said, we need not examine the other judgments at length. They are expressed in lawyers' language, include some very long sentences, and are not easy for a layperson to follow. Again, since I will be referring back to them, I will number them, this time using Arabic numerals to distinguish them from the propositions quoted earlier, which summarised the law as it was before this judgment, and for which I used Roman numerals. (I had to use different kinds of numbers, rather than letters, given that the protagonist in this case is identified as 'A'.) I will call them 'propositions', to distinguish them the rules Judge Laffoy applied, which I called 'principles'. That choice of words suggests bias on my part, but I think you will agree it is justified. The quotations from Judge Murray's judgment read as follows:

1. *In a criminal prosecution where the State relies in good faith on a statute in force at the time and the accused does not seek to impugn the bringing or conduct of the prosecution, on any grounds that may in law be open to him or her, including the constitutionality of the statute, before the case reaches finality, on appeal or otherwise, then the final decision in the case must be deemed to be and to remain lawful notwithstanding any subsequent ruling that the statute, or a provision of it, is unconstitutional. That is the general principle.*

2. *I do not exclude, by way of exception to the foregoing general principle, that the grounds upon which a court declares a statute to be unconstitutional, or some extreme feature of an individual case, might require, for wholly exceptional reasons related to some fun-*

damental unfairness amounting to a denial of justice, that verdicts in particular cases or a particular class of cases be not allowed to stand. ... I do not consider that there are any grounds for considering this case to be an exception to the general principle. Mr. A., like all persons who pleaded guilty to or were convicted of an offence contrary to s. 1 (1) of the Act of 1935 had available a full range of remedies under the law. They could have sought to prohibit the prosecution on several grounds including that the section was inconsistent with the Constitution. Not having done so they were tried and either convicted or acquitted under due process of law. Once finality is reached in those circumstances the general principle should apply.

3. It cannot be said, and the applicant does not contend, that there was any inherent injustice in convicting a person of having sexual intercourse with an under-age girl, something which has been forbidden by law for a very long time and was contrary to the law as applied at the time.

Proposition number 1 contains three surprises. First is the reference to 'a statute in force at the time'. I will come back to that later.

Second is that the principle Judges Henchy and Griffin laid down, Principle II above, has been changed. Having accepted the principle that actions based on a void statute were themselves void, Judges Henchy and Griffin allowed an exception. But the exception was to apply only in situations where something had been done under the authority of what seemed at the time to be a valid Statute, and which, once done, could not be undone – the egg that couldn't be unscrambled. In Chief Justice Murray's judgment, what Judges Henchy and Griffin described as an exception to a principle is promoted to being a principle in its own right. Literally, the exception has become the rule. And it is a rule that he says operates even in a situation where what had been done under the void statute could be reversed – where Judge Griffin's egg was still in its shell.

The third surprise is that Chief Justice Murray seems to restate Judge Hamilton's statement (III above), that 'the finality of proceedings ... should not lightly be breached', but actually reverses it. Judge Hamilton said that it was important to the administration of justice that a judgment (either on appeal or if no appeal was taken) should be regarded as final, and that this was a principle that should not lightly be breached. Chief Justice Murray says it is a principle that should not be breached. At first sight he seems to adopt Judge Hamilton's principle, but by deleting the word 'lightly', he gives it a fundamentally different meaning.

Chief Justice Murray's conclusion, that things done under an unconstitutional Statute that could be undone should be treated in the same way as things that cannot be undone, is not supported by any precedent. So far as I can follow his reasoning, he starts from an assumption that a decision of a court from which no appeal is taken or where the relevant rules do not allow an appeal, must be 'final'. He then proceeds to argue in a way that illustrates the logical fallacy '*petitio principii*', also called 'begging the question' or 'arguing in a circle'. In logic, we can prove something by assuming it is not so, and then showing that this assumption leads by logically valid steps to an absurd conclusion. If the steps are valid but the conclusion absurd, then the premise must be wrong, and therefore the contrary must be right. But if you try to prove something by assuming it is so, your argument goes round in a circle and cannot prove anything. Here, the circle seems to be:

Q: *Why cannot someone who has been convicted of a non-existent crime be released?*

A: *Because his trial has been concluded.*

Q: *Why do you say it has been concluded?*

A: *Because it cannot be reopened.*

Q: *Why can it not be reopened?*

A: *Because the Supreme Court has said so.*

Q: *Why has the Supreme Court said so?*

A: *Because his trial has been concluded.*

It is like the First World War song, 'We're here because we're here because we're here because we're here.'

Before we move on to Chief Justice Murray's proposition number 2, please consider the phrases 'a statute in force at the time' which appears in his proposition 1, and 'the law as applied at the time', which appears in proposition 3. At first glance they seem also to involve begging the question, because they assume the statute was in force at the time, rather than proving it. But this language goes beyond question-begging. It directly contradicts principle I above that Judge Laffoy applied in the High Court, that a provision of a pre-1937 Statute inconsistent with the Constitution was automatically repealed in 1937 when the Constitution was adopted, and ceased to be law from that date. That is not a principle laid down by judges, which judges may be entitled to change. It is contained in the Constitution itself, and can lawfully be changed only by a referendum of the people. This is made clear by Articles 15.4.2 and 50.1, both of which appear in the Glossary at the end of this book.

Right or wrong, the Supreme Court's decision in the *C.C.* case meant that Section 1 of the Criminal Law Amendment Act 1935 had been repealed when the people adopted the Constitution in 1937, and ceased to be part of Irish law from that date. It remained in the printed Statute Book up to the time the Supreme Court handed down the *C.C.* decision, but only because nobody realised that it had been repealed. Describing a repealed enactment as the 'law' or as a 'statute in force', fails to distinguish shadow from substance, illusion from reality. The illusion is that it was a valid statute and the reality is that, in accordance with the Constitution, it had ceased to be part of Irish law in 1937. To describe legislation repealed in 1937 as 'a statute in force' at the time of A's prosecution is to ignore the Constitution. An argument based on such a premise does not merely have a shaky foundation. It has no foundation. (A similar phrase, 'a statute in force at the time', appears in Judge McGuinness' judgment, and shows the same failure to distinguish between appearance and reality.)

Judge Denham's judgment puts forward a different proposition. She takes Judge Griffin's analogy of an egg that has been scrambled and cannot be unscrambled, but extends it further than he did. Judge Denham seems to argue, or to assume, that because some things done under an unconstitutional statute cannot be undone and must accordingly be accepted, it follows that in other cases, where other constitutionally improper things have happened – for example, a man imprisoned under non-existent legislation – the undoing process should not take place, even though it could.

Judge Denham acknowledges that what she surprisingly calls 'cold logic' might lead to a different conclusion. One has to wonder if applying logic is not part of a judge's job? Does describing it as 'cold' mean it can be ignored?

Judge Denham also seems to argue – though here the language lacks the clarity that usually characterises her judgments – that even though a section of an Act may be unconstitutional, if it remains on the Statute Book for long enough before being declared void, it acquires some form of legitimacy – in much the same way, it seems, as someone who unlawfully squats in another person's property for long enough becomes entitled to stay there. She does not quote any authority for that proposition, and I think the reason is that there is none. If that is indeed what she is saying, it is inconsistent with Articles 15 and 50 of the Constitution, mentioned above, which provide that a Statute inconsistent with the Constitution was repealed by the adoption of the Constitution in 1937, not from a later date when a judge identified the inconsistency.

Remedying Injustice

There is another important difference between the decision in this case and other decisions by the Supreme Court, where the Court had also declared legislation unconstitutional but had declined to undo decisions previously taken in good faith in the belief that it was valid. To explain it, I have to describe those other cases, where the other judges declined to unscramble the egg. One was when the Supreme Court decided that the system in operation for summoning juries was defective. The people who had served on juries up to then had been qualified, but other people who were also qualified had not received jury summonses, as they should have, and did not have the opportunity to serve on juries. The jurors that had tried previous cases had been selected from a pool that was smaller than it should have been. The Supreme Court decided that the verdicts in trials that had already concluded, with juries summoned under the defective system, should not be set aside. A new system for summoning juries was needed, but previous trials held under the old system had been heard by qualified jurors, the Defendants had not been deprived of their right to a fair trial before a qualified jury, and the decisions of those juries should stand.

The other major 'scrambled egg' the Supreme Court examined was a practice that had grown up in general elections. An identifying number appeared opposite the name of everyone who was listed in the Register of Voters. When you went to vote and received a ballot paper, the returning officer would cross out your name in his copy of the Register of Voters and write your identifying number on the counterfoil of your ballot paper. That meant that after the votes had been counted, someone who didn't like the look of your voting paper could note its number, and track down the matching book of counterfoils. There would be only one counterfoil with the same number as your ballot paper, and if the returning officer had written your identifying number on that counterfoil, a hypothetical researcher could then identify you from the Voters' Register as the person who had filled in that voting paper.

None of this was remotely likely to happen, but the Supreme Court decided that a practice that made it theoretically possible that a voter might be identified was inconsistent with the constitutional requirement that voting be by secret ballot (Article 16.1.4). The Court did not declare that all elections previously held, in which that illegal practice had been followed, were inoperative. That would have meant declaring every Dáil, including the then current one, illegal, and all legislation passed by them inoperative. 'Which,' as Euclid might say, 'is absurd.'

The third case was the one involving the Revenue, described above, where the Court did not direct the Revenue to distribute tiny refunds.

In the first two cases, unlike C.C., legislation was declared unconstitutional for technical reasons and there was no suggestion that any citizen had suffered injustice from its application. In the Revenue case, there had been injustice, but it was minimal. But Section 1 was not struck down for technical reasons. It was declared to be unconstitutional because the Supreme Court concluded (whether rightly or, as I hope I have convinced you above, wrongly) that it produced injustice and therefore could not be part of Irish law.

Having decided in the C.C. case that Section 1 was void because it produced injustice, the Court decided in the A case notionally to prolong its existence beyond the date in 1937 when it had been repealed. That is, they decided to extend the lifetime of a law that the Court had previously found to be unjust. Judge Griffin's scrambled egg could not be unscrambled. In the A case, the Court decided that a rotten egg should not be thrown out.

Previous Unjust Trials

I promised earlier to come back to quotation number 2 from Chief Justice Murray's judgment where he says that in exceptional cases a trial might be reopened but goes on to say that, not having challenged the validity of Section 1 at the time of the trial, A may not do so later. Judges Denham, McGuinness and Geoghegan, using slightly different words, agree with Judge Murray's new rule that once a trial has been concluded, whether justly or not, it cannot be reopened.

This is disturbing. Every legal system should recognise its own imperfection, acknowledge the possibility that it will make mistakes, and promise that if a mistake has been made, it will be remedied. A system that does not make and keep that promise is not one that citizens of a democracy can respect, or should accept. I quoted earlier the Latin maxim that expresses that core value: '*Fiat justitia, ruat caelum*' – 'Let justice be done, though the heavens fall'. The decision in *A v. Governor of Arbour Hill* is an unambiguous statement that someone who has suffered an unjust trial and conviction is not going to have that injustice remedied. Efficient administration of the courts is made more important than justice for the citizen. Of course, when I speak of 'the citizen', I do not mean only A, but other citizens who will come before the courts at some future time, and will be refused justice because their judges will be bound to apply the law the Supreme Court laid down in the *A* case.

Now, of course, if you accept the arguments in the last chapter that the *C.C.* case was wrongly decided, and Section 1 should still be regarded as part of Irish law, people convicted under Section 1, including A, were rightly convicted. If so, it is right that they should stay in prison. But doing justice to A by two wrong decisions that cancel each other does not seem a good way of running a judicial system.

Judge Hardiman makes the point that the facts in the A case show that he knew his victim's age, since she was a classmate of his own daughter and could not have pretended not to, even if that defence had been legally available. But he does not make that point in order to distinguish A from other people convicted under Section 1 whose trial may have been unfair. He makes it only to justify a finding that A did not have what lawyers call 'standing' to challenge his conviction. The argument is that since he could not have raised the defence that he believed the girl was of age, he did not suffer any injustice, and therefore has no right to complain, even if he was tried and convicted under non-existent legislation. Like his colleagues, Judge Hardiman does not open a door to rectify injustice suffered by people who have had an unfair trial. And, of course, this is not limited to prosecutions under Section 1, but applies to all prosecutions.

Blaming the Lawyers

Judge Murray's quotation number 2 seems to lay down another rule that I think should worry us all. He says A's legal team could have done what C.C.'s lawyers later did, that is argue that Section 1 was unconstitutional and seek to have it set aside. They did not do so, and he says A lost his chance. That is, a citizen should stay in prison, even he is there unjustly, because his lawyers let him down. It is interesting that in the United States, a country whose criminal law system is very far from being a model, people who have been convicted have been appealing, sometimes successfully, on the grounds that their trial was unfair because the lawyers appointed to represent them were inadequate. In Britain, as we all know, people of Irish origin who were unjustly convicted of terrorist atrocities were later released and their convictions were set aside. That they had been wrongly convicted was a scandal, the police conduct was appalling, and the judges failed in their duty to protect the innocent. But the British system admitted its failures and tried to remedy them. I find it disturbing that Ireland's Supreme Court has decided that people accused of a crime get one chance only to defend themselves. Even if it can later be shown that their trial was unfair and their sentence unjust, they have had their only chance, have failed, and have no further rights.

Incidentally, speaking of the Irish immigrants in Britain whose convictions were set aside, I found it strange that they eventually received an 'apology' from the then Prime Minister, the endlessly self-promoting Tony Blair, not from the people who should have apologised, the judiciary. You cannot apologise without admitting you have done something wrong. Blair hadn't, his 'apology' was meaningless, and that is why I put the word in inverted commas.

Indeed, I think it was worse than meaningless, because it pre-empted what should have happened, an apology from the judiciary, whose job is to see that people accused of a crime got a fair trial, had strikingly failed to do their job and owed an apology to the innocent men they had sent to prison. It would have been better for the administration of justice in Britain if one of the judges who had failed them in their long-drawn-out struggle against injustice, or a senior judge representing the judiciary, had publicly acknowledged its failure and apologised. Britain is not my concern, but it would be a good day for Ireland if our judges were to say 'I got it wrong and I am sorry.' It would be even better if the Supreme Court said it. Pretending always to be right means not acknowledging your errors. And that is a formula for repeating them.

Why Should We Care?

Even if you accept that the Supreme Court's decision in the *A* case was wrong in law, did they do justice? And, if they did, should we not be pleased with the result, rather than criticise it? The argument that justice was done is strong. The man known as 'A' raped a twelve-year-old girl, tried to invoke a technicality to avoid completing his sentence, gained a few days of freedom between Judge Laffoy's decision and the Supreme Court's, but was then returned to prison. That seems right. Even if the Supreme Court's decision means that other men who had previously been sent to prison under the same section are not allowed to seek freedom by claiming they thought their sexual partner was older, should we worry about that? They had sexual intercourse with under-age girls. Their punishment may seem excessive, but many will feel it is right that they should suffer some penalty.

I think there are many reasons to worry. First, citizens' confidence in the law and the judiciary is weakened when our highest court issues a decision supported by arguments that do not stand up to analysis. It is not just a question of the court reaching a decision that I, and I hope you, think is wrong. It is more serious. This is a decision that is inadequately reasoned, sets aside established legal principles, and creates a bizarre precedent. It casts doubt on the reliability of the Supreme Court. And if we cannot trust our Supreme Court, where can we place our trust?

Secondly, a judgment of the Supreme Court binds all other courts in future trials, in the same way as the Court's decision in *C.C.* deleted Section 1 from the Statute Books, even if the Court got it wrong. The decision in *A* has already been relied on as an authority in a number of Supreme Court cases.

Thirdly, we look to the Courts to give effect to the Constitution, Article 40.3.2 of which reads:

> *The State shall, in particular, by its laws protect as best it may from unjust attack and, in the case of injustice done, vindicate the life, person, good name, and property rights of every citizen.*

One of the duties of our courts is to enforce that provision, and to protect citizens from injustice. That includes injustice at the hands of organs of the State, and 'organs of the State' includes the judges. Protecting citizens from injustice was the principle that lay behind the decision in *C.C.*, and if the judges had been right in deciding that the section worked injustice, and if it was not exempt from their interference, they would have been right to declare it unconstitutional.

When a citizen claims in court that the State has infringed his or her rights, the outcome potentially affects all other citizens. It is easier for us to think of *A* as a repulsive child-rapist than as a citizen, but of course he is both. Few of us may expect to be prosecuted for raping a child, but any citizen may be prosecuted under an unjust Statute, denied a fair trial and sent to prison, or ordered to pay a heavy fine. And we now know that if that does happen to any of us, then, even if the statute under which we were imprisoned or impoverished is later declared unconstitutional we will stay in prison, or will not get our money back. It will not matter that we were prosecuted under legislation that was unconstitutional, or even that it was declared to be unconstitutional because it was unjust. We had one chance, and we blew it, or our lawyers did. Under the rules laid down in the *A* case, we are not entitled to a second chance.

There is a further cause for worry. The decision leaves the Supreme Court vulnerable to the suggestion that its judges put too much emphasis on the operation of the court system, and not enough on its function, which is to do justice, whether between citizens or between a citizen and the state. Admittedly, in quotation number 2 above, the Chief Justice acknowledges that there may be exceptions to the principle he announced in quotation number 1, if applying it might result in a denial of justice. But the fact that he and his four colleagues were not prepared to entertain A's claim that he was jailed for doing something that at the time he did it was not a crime, indicates we should not rely on that acknowledgement.

The outcome of any such case shifts the balance between the power of the state and the rights of citizens. Our constitutional rights to claim our liberty and the protection of our good name (so that, for example, we will not labour for the rest of our lives under the stigma of an unjust conviction) still exist in theory, but we must wonder what they are worth if judges will not enforce them.

There is still a further reason to worry, as though those I have already given were not enough. I tried to show above that the earlier decision of the Supreme Court in the *C.C.* case was wrong. We looked at arguments that at first sight seemed valid, even if they seemed less so under scrutiny. The level of the reasoning in the *C.C.* case is respectable, even if you agree that the conclusion is wrong. The judgments in the *A* case are unconvincing on even a superficial reading.

In summary, this is a judgment of the Supreme Court that seriously abridges the rights of citizens, changes the law to do so, and is supported by arguments that do not stand up to analysis. I think it will affect public confidence in our legal system, and I think it ought to. Its impact is increased by the link with the decision in the *C.C.* case, so the effect is cumulative.

Different Approach? An Afterword

It is interesting to note that A's application to be released would probably never have been made, and judicial embarrassment would have been avoided, if the judges had adopted a different approach to the consequences of their decision in the *C.C.* case, when they found Section 1 to be unconstitutional. Their practice is to make a declaration that an Act or Section is inconsistent with the Constitution, and therefore invalid in its entirety. Judges do not treat the Act or Section like an apple, part of which should be cut out because it is rotten but the rest of which is sound and may be eaten. They view it as a rotten egg, which must be thrown out. They have justified this by invoking the concept of 'separation of powers'. They say legislating is the function of the legislature, the Houses of the Oireachtas, and of course that is right. They go on to argue that if they, the judges, were to examine a piece of legislation, cut out the unconstitutional bits, and leave the sound part, that process would produce new legislation, different from what the legislature enacted. At best, they say, this would risk trespassing into an area of government occupied exclusively by the Houses of the Oireachtas. That argument seems reasonable, and to the extent that it suggests some respect for the functions of the Oireachtas it should be welcome. But is it right? Article 15.4 of the Constitution provides:

> *Every law enacted by the Oireachtas which is in any respect repugnant to this Constitution or to any provision thereof, shall, but to the extent only of such repugnancy, be invalid.*

Clearly, if the judges decide a piece of legislation has an unconstitutional objective – for example, to deprive citizens of a constitutional right – they would be right to invalidate the entire. Something similar would apply to a defective Section of an Act that was otherwise valid: they would 'strike down' that Section only, as they did in the *C.C.* case, and leave the rest of the Act standing. The same would apply to a defective sub-section of an otherwise valid Section. However, the words 'but to the extent only of such repugnancy' seem to mean that if any piece of legislation, whether it is a Statute or a Section of a Statute, is worded in such a way that it is possible to cut out the bad bits, and leave the rest, then that is what the judges ought to do.

If so, even if they were right in saying Section 1 of the Criminal Law Amendment Act 1935 included some 'bad bits', they should have looked at it so see whether it contained some 'good bits', too. If the judges in the *C.C.* case had compared Section 1 to an apple, and cut out the 'bad bits' leaving the rest to stand, instead of like a rotten egg, to be discarded, enough of the Section might have been left to leave A with no valid grounds for making his application.

And they would have served us better.

3. The 'Abbeylara Case'

As explained in Chapter 8, the background was as follows. John Carty was killed by police gunfire in Abbeylara, County Offaly. The Oireachtas decided to try to find out why he had died, and established a Committee of Enquiry to investigate and report. Police officers who would face questioning by the Committee applied to the High Court for an order preventing the Committee from going ahead with its enquiry. They succeeded in the High Court, and that decision was appealed to the Supreme Court, where it was modified, but in effect affirmed.

From early on, it was clear that the Committee had been set up without regard for formalities that should have been observed. The judges decided that the job of setting up the Committee had been handled so incompetently that it had no standing. They didn't stop there. They went on to decide that the Dáil did not have the constitutional power to hold an enquiry if it might lead to a conclusion damaging to anyone's good name. That amounted to a blanket ban on any enquiry by the legislature, since any enquiry that reached a conclusion could be interpreted as criticising somebody. A result that nobody could say pointed a finger of blame at anybody would be useless.

For technical reasons, the litigation was taken by the Gardaí as 'Applicants', not Plaintiffs, against a group of TDs and Senators as 'Respondents', not Defendants. It was first heard in the High Court. It raised important issues, so, instead of it being heard by one High Court judge sitting alone, what is called a

'Divisional Court' was set up to hear it, consisting of three judges. The three were judges that practising lawyers would have seen as 'heavy hitters', judges whose views carried weight. They decided, first, that the process of establishing the enquiry had been so mishandled that the Committee had no standing, Secondly, they held that the Dáil had no power to hold such an enquiry. They did not deliver separate judgments. Judge Morris, who was then President of the High Court and has since retired, delivered the sole judgment.

The members of the Committee appealed this decision to the Supreme Court, where five judges delivered separate judgments. Judges Murray, Denham and Geoghegan in effect agreed with the High Court decision. (The difference between their decision and the High Court's is not significant for our purposes.) Judge Keane, who was then Chief Justice, and Judge Francis Murphy (both of whom have since retired) disagreed, but were in a minority, so the Supreme Court in effect affirmed the High Court ruling.

The report of the case, including six judgments, takes up nearly 167,000 words, about twice the length of this book. If I were to summarise and criticise all the points made by different judges, as I did in commenting on the *C.C.* and *A* cases, a lay reader would probably become hopelessly bogged down. Instead, I will set out how I would have decided the case if I had been one of the judges. In doing so, I will also try to show how judges might write judgments that would lay down legal principles and be understood by people who have not spent years studying law. Since my 'judgment' is effectively a criticism of the majority decision in this case, I do not follow the normal rule of judges, which is to adjudicate only on the points they need to address in order to reach a decision on the issues, and to refuse to address any other points. It is therefore longer than it would be if I were a real judge. However, I will focus only on the principle of the powers of the Oireachtas, and not go into the reasons that led all the judges to agree that the Committee of Enquiry had been set up in such a hamfisted way that it should not be allowed to proceed.

'Judgment' of 'Judge Williams' in Maguire and Others v Ardagh and Others

Background

The Applicants in this action are all members of An Garda Síochána. They have been called before an enquiry established in order to ascertain what happened in a matter in which they were involved as members of An Garda Síochána. I will consider later in this judgment the relevance of this country being a democracy, and at this point it is enough for me to note that in any country actions or omissions of the police force are a matter of legitimate interest and concern to citizens, and public confidence in the police is essential to their being able to function effectively. If the conduct of the Gardaí or members of the Gardaí is questioned, there is a public interest in that conduct being examined.

It is also in the interests of the Gardaí. No police force in a modern democracy can function without the consent of the community it polices. That consent depends on the community feeling confidence in its police force, and confidence depends on the community seeing the police force as accountable. A successful attempt by some members of the Gardaí to avoid accountability would endanger community consent to the functioning of the force.

While the Applicants have the rights of citizens, they are also members of a force whose duty is to serve the People. Before I could properly make an order to prevent the proposed enquiry from going ahead, I would have to balance the public interest in its taking place against any private interests that may be affected by it. In my view, the interest and right of the People to be reassured, through a public enquiry, about how they are policed has great weight. The courts should be reluctant to make an order whose effect would be to protect the Gardaí or any individual Garda from having to explain and justify their actions, or to grant them immunity from public scrutiny.

This of course assumes that the People do have such a right, and that it is exercisable by them through their elected representatives. For reasons I will explain later in this judgment I hold that they do have such a right and that it is so exercisable.

I propose to address the issues in this case by answering the following questions:

1. Does the legislature have power to hold or authorise an enquiry such as this?

2. If so, does the body holding an enquiry have the right to summon people to appear before it and answer questions?

3. If so, subject to what limitations? Or, to put it another way, what rights have people who are required to give evidence before such a body?

Preliminary Considerations

(a) Expediency

First, I should exclude one issue from my judgment. It has been suggested that tribunals and Dáil enquiries are not an effective way of ascertaining facts, that their findings are not available as evidence in other proceedings, and that they do not represent good value for the money they cost. That is not an issue on which a judge is entitled to express a view. It is the duty of the judicial organ of government to ascertain, if asked, whether a tribunal or enquiry has been established by a body with the constitutional power to do so; if so, whether that power has been validly exercised; and whether the tribunal or enquiry is being conducted lawfully. Whether it is expedient to establish a tribunal or enquiry, or prudent to do so having regard to its likely cost, are political questions, for decision by other organs of government. They are not questions on which a judge can express a view without entering territory where, constitutionally, he is a trespasser.

(b) Presumption in Favour of Legislature

There are valid reasons why the courts should be reluctant to answer the first question in the negative. In general, it is right for each of the three organs of government to be self-governing within the limits of the Constitution, and none of them should seek to dictate to the other or others how it should perform its constitutional functions. Legislating, and deciding in what areas legislation is needed, and what form it should take, is the duty of the Oireachtas. How it gathers information to enable it to perform that duty is primarily a matter for it to determine, without interference by any of the other organs of government. Furthermore, Article 28.4.1 of the Constitution states:

The Government shall be responsible to Dáil Eireann.

It is *prima facie* for the Dáil to determine how to exercise its function of holding the Government responsible to it. A public enquiry is one such way. Such an enquiry, under the auspices of the Dáil, into how an entity such as the Garda Síochána, under the control of the Government, performs its functions seems a particularly suitable way – in so far as I may properly comment. The courts should be slow to interfere in such a process unless it is being conducted unlawfully.

I will now address the three questions I posed above.

1. Does the legislature have power to hold or authorise an enquiry such as this?

The Applicants argue that the Constitution does not give the legislature power to hold an enquiry such as the one they challenge. They contend that such a power would exist only if the Constitution granted it, and that in the absence of such authority the power to hold an enquiry does not exist.

Audi Alteram Partem

In my opinion, this court does not have jurisdiction to entertain that argument in these proceedings. If the court were to make a finding such as the Applicants seek, that the Oireachtas and/ or its constituent Houses lack the power to hold or authorise enquiries, that, clearly, would operate to prevent the Dáil from doing something that it has been doing up to now. That is, an order of this court would deprive the Dáil of a function it has been exercising, and would thereby curb its powers. One of the fundamental principles of justice is that no order should be made that has adverse consequences for any person or body without that person or body being given the opportunity to argue against it. That principle is summed up in the Latin maxim 'audi alteram partem' – 'hear the other side'. This court would ignore that principle if it made an order limiting the powers of the Dáil without first giving the Dáil an opportunity of arguing against it.

The Respondents in these proceedings are members of the Dáil or Seanad, and have been nominated (albeit invalidly) to conduct the proposed enquiry. There is no suggestion that any of them, even if they had been validly appointed, has been nominated to represent either the Oireachtas or the Dáil before this court on the issue of the power of the Oireachtas or Dáil to hold enquiries. Of course, given that their purported appointment to conduct an Enquiry was invalid for the purpose intended, it could not be operative for another, presumably unintended, purpose, such as representing the Oireachtas or either of its Houses on the issue of their constitutional powers.

It might be difficult for a Plaintiff to frame proceedings in such a way that the Oireachtas or Dáil would be a party, but that would not justify me in abandoning the audi alteram partem principle.

It may be argued against this view that the courts do from time to time make decisions whose effect is to delete from the legal code of this country legislation that is inconsistent with its Constitution, and that it does so without hearing the legislature. But that is a different process. What the courts decide in such cases is a result of examining the Constitution and the impugned legislation, interpreting both, and deciding whether they are compatible. That is clearly a judicial function. There is no need to ask the legislative organ to participate, and its views on the interpretation of legislation would be irrelevant. Indeed, inviting comment from the legislative organ might be an invitation to it to trespass beyond its constitutional function of making laws, into interpretation, which is the function of the Courts. That process is entirely different from one where the court is asked to limit the powers of someone who is not a party to the proceedings, and where to make the order sought would be inconsistent with *audi alteram partem*. Moreover, a finding by the judicial organ of government that in a specific instance the legislative organ has exceeded its powers does not limit or affect the general capacity of the legislative organ to perform its constitutional functions. However, in order to resolve this issue finally, I will address it.

Constitutional Powers

The argument that there is no express provision in the Constitution giving authority to the legislature to hold enquiries is correct. The Applicants argue that such a power cannot exist unless it is either implicit – implied though not stated – or inherent – part of the normal powers of a legislature. They say there is nothing in the Constitution that could be regarded as implying power to hold an enquiry. I reject that argument. Article 15.2 of the Constitution provides (irrelevant material omitted):

> *The sole and exclusive power of making laws for the State is hereby vested in the Oireachtas: no other legislative authority has power to make laws for the State.*

Article 15.2 means that the Oireachtas has constitutional authority to pass legislation subject to one limitation only: if its legislation is inconsistent with the Constitution, it is void. That is specifically provided in Article 15.4.2, as follows:

> *Every law enacted by the Oireachtas which is in any respect repugnant to this Constitution or to any provision thereof, shall, but to the extent only of such repugnancy, be invalid.*

This means that unless a law passed by the Oireachtas can be shown to be inconsistent with the Constitution, it is a valid exercise by the Oireachtas of the power vested in it by Article 15.2. For the Courts to say, 'the Constitution does not specifically empower the Oireachtas (or any other body) to do certain things, and therefore it may not do them', would be inconsistent with Article 15 and with the scheme of the Constitution. The Constitution does not pretend to present an exhaustive list of what the Oireachtas may do. Instead, Article 15 authorises the Oireachtas to legislate *inter alia* to give itself powers to do things the Constitution does not specifically authorise it to do, provided those things are neither specifically prohibited by the Constitution nor inconsistent with the functions of the Oireachtas.

Common Sense

This approach seems to me to be consistent with common sense and with good government in a way that no other would be. The Garda Síochána has certain rights, powers and immunities, because the Oireachtas has decided it should have them in order to perform its function as a police force. The presence of some Gardaí, in control of firearms, at Abbeylara when Mr. Carty met his death was lawful because it was authorised in legislation passed by the Oireachtas. It is part of the duty of the Oireachtas to keep an eye on how the Gardaí use the powers entrusted to them, including whether they abuse them, so that the Oireachtas can decide whether Garda powers should be continued, extended or curtailed. The Gardaí are part of the executive organ of government and the Oireachtas might reasonably decide that in exercising its lawmaking functions it should not rely on a report of an investigation by the Executive on the conduct of the Gardaí. If so, the Oireachtas may feel bound to take on itself the duty of investigating a matter of legitimate concern to it in its performance of its function as sole and exclusive lawmaker. For the courts to say that the Oireachtas may not enquire directly, or through some of its members, into the activities of the Gardaí would risk frustrating the Oireachtas in doing its constitutional job.

I think it would also be inconsistent with common sense and with proper governance of the state if this court were to decide that the conduct of the Gardaí was not open to examination. But that would seem to be the consequence of prohibiting the Oireachtas from conducting such an examination, because no other organ of government could do so effectively and independently. The right that should exist in a democratic society to hold the police force to account would have been lost, and the People would be the losers.

Public Interest

This relates to an issue I mentioned earlier. If something happens that may cause public disquiet, such as a citizen being shot dead by members of the Garda Síochána, the People may wish or need to be adequately informed. (I use the word 'People' with a capital 'P', here and elsewhere in this Judgment, to indicate that I am referring to the people in the sense in which that word is used in the Constitution.) Article 5 of the Constitution identifies this as a democratic state, and democracy requires that the People should have whatever knowledge or information they may consider they need in order to exercise their powers. Indeed, the extent to which the People are informed about how their country is governed is one of the measures of the health of any democracy. Article 6 of the Constitution provides:

> *1. All powers of government, legislative, executive and judicial, derive, under God, from the people, whose right it is to designate the rulers of the State and, in final appeal, to decide all questions of national policy, according to the requirements of the common good.*

> *2. These powers of government are exercisable only by or on the authority of the organs of state established by this Constitution.*

The provision that it is the right of the People to decide all questions of national policy carries as a necessary corollary or precondition, that the People are adequately informed, so as to be able make such decisions. That is, the general rule (to which there may be exceptions) is that if matters relevant to national policy become known to any person who exercises any of the powers of government listed in the Article, that person has a duty to ensure that such matters are disclosed publicly. I repeat that there may be exceptions to this rule, but the onus of establishing an exception lies on the person asserting it. This is a further argument in favour of the proposition that any enquiry by the Dáil or Oireachtas should be conducted in public. If the courts should be reluctant to abridge the powers of another organ of government (as they should) they should be even more reluctant to make a ruling whose effect would be to deprive the People of access to information on a matter of interest or concern to them. It would be strange if the courts, whose power to interpret the Constitution derives from the People, were to interpret it so as to deprive the People of access to information they might feel they should have, and are entitled to have. (The expression, 'biting the hand that feeds you' comes to mind.) This seems to me to be a powerful additional argument (if one were needed) against this aspect of the Applicants' case.

That disposes of my first question. The second was:

2. Does the body holding an enquiry have the right to summon people to appear before it and answer questions?

I think what I have said above answers that question. An enquiry that does not have such a power would be meaningless. If the power exists, the necessary machinery to make it operative must also exist. My third and last question was:

3. If so, subject to what limitations? Or, to put it another way, what rights have persons who are required to give evidence before such a body?

If an enquiry does go ahead, it may uncover that one of the Applicants acted in a particular way. It may be suggested that he (all the Applicants are male) was wrong in so acting. In *re Haughey* it was held that a person whose good name came under question in the course of an enquiry had a right to certain protections, including being represented by counsel. I propose to consider that decision further. Article 40.3.2 of the Constitution reads as follows:

> The State shall in particular by its laws protect as best it may from unjust attack and, in the case of injustice done, vindicate the life, person, good name and property rights of every citizen.

The State is required to protect as best it may the good name of citizens but only from unjust attack, and to vindicate a citizen's good name, again as best it may, but only 'in the case of injustice done'.

Indeed, I think that is obvious. Someone who has an undeserved good reputation is not entitled to constitutional protection or vindication of it. If a citizen has done something that others did not know he had done, and which they might think he should not have done, and if that fact is uncovered, his reputation may suffer. That does not in my opinion entitle him to invoke Article 40.3.2. His good name has not come under unjust attack, and he has not suffered injustice. In order to be entitled to the protection of the Article, a citizen must show two things. The first is that his good name has come under attack, and the second is that the attack is unjust.

Nor in my opinion are the words 'unjust' and 'injustice' to be construed as meaning 'otherwise than by a decision of the courts, administering justice in accordance with Article 34'. It may be argued against this that finding facts is the function of the courts and its judges, and that no other body may do so. I do not think such an argument is tenable. Article 34 provides that the courts have jurisdiction 'to determine all matters and questions, whether of law or fact, civil or criminal'. It does not say that only the courts may do so, and such an interpretation would lead to absurdity. To take two examples: it would mean that the death of a citizen would have to be pronounced by a judge, not a medical doctor; and that scientific research, whose purpose is, clearly, to determine questions of fact, could lawfully be carried out only under judicial supervision.

The onus of proof that an attack on a citizen's good name is unjust must fall on the person alleging it. If the issue is disputed, it must be determined by the courts, in accordance with Article 34.

Inherent in the Applicants' case is an assumption that an enquiry or tribunal which may lead to damage to anybody's reputation should be conducted, if not actually by a judge, then so far as possible in the way a judge in court would conduct it between litigants, and that any departure from that concept is unlawful if it might result in injury to the good name of a citizen. Let us look at how far the court process protects the good name of citizens.

Protection of Citizens' Good Name in Litigation

There is little protection for witnesses in Ireland's court system. Cross-examination is often an ordeal for witnesses. Advocates legitimately cross-examine in a way intended to persuade judges and juries that a witness whose evidence is unfavourable to their case is a perjurer, forgetful, or stupid if he is a witness of fact, and incompetent if he is an expert witness. The reputation of a witness who has been exposed to such a cross-examination may be permanently and incurably injured. This may happen even if the decision indicates that judge or jury believed his evidence. It is much more likely if the decision suggests otherwise. The courts offer no protection against such injury to the reputation of witnesses, other than limited protection in the shape of the opposing advocate, and his duty is to his client, not to the witness. Nor do the courts consider whether any such injury to the reputation of a witness is just or unjust, either in civil or in criminal litigation.

The questioning of complainants in trials for rape or other sexual offences is another example of the limited protection the courts afford witnesses, but I do not need to examine it for my present purposes.

I look next at how the evidence of a witness in litigation, whether civil or criminal, may affect the reputation of somebody else. There are limitations on the right to cross-examine. Only a party to litigation may cross-examine a witness, and in general a party may cross-examine only witnesses called by the other party. If I am a party to litigation and I call a witness who says things about me that injure my good name, I am unlikely to be allowed to cross-examine him in order to defend my reputation, unless I can persuade the judge to allow me to treat him as a 'hostile witness', which, for good reasons, judges rarely do. If I am a party to litigation and a witness called by the other side impugns my good name, I or my counsel may cross-examine him, but only if what he has said about me is relevant to the issues. For example, if the litigation is about a commercial contract and a witness on the other side accuses me of sexual immorality, I will not be allowed to cross-examine him on that accusation unless I can show that it is relevant to the issues the judge has to decide.

Of course, if the witness impugns the good name of someone who is not a party to the litigation and is therefore not represented in court, he (or she) will have no right or opportunity to cross-examine or rebut his accusations. In such cases the person whose good name has been injured will have to look to the second aspect of Article 40.2, the right to seek to have his good name vindicated against unjust attack. Even if the attack was unjust, he will have difficulty in framing an action. He may not sue the witness who has spoken ill of him, because the law does not permit such an action. Even though a witness may have spoken with malice (whether in the normal meaning of that word, the technical legal meaning, or both) his evidence has the protection of 'absolute privilege'. Media reports have the protection of qualified privilege, which in practice means that if a newspaper, radio or television station or one of the 'social media' accurately reports defamatory, even malicious, statements made by a witness in a court action, the medium concerned faces no legal liability. If someone believes his good name has been damaged by what a witness in court has said under oath, or by a newspaper report of it, his prospects of being able to vindicate it are nebulous.

The courts impose these restrictions on the right to cross-examine, on the right to sue a witness for what he says under oath, and the right to challenge media reporting, in the interests of the administration of justice. If they are constitutionally justified, as I think they are, it can only be by the words 'as best it may' in Article 40.2. The constitutional function of the courts, of doing justice between litigants or between the State and a person accused of crime (Article 34) has priority over the possibility of damage to a citizen's reputation.

This is the extent of the protection available to a citizen whose good name may be attacked in court, whether as a witness or because of how a witness, or, indeed, an advocate, speaks of him. It does not seem to me reasonable to argue that a citizen should be entitled to a higher standard of protection from a non-judicial enquiry or tribunal. Nor in my opinion should he be entitled to prevent such a tribunal or enquiry proceeding on the ground that if his good name comes in question, the tribunal will probably not afford him more protection than he would enjoy if the same thing had happened in court proceedings. The function of a tribunal is not to do justice but to inform the legislature on matters it considers necessary for it to perform its constitutional function of legislating and/or to exercise the powers vested in the Dáil by Article 28 of the Constitution. It is not for the courts to say that more weight should be attached to their function of doing justice than to the Oireachtas' function, or to hold an enquiry authorised or conducted by the Oireachtas to a higher standard than the courts themselves accept. In homely language, the courts should not tell the legislature, 'Don't do as I do: do as I say.'

To the extent that re Haughey may be read as requiring a tribunal or enquiry to give greater protection to the good name of a citizen than the protection (limited, as I have shown) the courts give, it was in my opinion wrongly decided. It follows that in a tribunal or enquiry there is not an automatic right to confront witnesses and cross-examine them. If someone alleges that what a witness has said affects his good name, it is for the people conducting a tribunal or enquiry to decide how much scope they should allow him or her to defend his or her reputation. The Respondents are legislators, either TDs or Senators. I am bound to assume such people will decide fairly and wisely. If someone feels they have not, and he has suffered injustice as a result, he has access to the courts. However, in order for a judge to be justified in interfering with the conduct of a tribunal or enquiry, it would have to be shown that the reputation of the witness was (a) attacked, (b) in a way that involved injustice and (c) would not have happened in a judicial hearing.

It occurs to me that if there is no automatic right to confront and cross-examine witnesses during an enquiry or tribunal, it seems to follow that there can be no automatic right to be represented by lawyers. However, I am not so deciding in this case, and would not do so without first hearing argument.

Historical Argument

The argument that the Oireachtas, and in particular the Dáil, has power to hold enquiries is supported by considering the present Constitution in its historical context. It is a successor to the Constitution of 1922, whose origins lie in the 'Articles of Agreement for a Treaty between Great Britain and Ireland' signed on 6 December 1921. Articles 1 and 2 of the Treaty read as follows:

> *1. Ireland shall have the same constitutional status in the Community of Nations known as the British Empire as the Dominion of Canada, the Commonwealth of Australia, the Dominion of New Zealand and the Union of South Africa, with a parliament having powers to make laws for the peace, order and good government of Ireland and an*

Executive responsible to that Parliament, and shall be styled and known as the Irish Free State.

2. Subject to the provisions hereinafter set out, the position of the Irish Free State in relation to the Imperial Parliament and Government and otherwise shall be that of the Dominion of Canada, and the law, practice and constitutional usage governing the relationship of the Crown or the Representative of the Crown and of the Imperial Parliament to the Dominion of Canada shall govern their relationship to the Irish Free State.

While the issue is not specifically addressed, it seems to me that the intention and effect of those provisions was that the Parliament of the emerging Irish Free State was to have the same powers as its predecessor as Ireland's Parliament, the Imperial Parliament, which unquestionably had the power to authorise and hold enquiries such as the one in contemplation here – as did those of the other territories listed in Article 1. That view is strengthened by Article 16 of the Treaty, which specifically limited the powers of the new Parliament in one respect, thus impliedly confirming that in all other respects it would enjoy the same powers as its predecessor. This construction of Article 16 accords with common sense and established principles of construction. ('*Expressio unius exclusio alterius est*'.) If under the 1922 Constitution the Dáil and/or the Oireachtas had such power as successor the to Imperial Parliament, specific language would have been required to have terminated it in 1937. The Constitution does not contain any such language. (See Article 49.)

Additional Observation

The foregoing answers the three questions I posed near the beginning of this judgment, and determines the issues they raised, but I would add this. The effect of my decision is that the People's elected representatives in the Oireachtas may enquire into the activities of the State's police force and require them to account for their actions, and may do so in public. That conclusion is consistent with Article 5 of the Constitution, which declares the State to be democratic, and with Article 6.1.

Each of these Articles is fundamental. Within a house or other building, some walls serve only to divide the building into separate rooms, and may readily be removed or altered, while others are structural, or load-bearing, and cannot be disturbed without endangering the structure. These two are among the Articles of Ireland's Constitution that are like structural walls in a house; they cannot be interfered with without endangering the entire. I do not think a decision prohibiting the Dáil or Oireachtas from holding or authorising enquiries would be compatible with either of them. In particular, the effect of Article 6.2. seems to be that if the Oireachtas did not have power to enquire publicly into the activities of our police force, no other body could do so, and the State Police Force would not be publicly accountable to anyone. I think it would be hard to reconcile such a situation with the provisions of Articles 5, 6 or 28, or with the democratic nature of this State. However, it is not necessary for me to decide this question in these proceedings, and I do not do so.

(End of 'Judgment')

Consequences of the Abbeylara Decision

None of the judges who constituted the majority in the *Abbeylara* case agreed with any part of the above 'Judgment'. If you find its arguments persuasive, I think you will have to conclude that they were wrong. But let us look at the consequences of the decision.

Obviously, it ended the Dáil's attempt to find out what happened in Abbeylara when a citizen was shot dead by a Garda or Gardaí. It also meant that the Dáil has been prevented from carrying out other enquiries its members may have thought necessary. It is easy to see the abridgement of Dáil powers simply from the point of view of the TDs who compose it, and of the government of the day, but that would be a superficial view, neglecting the fact that the Dáil, like the courts, exists for the

People (following the example of the 'Judgment' above, I use a capital P). When the powers of the Dáil are abridged, its ability to serve the People diminishes. When the powers of the Dáil are wrongly abridged, the Dáil, its members and the government are the obvious losers, but the People suffer, too, even if in a less obvious way. I do not think the judges of the Supreme and High Courts who decided the *Abbeylara* case gave that enough weight. When the courts restrict the powers of the legislature, it is easy to see this as part of a struggle for power between the judiciary on the one hand and the legislature and executive on the other, a struggle that is not acknowledged and perhaps not even consciously recognised on either side, and would probably be denied on both. But when one of the antagonists deprives another of a power that it has exercised on behalf of the People, the People are the losers. I think the Supreme Court did that in the *Abbeylara* decision.

4. McKenna v. Ireland

This is the case where the Supreme Court forbade the Government to campaign in favour of an amendment to the Constitution and forbade the Dáil to vote funds for that campaign. Let me start my explanation of why I think the majority decision was wrong by quoting some of what Judges Keane and Egan, who would have dismissed Ms. McKenna's claim, said.

Discussing provisions in the Constitution for its amendment, Judge Keane said:

> *These provisions are at the heart of the structures of parliamentary democracy which we have inherited, recognising as they do the primary role of the executive and the popularly elected assembly, to which it is responsible in the raising and expenditure of monies. The extent to which and the manner in which the revenue and borrowing powers of the State are exercised and the purposes for which the funds are spent are the perennial subject of political debate and controversy but the paramount role of those two organs of state, the Government and the Dáil in this*

area is beyond question. For the courts to review decisions in this area by the Government or Dáil Eireann would be for them to assume a role which is exclusively entrusted to those organs of state, and one which the courts are conspicuously ill-equipped to undertake. While the expenditure by the Government of £.5m in this case has given rise to debate and controversy, it is not the function of the courts under the Constitution to enter into, still less, purport to resolve such disputes.

In his dissenting judgment in the Supreme Court, Judge Egan said:

The money was voted to the control of the Government under the heading "Divorce Referendum" and could, of course, only be applied for a purpose or purposes which would come under that heading. Apart from that, there is no direction, statutory or otherwise that it must be apportioned or applied in any particular manner. Apart from such a direction in clear terms it is a matter solely for the executive arm of government to decide how the money should be expended. Its decision is not for the scrutiny of the judicial branch of government.

In his judgment in favour of Ms. McKenna, Chief Justice Hamilton quoted from a judgment of the late Judge Costello in another case, sharing the views of Judges Keane and Egan, but he did so only to disagree. Judge Costello had said:

The extent of the role the Government feels called upon to play to ensure ratification is a matter of concern for the executive arm of government, not the judicial. The Dáil decides what moneys are to be voted for expenditure by the Government on information services (which would include an advertising campaign in support of an affirmative vote in a referendum). Should the Government decide that the national interest required that an advertising campaign be mounted which was confined to extolling forcibly the benefits of an affirmative vote, it would

> *be improper for the courts to express any view on such a*
> *decision.*

As I said, the majority in the Supreme Court disagreed with Judges Keane, Egan and Costello. Each judge expressed his or her reasons for their decision in different words, but the following is a fair summary of their shared view.

> *Both the legislature and the government are limited in what they may do, because they are not allowed to act in a way that involves 'constitutional injustice'.*
>
> *Deciding whether any decision by legislature or government is in accordance with 'constitutional justice' is the function of the Courts, and only the Courts, and the Courts may annul any legislative or executive decision that they consider to be unjust.*
>
> *'Constitutional justice' requires the government and Dáil to 'hold the scales equally between those who support and those who oppose the amendment'.*
>
> *Spending public money in support of the proposal would therefore be 'constitutionally unjust', and is prohibited by the Court.*

Each of those propositions seems reasonable on its face, and they appear to hang together in a logical progression. I think the first two are valid, with reservations, which I will discuss later. But let us look at the third and fourth more closely, to see how they stand up if we relate them to two other questions. One is:

1. Were the judges right to classify a referendum campaign as a contest between different groups of people, on which the government could not 'take sides' without infringing the concept of 'constitutional justice'?

The other is:

2. Does their decision affect adversely the ability of a government to function?

Sadly, the answer to this second question is fairly obvious. Let me clarify that I am not saying the courts should never make a decision that makes it harder for another organ of government to do its job. That would be inconsistent with the principle that judges must do justice, whatever the consequences – *fiat justitia ruat caelum*. But I do say that if they are deciding a case, particularly one where they are called upon to interpret the Constitution, and their decision could limit the ability of another organ of State to serve the People, they should consider carefully whether it is right to interpret the Constitution in a way that produces that result.

The argument that if there are two opposing 'camps' of citizens, one supporting a change in the Constitution and advising fellow-citizens to vote for it, the other opposing it and advising people to vote no, the government of the day should not take sides, seems plausible. But it assumes the right and only way to view a referendum is as a conflict between two opposing groups of citizens. Is that assumption justified? Is a Bill to amend the Constitution simply the occasion for a conflict between two sides? Or may it be an issue of principle?

Those questions are not considered in any of the majority judgments. We do not know what arguments the lawyers on each side advanced, except to the extent that the judgment addresses some of them, but it seems from what the judges said that the issue of principle may not have been raised on either side. If not, it is understandable that the judges did not focus on it. It is an issue of a political kind, not one that judges come across in their work, or on which they are entitled to express a view, let alone to decide. But the effect was that they assumed that a referendum to amend the Constitution, like the conflicts between litigants that judges decide, could be expressed as a simple competition between opposing groups, and that the role of the Government and Dáil was to throw in the ball, and let the opposing teams get on with the game.

It seems odd that they made such an assumption. Judges would not decide a dispute about the construction of a building without trying to understand the principles and rules governing such work. If a dispute within the financial services sector came before a conscientious judge, he would not decide it without seeking to educate himself on how that sector operates. But in the *McKenna* case, where the issues were political, the majority judgments indicate that the judges assumed they understood them, without needing any explanation.

With this in mind, let us take a deeper look. Any proposal to amend the Constitution starts because the executive, the government of the day, forms the view that the Constitution as it stands does not serve as well as it should the objective of attaining 'the common good' and requires amending in order to do so more effectively. Of course, the Government cannot take this further without the support of a majority of the Dáil, but under our system that majority is available. Thus, the view that the People will be better served by an amended Constitution is shared by Government and the Oireachtas, the nation's legislature and executive.

Some citizens may disagree with the opinion of the executive and legislature, and views may be expressed, even stridently, on both sides, as pro and anti groups form and campaign on each 'side'. But this is not inevitable. For example (admittedly, after the *McKenna* judgment), there was practically no disagreement in 2011 when the Constitution was amended to allow for reductions in judges' salaries in line with those of other public servants. Nor does it seem right to assume a faction fight is the essence of what happens when the People consider a proposal to amend their Constitution. I think if we look at it rightly, the essence of this referendum was as follows.

The Legislature and Executive, the bodies which in accordance with the country's democratic process the People nominate to run the country, have a duty to seek to promote the 'common good'. The responsibility to think carefully about how to do so falls on the Government with particular weight, on the Legislature also, and on the judiciary much less, if at all. Identifying the common good and trying to attain it is the function of politicians, not judges. In doing its job, the Government came to believe that one constitutional provision seemed not to accord with the objective of attaining the common good. The Constitution provided that people who had married and separated might not enter into a new marriage with a different partner. It also included and still includes a number of provisions aimed at protecting and advancing 'The Family' and family life. Since it was adopted, the judicial organ of government decided in a series of decisions that these provisions apply only to a 'family based on marriage', not to people who may be living in families but who are not married, or to the children of such people.

The government must accept the decision of the courts, interpreting the Constitution in accordance with their constitutional function. But it is its constitutional function to govern the country as best it can, under the law. In doing so, it identified an adverse effect on Irish citizen-babies born into non-marital families who have come into the world without constitutional protection that other newly born citizens enjoy. The government formed the view that as it stood, and as construed by the courts, the prohibition on divorce produced injustice for those young citizens, and should be deleted, so that the Constitution would better serve the common good.

The Government may also have considered whether it is the role of a political community, as distinct from a religious one, to impose on its members restrictions on a right to marry, such as our Constitution contained, and concluded it is not. In any event, it concluded that the constitutional prohibition of divorce was not conducive to the 'common good'. In discharge of its constitutional duty, the Government put in train the process to amend the Constitution, to eliminate a perceived injustice, and so that it would better serve the People, and be more conducive to attaining the common good.

In this instance, the Government also considered practical issues, including whether enough voters would accept its recommendation to carry through what it saw as a necessary reform. It considered a previous attempt to amend the Constitution, that was defeated. One factor in that defeat was a strong 'no' campaign, using the dubious slogan: 'hello, divorce, goodbye daddy'. The Government decided that it would be right for it, in furtherance of its duty of seeking to promote the common good, and in discharge of its duty to the People, to spend public money on a campaign for a change in the Constitution, in order that voters would fully understand the issues, and to rebut false arguments that might be advanced by opponents of change. The Government asked the Dáil to authorise it to do so, because spending money in that way required Dáil approval, and explained to the Dáil its reasons for seeking that authority. Having understood them, the Dáil gave the Government the authority it sought, limiting the amount of money the Government might spend.

If this is an accurate description of what happened, to equate it with a sporting contest requiring a 'level playing field' is to misunderstand – indeed, to trivialise – the role and function of Government and Dáil. The decision of the Supreme Court in the *McKenna* case seems to me to have been based on a misunderstanding by the majority about the nature of a proposal to amend the Constitution. Indeed, I think it would be more accurate to call it a wrong assumption than a misunderstanding, because the majority judgments show little interest in seeking to understand. It also involves a striking failure to show what a Supreme Court judge many years ago described as 'the respect one great organ of state owes to another'.

This is not to argue that the courts should never interfere in a referendum. There was one years ago, rejected by the People, to alter the voting system for Dáil elections. Most citizens believed the motive of the Government of the day was the selfish one of seeking to improve the electoral prospects of a political party, not the worthy one of seeking to attain the common good. If a future Government wanted to spend public money on promoting a questionable referendum, it might be right for the Courts to intervene, though the onus of proof would be high.

Before I move on, I think I should make specific comment on one sentence that appears in the judgment. Former Judge O'Flaherty said:

> *The public purse must not be expended to espouse a point of view which may be anathema to certain citizens, who, of necessity, have contributed to it.*

I describe this as strange, because the Judge describes accurately what happens in a democracy, and then goes on to say that it must not happen. Inevitably, taxpayers contribute to causes they do not approve. Pacifists pay taxes that support armed forces, strict Catholics who would not use birth control themselves pay indirectly for providing it to others, and we all pay for excessive pensions and perks for politicians. That is what happens in a democracy. It may happen less than under a tyranny, but democracy requires taxpaying citizens to accept the fact that their tax contributions may be spent on things they do not approve. A country where taxpayers had a veto over how tax revenue was spent, as Judge O'Flaherty seems to suggest, would be ungovernable.

It also seems to me strange that the courts support citizens who object to the Government spending money and to the Dáil voting to allow the Government to spend money, on promoting something that is the official policy of the Dáil and Government, simply because those citizens disagree with Government policy. But that is the effect of the *McKenna* judgment.

5. *Damache v. DPP*

As in *Abbeylara*, I comment on this decision primarily by another 'dissenting judgment'. This was initially because of how I became aware of the decision, but on thinking about it, I decided I could not find a better way of explaining why I disagree with the Supreme Court's decision. I also hope the text of my 'judgment' illustrates and supports the suggestion in Chapter 1 that judges could be better at laying down the law in language citizens understand.

In March 2012, when I was on the point of going away on a three-week holiday, I read in *The Irish Times* that the Supreme Court had declared void a Section of an Act that allowed a senior police officer to authorise a search of a citizen's home. The judgment was not reported in full, only the result, but the facts seemed clear from the report. A police officer who was involved in the relevant investigation had authorised a search of the Plaintiff's home, and the Supreme Court had held that he had no power to do so and that the Statute purporting to give him that power was invalid.

At the time, I was examining the other judgments of the Supreme Court discussed above, in which I thought the Court had acted in excess of its powers, and I suspected that this case fell into the same category. The newspaper report gave me an opportunity to conduct an experiment. In the other decisions I had criticised, I had the text of the judgment in front of me, and was in a position to pick holes in the reasoning. This time, I was going away, and would not read the judgment until I returned. I thought it would be interesting in the meantime to identify the principles that I thought should apply in such a case and form a view on how the issue should have been decided. Needing to travel light, the only reference I would bring with me would be the Constitution, and I would apply it, together with my under-standing of the legal principles involved, to the facts as report-ed. If my initial guess that the Court had exceeded its powers was confirmed by that exercise, then I would write a 'judgment' setting out why I thought so, and on my return compare it with what the Court had said. Of course, I would not write my own 'judgment' if, on examining the principles, I agreed with the de-cision. (That did not happen.) My 'judgment' would be based on the text of the Constitution, not on how judges have interpreted it over recent years, but I felt it would not necessarily suffer as a result.

I would not know what arguments each side had deployed. In one way, that would be a drawback, but I did not think it was necessarily an unmixed disadvantage. Advocates can illuminate issues for the benefit of judges, but they can also narrow the judges' focus, leading them to overlook issues that the advo-cates fail to mention. (That may be what happened in C.C.: per-haps the lawyers representing the State did not raise Article 45 of the Constitution in their submissions to the Court, and the judges overlooked its relevance.)

Here is the result of that exercise. I have added basic information that I did not have when I wrote it, such as the text of the Section the Court declared unconstitutional, and names and dates, and my original hand-written text has gone through the same editing process as everything else in this book, but I have not added or subtracted anything of substance.

'Judgment' of 'Judge Williams' in Damache v. DPP

On 9 March 2010 the Plaintiff's dwelling was entered and searched by officers of the Garda Síochána under the authority of a warrant issued by Detective Superintendent Dominick Hayes the previous day. In this action, the Plaintiff challenges the legitimacy of the search and the warrant, on two grounds. The first is that Superintendent Hayes was involved in the investigation that led members of the Garda Síochána to want to search the Plaintiff's dwelling and therefore lacked the independence that someone considering issuing such a warrant should bring to such consideration. The second is that the Statutory provision, Section 29(1) of the Offences against the State Act, 1939 (as inserted by Section 5 of the Criminal Law Act, 1976), under which a Garda Superintendent may authorise a search, is unconstitutional. The Plaintiff contends this is because it is inconsistent with Article 40.5 of the Constitution and because constitutional justice requires that such authority may be given only by a judge. The rationale of my decision indicates that I should consider those two grounds in reverse order.

I should first make it clear that I am not holding that if Gardaí arrive at a citizen's dwelling, whether equipped with a warrant or not, and enter it without resistance or objection from its occupant(s), such entry should be deemed to be forcible. For the purpose of this action I will assume it, in the Plaintiff's favour.

Alleged Unconstitutionality of s. 29

The impugned section reads as follows:

> *Where a member of the Garda Síochána not below the*
> *rank of superintendent is satisfied that there is reasonable*
> *ground for believing that evidence of or relating to the*
> *commission or intended commission of an offence under*
> *this Act or the Criminal Law Act, 1976, or an offence which*
> *is for the time being a scheduled offence for the purposes*
> *of Part V of this Act, or evidence relating to the commis-*
> *sion or intended commission of treason, is to be found in*
> *any building or part of a building or in any vehicle, vessel,*
> *aircraft or hovercraft or in any other place whatsoever, he*
> *may issue to a member of the Garda Síochána not below*
> *the rank of sergeant a search warrant under this section*
> *in relation to such place.*

Broadly, and sufficiently for my purpose, the effect of the Section is that a Garda Superintendent or a Garda officer of higher rank may issue a search warrant if he believes one is needed, and it should be executed by a Garda Sergeant or officer of higher rank. The Section does not require that the issuing officer is not connected with the investigation that gives rise to the warrant.

Article 40.5 of the Constitution provides:

> *The dwelling of every citizen is inviolable and shall not be*
> *forcibly entered save in accordance with law.*

Article 15. 2, to which I will also refer in this judgment, provides:

> *1° The sole and exclusive power of making laws for the*
> *State is hereby vested in the Oireachtas: no other legisla-*
> *tive authority has power to make laws for the State.*
>
> *2° Provision may however be made by law for the creation*
> *or recognition of subordinate legislatures and for the pow-*
> *ers and functions of these legislatures.*

The first thing that must strike anyone who approaches the interpretation of Article 40.5 is that it consists of a single sentence, and the first part is inconsistent with the second. If the dwelling of every citizen is inviolable, then it may not be forcibly entered, by anyone, under any circumstances. That is what 'inviolable' means. If it may be forcibly entered in accordance with law, then it is not inviolable.

Which is it? For reasons set out below, I conclude that overwhelming public interest must in certain circumstances override the reluctance of a citizen to see his dwelling forcibly entered, and accordingly it must be the second. The first would lead to the following consequences, which seem to me to be absurd.

1. A local authority could not enter a dwelling against its occupant's objections to abate a nuisance, even one that threatened public health.

2. The Fire Service could not enter the dwelling of an absent citizen to deal with a fire there, even though it threatened to engulf adjoining dwellings. The concept of 'implied consent' by an absent owner to the Fire Service breaking in does not get around this. 'Implied consent' can exist only where there is a right to withhold consent, and I am satisfied that the owner of a burning terraced house or of a flat in an apartment complex does not have the right to imperil his neighbours' dwellings by refusing to admit the Fire Brigade to quench there a fire that poses a threat to other people's property or lives.

3. A landlord of a dwelling could never eject a tenant, because in order to do so the landlord or court officials would have to enter the dwelling, and neither would be entitled to do so if it was inviolable. Nor could a mortgagee eject a non-paying mortgagor of a home. All Possession Orders of homes made up to now in favour of landlords and lenders would have to be declared *ultra vires*. Residential landlords would cease to exist, because no home-owner would be willing to rent to a tenant who could not be ejected. Similarly, no bank or building society would lend on the security of a mortgage of a residential property. It is hard to see how the bulk of the population could hope to be housed.

The terms of the 'social contract' citizens make with each other when they live in a community may have to be implied, if they are not clearly stated. I am satisfied that the social contract in force in this country does not entitle any citizen to insist on the inviolability of his dwelling to the peril of his neighbours. I hold therefore that in spite of its use of the word 'inviolable', Article 40.5 must be construed as permitting the Oireachtas (the Nation's sole and exclusive lawmaker, under Article 15) to make laws under which the dwelling of a citizen (and *a fortiori* of a non-citizen) may be entered forcibly. I interpret the word 'inviolable' in this context as guidance to the Oireachtas about the importance of a citizen's right, qualified though it may be, to privacy and freedom from intrusion in his home. It suggests, for example, that the Oireachtas should legislate on this issue, and not delegate the power to do so to one of the subordinate legislatures Article 15 contemplates. It does not create any limitation on the exercise by the Oireachtas of its legislative function. In this context, the function of the Oireachtas is to decide by whom, in what circumstances, and subject to what conditions and protections, a citizen's dwelling may be forcibly entered, and to give effect to that decision in legislation.

Even if Article 15 did not by necessary implication identify the Oireachtas as the organ of government that should decide the conditions for forcible entry of a citizen's dwelling, common sense would do so. Given that the right to an 'inviolable' dwelling is not and cannot be absolute, it must be the constitutional lawmaker that decides to what extent that right is to be limited and what circumstances over-rule it. The balance between a citizen's privacy and immunity from interference in his home and the claims of the common good may have to be adjusted as circumstances change. For example, restrictions on the power of authorities to enter a citizen's dwelling that apply in normal times might need to be relaxed in times of national emergency. Or it might appear that excessive limitation on a right to enter a citizen's home was making it easier for some citizens to commit crimes in or from their homes, or to act there anti-socially with impunity, and that a different balance should be struck between private rights and public interest. Or that a power vested in the Executive by legislation to enter the homes of citizens was insufficiently limited or was being abused, and needed to be curtailed. Drawing, and if need be adjusting, a balance between private rights and interests and the common good is clearly the function of the law-making organ of government, whose members are elected by citizens and answerable to them for how they have exercised their legislative power.

Hypothetically, if the Oireachtas had failed to legislate in this area, the courts might apply common law principles, and the courts' rulings would constitute the law until replaced by legislation. But the courts have no authority to say what shape such legislation might take. The Oireachtas might decide to protect the interest of citizens in privacy and safety from disturbance in many different ways. For example, it might confine the power to authorise a search to a limited class of people, such as senior Garda Officers, judges – or even legislators. Or it might list conditions that must be met before a lawful search could take place. It might combine those two, prescribing that only a limited class of people might authorise a search, while also laying down criteria to be met. Or it might approach legislating on the issue in a completely different way. Under the Constitution, it is for the Oireachtas, and only the Oireachtas, to decide what conditions, if any, should be complied with before a citizen's dwelling may be entered. A judge has no authority on this question, and could not express an opinion on it without infringing the principle of separation of powers.

Constitutional Limits on Forcible Entry?

Given that legislating is a matter for the Oireachtas, the next question is: what limit, if any, does the Constitution impose on the powers of the Oireachtas to legislate for forcible entry of a citizen's dwelling? Or, rather, since it is not the function of a court to decide issues not properly before it, the question should be rephrased as: 'does constitutional justice allow the

Oireachtas to legislate for forcible entry of a citizen's dwelling without the authority of a judge or other independent person?'

Expressed in those words, the question answers itself. A local authority seeking to eliminate from a citizen's dwelling something that constitutes a threat to public health may or may not have time to make an application to the courts or seek the approval of an 'independent' person. If the Fire Brigade is called to quench a fire in an adjoining dwelling that threatens to engulf the caller's home, it certainly will not. Neither the local authority nor the Fire Service can be described as 'independent' in this context. Each has its own 'agenda', public health or quenching fire. Neither can strike an impartial balance between the importance of their operations and the interests of the private citizen whose dwelling they propose to enter.

Clearly, therefore, there are situations where there must be a right for appropriate people to enter a citizen's dwelling withouit his consent, forcibly if need be, without judicial or other independent authority. The Oireachtas is vested with sole authority to legislate for those situations.

Is there a difference in principle between legislating for forcible entry by one agency of the Executive, the Fire Service, in discharge of its fire-fighting functions, and forcible entry by another agency of the Executive, the Garda Síochána, in discharge of its function of protecting citizens and the State by preventing or detecting crime? The Fire Brigade's entry will almost certainly be in an emergency. The Gardaí's may or may not be, but if they fear that a serious crime is about to be committed, or may have been committed, or material they need to take possession of in order to do their job may be destroyed or taken out of their reach if they do not intervene promptly, they may also need to act urgently. There are obvious differences in practice. For example, the Fire Brigade will almost inevitably damage any property they may enter, and the Gardaí will not necessarily do so. But are there real differences in principle between the two? It is not easy to see any.

I would reformulate this question as: 'Does forcible entry by the Gardaí of a citizen's home in order to conduct a search differ from forcible entry by the Fire Brigade in order to quench a fire in ways or to an extent such that the former should require judicial or other 'independent' approval while the latter does not?' In trying to answer that question, it will be useful to examine how the Gardaí might seek judicial or other independent approval and in what circumstances it might be given or withheld, assuming such approval was needed.

Judicial Functions

The role of a judge on any disputed issue is to decide between parties in conflict, after hearing both sides. *Audi alteram partem* ('hear the other side') is a fundamental requirement of natural justice, as this Court has pointed out on many occasions. Judges may on occasion grant applications made *ex parte*, that is in the absence of one party to proceedings, but a final determination on the issues is never made unless both (or all) parties have had an opportunity to be heard. On an application for a search warrant, it is impossible for both sides to be heard. If the person whose home the Gardaí wish to search becomes aware of their wish before the search happens, it is almost certain that if a search does later take place, it will be useless. It is essential to the operation that the occupant of the 'target' dwelling does not know it is a target until the search takes place. So, a person asked to authorise a search cannot apply that fundamental principle of justice. That is, he or she cannot act as a judge.

There is another objection in principle to an argument that judicial approval should be required for a Garda search of a citizen's dwelling. Ours is a constitution based on the concept of separating the legislative, executive and judicial functions and powers – though some may question the extent of the separation between the first two. To involve one organ of government in the decision-making of another is in principle, and usually in practice, for the benefit of neither. That is, it is not for the benefit of those whom each is bound to serve: the State and its citizens. This objection in principle translates into practical difficulties if we think about how a system of judicial approval for search warrants must operate in practice. In the first place, as I pointed out above, any judicial hearing must be tainted by the impossibility of observing *audi alteram partem.*

Secondly, if judges were to set standards of proof adequate to protect the putative inviolability of a citizen's dwelling, some requests for search warrants would inevitably be refused. From the point of view of the Gardaí and of the executive organ of government of which they are part, that must mean that they have been frustrated in trying to do the job that the Constitution requires them to do, of maintaining public order and detecting and prosecuting crime, by the interference of another organ of government, exercising what a British Prime Minister famously described as 'power without responsibility'. That is not a desirable situation from the point of view of the Executive. Nor is it desirable from the point of view of the judicial branch that the Executive may blame it for frustrating the performances by the Executive of its constitutional function.

Thirdly, if a search has been judicially authorised and has taken place in circumstances where it should not have, the involvement of a judge in that process may deprive injured citizens of a remedy they should have. Assume, for example, the Gardaí advance an inadequate case for a search warrant, and the judge who hears it – and of course hears one side only – does not recognise the inadequacy, because the Garda representative puts forward a plausible case. A citizen whose dwelling has been 'violated' in such circumstances ought to have the right to seek a remedy against those responsible. But it will certainly be hard and may be impossible for him to claim such remedy if the unlawful search was authorised by a judge.

This could operate to his detriment in either or both of two ways. A citizen whose dwelling had been wrongfully violated, and who should be entitled to compensation, might lose his right to claim compensation if the violation took place under the order of a judge. And if a search had been judicially authorised, someone (whether a citizen or not) who was being prosecuted and wanted to argue that evidence gained in an illegal search should be excluded, could be prejudiced if the evidence had been obtained with a judge's approval. Thus, the involvement of a judge in the process might well operate to the unjust detriment of a citizen and/or a Defendant in a criminal trial, and, unjustly, in favour of the executive organ of government.

Finally, there must be a risk of objective bias at the least in any criminal trial that takes place after a questionable search has been carried out with judicial approval. An impartial observer might reasonably fear that if a search warrant has been authorised by one judge, his colleague, the trial judge, would be less inclined to set it aside, or to exclude any incriminating evidence it may have uncovered, than if the search had been authorised by an exclusively administrative decision. Furthermore, there may be a danger in a criminal trial that jurors may be influenced against an accused if they knew that a judge, not merely a Garda officer, had decided that the evidence justified allowing the Gardaí to enter his home against his will and carry out a search there.

For all these reasons, I hold that constitutional justice does not require that only a judge may authorise a search of a citizen's dwelling. That disposes of the Plaintiff's second ground.

The First Question

That leaves the Plaintiff's first argument, that if a decision to approve forcible entry of a citizen's dwelling to conduct a search there is to be taken by a member of the Garda Síochána, it must be taken by an officer unconnected with the investigation giving rise to the proposed search, and that a legislative provision that does not so provide is constitutionally defective. The Plaintiff claims that the Garda Superintendent who authorised the search was involved in the investigation in the course of which the search took place, and therefore lacked objectivity, and that seem not to be disputed.

Court's Jurisdiction?

I have first to consider what jurisdiction the Courts have in relation to the complaint. As I have said earlier, the Oireachtas has sole constitutional authority to legislate for forcible entry into a citizen's dwelling. It has done so. It has chosen to vest in a Garda Superintendent the power to authorise a search, and has not chosen to specify that the Superintendent should not have been involved in the relevant investigation. Unless it is shown that legislation is unconstitutional and therefore invalid (Article 15.4), the duty of the judicial organ of government is to enforce decisions of the legislative organ. Judges should do so without comment or criticism of the legislation or its authors, in accordance with the principle of the separation of powers, just as the legislature should refrain from comment on judicial decisions. (Of course, this does not exclude criticism in a private capacity by legislators of judicial decisions or by judges of legislation.)

If the decision to approve a search were judicial in nature, it would be right that it should be made by a judge, whose independence could not be questioned. It is not. It is executive in nature, the legislature has not required it to be made by an 'independent' member of executive personnel, and no grounds have been advanced – or in my view could be advanced – for saying that the legislature in so deciding has breached any provision of the Constitution. A judge considering legislation that comes before him might have a sense that it could have been better worded, or that it should have included protections or safeguards for people who might be affected by it. But that would not entitle the judge to interfere with a decision of the legislature, unless it can be shown that the legislation breaches a specific provision of the Constitution. As a citizen, I might prefer that a decision to breach a citizen's privacy in his home should be made by a completely independent person, if that were possible, but I would not be entitled to express my hypothetical preference in my role as a judge. Still less would I be entitled to impose it on the legislature, in the absence of a specific provision in the Constitution. None such has been shown.

Furthermore, in my view this argument ignores reality. The Garda Síochána is part of the executive organ of government and, like most if not all components of that organ, it is a hierarchy. Any police force operates on the basis that individual

officers comply with policy and with orders from their superiors, and do not exercise independent judgment contrary to
whatever may be current policy, or orders from 'on high'. Its
members are not merely expected to comply with the decisions
of their superiors. They are required to do so.

Moreover, it is almost inevitable that any senior member of
the Garda Síochána asked to make such a decision will know
some of the officers involved in the investigation. If the investigation involves a senior police officer, it is likely that he or
she and any proposed 'deciding officer' will know each other at
least well enough that, if the 'deciding officer' had been a judge
hearing an action instead of a policeman deciding whether to
approve a search, it would have been his duty to recuse himself.
Moreover, any senior police officer facing the duty of making
such a decision must be aware that his superiors in the Gardaí
would not look kindly on an officer who frustrated his colleague's conduct of an enquiry by refusing to approve a search
of a suspect's home. The same is probably true within the Department of Justice, whose Minister's satisfaction or displeasure
would be likely to affect the career prospects of any 'deciding
officer'. Accordingly, limiting decision-making on the issuing of
a warrant to a police officer not connected with the investigation, or to an official in the Department of Justice, might give
the process a false appearance of independence, but would not
achieve independence.

Further Observations

What rights has a citizen who has had the unpleasant experience of seeing his dwelling forcibly entered by the Gardaí in circumstances that did not justify the intrusion? I think the answer
must depend on the circumstances. If the entry was the result
of an abuse of a power vested in the Gardaí by the Oireachtas,
the citizen is entitled to pursue a remedy through the courts.
But if a power created by the Oireachtas has been validly exercised, the citizen has not suffered an actionable wrong. The
courts should not intervene to vindicate him. Still less should

they interfere with legislation that has been validly passed by the State's sole legislative authority.

I would add this general comment. Each of the three organs of government has devised ways of going about their respective jobs in order to do them effectively. For example, the Houses of the Oireachtas normally debate the purpose and principles underlying a Bill at Second Reading, and look at the detail of the legislation at Committee Stage only if they have first approved its general scheme. Similarly, judges require proof, usually under oath, of relevant disputed facts, reject hearsay, and insist on hearing both (or all) sides to a dispute. The Executive operates under a hierarchical system, where officials are expected to comply with policies laid down by their 'superiors'. It would be an error for any organ of government to assume that a *modus operandi* that it has chosen to adopt in order to perform its function, or even one that it may regard as essential to its function, is equally useful to the performance by other organs of their (different) functions. It would be an even greater error to assume that such a *modus operandi* would not merely be useful but should be compulsory for a different organ of government.

(End of 'Judgment')

When I returned to Dublin and read the text of the Section that the *Damache* decision set aside (quoted above), I was not impressed. The Constitution recognises the right of a citizen to limited immunity from forcible entry of his home, and legislation should recognise that the Constitution views forcible entry of a citizen's dwelling differently from forcible entry of any building that was not a citizen's home – 'any building or part of a building or any vehicle, vessel, aircraft or hovercraft'. The Section fails to recognise that distinction, and the Oireachtas is to blame for ignoring it. But that does not render the Section unconstitutional, and I think a challenge to it on that ground should fail.

I also came to realise as I studied the Section that it starts from a very questionable assumption: that a senior police officer is not merely competent to decide whether a citizen's dwelling may be forcibly entered and searched, but that he or she needs no guidance from the Oireachtas about what criteria should be applied in making such a decision. Except in cases of 'hot pursuit', I think a search of a citizen's home, which inevitably interferes with his or her constitutional (though not absolute) right to enjoy it without intrusion, should not take place unless a senior police officer believes, on credible information, certified in writing, (a) that the search is likely to lead to the detection and prosecution, or prevention, of a serious crime, (b) that if the search does not take place there is a real likelihood that the crime will take place, or go unpunished, as the case may be, and (c) that there is no practical alternative.

I also think a police officer who authorises a search when he or she should not have done so, because criteria that the Oireachtas laid down (or, rather, should have laid down) have not been met, should be liable to disciplinary action. If the decision can be shown to have been irresponsible, the citizen whose dwelling has been forcibly entered should be entitled to compensation. But my primary criticism of the Section is that it gives a police officer discretion to make a decision that may affect important rights of a citizen, without giving guidance about how that discretion should be exercised or placing any limit on it.

However, these are the comments of a citizen criticising how the Oireachtas has done its job. That the Oireachtas has done a poor job of legislating does not entitle the courts to interfere with the result. The courts may interfere with legislation if it infringes the Constitution, but not otherwise.

The Supreme Court Decision

When I read the single judgment, delivered by Chief Justice Denham, I was both disappointed and then, as I began to recognise what a profound change it made in our jurisprudence, dismayed. I explain in Chapter 9 why I was dismayed. Why was I disappointed? Not because her decision differed from my view. I knew that before I started. It was essentially because it seemed to me that she had failed to examine, still less to analyse, the Articles of the Constitution I quoted above in my 'Judgment'. Instead, she started from an assumption that Article 40.5 of the Constitution vests in a citizen absolute rights in relation to his or her dwelling, which the courts should protect. That is, she assumes a citizen's dwelling is 'inviolable'. She rejects, apparently without even considering, the proposition that the Constitution authorises the Oireachtas to decide in what circumstances the common good and needs of the community should override a citizen's natural wish to protect the privacy of his home. Her judgment seems to me almost to ignore the words 'save in accordance with law'.

I was also disappointed that she declared legislation to be unconstitutional without identifying any Article of the Constitution and showing how the legislation was inconsistent with it. The judgment seems to be based on an assumption that the courts are authorised to supervise the performance by the Oireachtas of its function of making laws. The concept that the courts' power is limited by the text of the Constitution seems not to have been considered.

My further criticisms of the judgment are probably best described by quoting some sentences it contains, and commenting on them in turn. This may risk being unfair, because sentences may be quoted out of context, but I do not think my quotations will be unfair and I will try to ensure that my comments are not, either. For ease of reading, I will put the extracts from the judgment in italic print, and my comments in normal font.

Quotations

> *The principle that the person issuing a search warrant should be an independent person is well established.*

> *The issuing of a search warrant is an administrative act, it is not the administration of justice. Thus a search warrant is not required to be issued by a judge. However, it is an action which must be exercised judicially.*

*There are two aspects of the issuance of a search warrant
which are important. First, that a search warrant be issued by an independent person. Secondly, that such a person must be satisfied on receiving sworn information, that
there are reasonable grounds for a search warrant.*

*The procedure for obtaining a search warrant should ad-
here to fundamental principles encapsulating an independent decision maker, in a process which may be reviewed.
The process should achieve the proportionate balance
between the requirements of the common good and the
protection of an individual's rights. To these fundamental
principles as to the process there may be exceptions, for
example when there is an urgent matter.*

Comment

It seems sensible to look at these together. At first sight, each
seems unobjectionable, but when we look at them more closely,
we see that they are inconsistent with the Articles 15 and 40.5 of
the Constitution, which, read together, provide that it is for the
Oireachtas, as the only constitutional lawmaker, to decide what
principles should apply to issuing a search warrant, and that
the judiciary have no constitutional authority to advise, and still
less to decide, what principles the Oireachtas should apply.

When the judgment says the alleged principle is 'well established', it assumes judges have an authority that the Constitution does not give them. Article 40.5 of the Constitution
protects a citizen from having his dwelling entered unlawfully.
Article 15 authorises the Oireachtas to make laws. Those laws
must respect citizens' rights, including their rights in their
dwellings, but it is for the Oireachtas, and only the Oireachtas,
to decide what principles should they should apply in framing
laws. Judges decide whether laws the Oireachtas has passed are
consistent with the Constitution, but have no authority to decide how the Oireachtas should frame the laws it is mandated
to make. Nor are they authorised to express opinions on how
the Oireachtas should do its job.

It seems Judge Denham and the other judges she quotes think, first, that a search should be authorised only by an independent person and secondly that someone who authorises a search should act 'judicially'. Each of these might be a means of protecting citizens from being disturbed in their homes by searches that should not take place,. But neither is constitutionally mandated, and the judges' opinions do not bind the Oireachtas. A 'principle' laid down by people who have no authority to do so should not be described as 'well established'. Indeed, on an issue that is within the exclusive authority of the Oireachtas (Article 15.2), judges should not express an opinion.

Nor does the view that while issuing a search warrant is an administrative action it is one that must be exercised judicially stand up to analysis. Judicial decisions should be taken by a judge, and unless there are convincing reasons to the contrary, administrative acts should be undertaken by administrators – that is, in this context, people working for the Executive. There is no reason in principle why an administrator should act judicially. Moreover, given that the decision we are talking about is whether or not to issue a search warrant, and it is impossible to hear both sides, as a judge must, there are strong reasons for saying that the decision should not even appear to be taken judicially, because to give that impression would be deceptive.

Incidentally, a respected lawyer with whom I discussed this issue briefly argued that the Supreme Court was right in principle in saying that a Garda Superintendent should not issue a search warrant in a case where he was active because 'nemo judex in causa sua' – 'nobody should act as a judge in his own cause'. That would be right if the decision was judicial, but does not apply if it is not.

Quotation

> In the circumstances of this case a person issuing the search warrant should be independent of the Garda Síochána, to provide effective independence.

Comment

The judgment does not offer any suggestion about what kind of person or office-holder might meet the criteria of being qualified to authorise a search of a citizen's dwelling, and also independent of the Gardaí. In the absence of such guidance, it must be very difficult for the Oireachtas to identify such a person. Moreover, when, in the course of doing their job, the Gardaí want to enter a citizen's dwelling, they must also want to do so without any possibility that its occupant may know in advance that they may shortly call with a search warrant. It would seem impractical to expect them to do their job while at the same time inhibiting them by requiring them to disclose their intention to anyone independent of the Force. Further, how does this person or office-holder acquire the authority to issue a warrant, or authorise its issue? It can only be by Statute passed by the Oireachtas. So, if we decode this sentence, it seems to say to the Oireachtas that if it wants to give the Garda Síochána a possibility of searching a citizen's dwelling, it must first identify people who are independent of the Gardaí, and also competent to decide on the issuing of a warrant, and then pass legislation giving them the necessary authority. Only then will the Court decide whether to approve the Oireachtas's choice.

Quotation

> Article 40.5 of the Constitution of Ireland states "The dwelling of every citizen is inviolable and shall not be forcibly entered save in accordance with law." Thus, the Constitution protects the inviolability of the dwelling.

Comment

As I have shown in my 'Judgment' above, the Constitution offers only limited protection for 'the inviolability of a dwelling' and, properly analysed, says that a dwelling is not inviolable, because the Oireachtas may legislate for its forcible entry without the consent of a citizen-occupier. Chief Justice Denham supports the view that a citizen's dwelling is inviolable by quoting judges who have taken positions strongly protective of citizens' rights, starting with Sir Edward Coke in 1604, and also quoting judges from other jurisdictions. But, impressive though they may be, they do not have authority to alter the Constitution that we, the Irish People, adopted in 1937. When the People vested in the Oireachtas the right to decide in what circumstances State and other authorities might enter a citizen's home, the views of judges uttered prior to that date or in other legal jurisdictions became irrelevant.

Quotation

> In *The Director of Public Prosecutions v. Dunne [1994] 2 I.R.537 at p. 540 Carney J.* stated: "The constitutional protection given in Article 40, s. 5 of the Constitution in relation to the inviolability of the dwelling house is one of the most important, clear and unqualified protections given by the Constitution to the citizen."

Comment

One reads the words 'clear and unqualified' with amazement, both at what Judge Carney said and at the Chief Justice quoting them with approval. To anyone, lawyer or not, who reads Article 40.5, the word 'clear' is strange, because the wording of the Article is contradictory and ambiguous. 'Unqualified' is even more surprising, because the Article specifically provides that a citizen's dwelling may be forcibly entered 'in accordance with law'. If that is not a qualification of its 'inviolability', what is it?

Quotation

> The Oireachtas may interfere with the constitutional rights of a person. However, in so doing its actions must be proportionate.

Comment

This is unobjectionable as a general statement of principle. But it assumes the existence of a constitutional right. We need to ask what constitutional right is at issue? It can only be a citizen's right not to have his or her dwelling forcibly entered 'save in accordance with law'. It cannot be an unqualified right never to have one's dwelling forcibly entered, because such a right does not exist. The words 'save in accordance with law' can refer only to legislation to be passed by the Oireachtas setting out in what circumstances people may enter a citizen's dwelling against his will. If a search takes place in compliance with such legislation, it cannot infringe any constitutional right of a citizen, because whatever right exists is subject to legislative curtailment. Since a search authorised by the Oireachtas, and therefore carried out 'in accordance with law', does not infringe a constitutional right, the question of proportionality does not arise.

Quotation

> *The Constitution in Article 40.5 expressly provides that the dwelling is inviolable and shall not be forcibly entered, save in accordance with law, which means without stooping to methods which ignore the fundamental norms of the legal order postulated by the Constitution. Entry into a home is at the core of potential State interference with the inviolability of the dwelling.*

Comment

This calls for three comments.

1. As the 'Judgment' above shows, Article 40.5 of the Constitution does not 'expressly provide that the dwelling is inviolable'. The Article consists of a single sentence, the second part of which takes away the 'inviolability' that the first seems to grant.

2. The judgment does not identify 'fundamental norms of the legal order postulated by the Constitution' that the Chief Justice relies on, leading a reader to infer that, like 'unspecified personal rights', they exist in the minds of the judiciary, and may be augmented as time goes by. It quotes statements by foreign judges about how they think the dwell-

ing of a citizen (presumably, a citizen of their own country, under the laws of that country) should be protected from invasion. They are irrelevant in interpreting the Irish Constitution. There are also, of course, views expressed by Irish judges, which the judgment quotes, with approval. Such views, on a topic where the Constitution authorises the legislature, not the judiciary, to legislate, have no authority. Indeed, they are open to the criticism that judges who made them have trespassed into an area that the Constitution reserves for legislators. To elevate that collection of views into 'fundamental norms of the legal order postulated by the Constitution' is, in the periphrasis of Swift's Houyhnhnms, 'to say the thing that is not'. Of course, I do not accuse the Chief Justice of deliberate untruth. But the Constitution specifies that it is for the elected representatives of the People in the Oireachtas to make laws governing such matters as when search warrants should be issued, and who should authorise them. Judges have no authority to set aside a constitutionally legitimate exercise by the Oireachtas of that power. The Section they set aside was a legitimate, though inept, exercise of a power the Constitution vests in the Oireachtas, as 'sole lawmaker'.

3. The words 'stooping to methods' are unjustified. This is a phrase used with one meaning only: to criticise sly or underhand behaviour. What the Oireachtas did here was to lay down openly, in a Statute all could read, that a Garda Superintendent had the power to authorise a search of a citizen's home. Can that fairly be described as sly or underhand? How can such a description be attached to a Garda Superintendent who acts in accordance with the Statute? To my mind, the use by the Chief Justice of such prejudicial language, which she would rightly rebuke if it were used in court by an advocate, is a cause for further concern.

Glossary

Definitions

The Superior Courts: The High Court, currently with thirty-seven judges and the Supreme Court with eight, are the 'Superior Courts'. The High Court hears appeals from the next highest court, the Circuit Court, and also deals with litigation commenced in the High Court itself. There is no limit on the amount of damages it can award. The Supreme Court deals only with appeals, mostly from the High Court, usually relies on transcripts of the evidence given at the oral hearing, and rarely if ever hears witnesses. Practice requires it to hear every appeal lodged. Unlike the US Supreme Court, it does not refuse to hear appeals.

Bench: a general term including all judges.

Barrister: a general term including Junior barristers and 'Senior Counsel'. They are collectively called 'the Bar'.

Judgments and Orders. An Order of the Court is a direction embodying the decision of a judge. For example, 'The Defendant is to pay the Plaintiff €40,000 plus the costs of the Plaintiff when taxed and ascertained.' A judgment is the judge's explanation of how and why he arrived at the conclusion that his Order gives effect to. It is often written and read out in court. If not written in advance, it is called 'ex tempore'.

Plaintiff and Defendant: a Plaintiff is the person who initiates litigation, seeking damages or other relief from the court. The Defendant is the person from whom the Plaintiff seeks the relief. (In some types of proceeding the parties are called 'Applicant' and 'Respondent', but they are less common.)

Appellant. A party to litigation who appeals to a higher court a decision reached in that litigation. The other party to the appeal is known as the *Respondent*.

Pleadings: the documents the Plaintiff and Defendant or their lawyers exchange in preparation for a hearing. Strictly, the only Pleadings are:

Summons, issued by the Plaintiff, setting out in general terms what the Plaintiff complains about.

Statement of Claim, issued by the Plaintiff setting out in detail the facts and legal principles the Plaintiff intends to rely on at the court hearing.

Defence, issued by the Defendant, setting out how much (if any) of the Plaintiff's case he accepts without proof, what he disagrees with and the facts and legal principles he intends to rely on.

Reply, issued by the Plaintiff, usually a purely formal document.

Sometimes the Defendant wants to pursue a claim against the Plaintiff, in which case, instead of a Defence, he will issue a *'Defence and Counterclaim'*, and the Counterclaim will usually take the same form as a Plaintiff's Statement of Claim. The Plaintiff will then issue a further document called *'Defence to Counterclaim'*, a *Reply* (see above) will follow and Pleadings will be complete.

For convenience, other documents exchanged between the parties leading up to a hearing are generally included under the heading 'Pleadings'.

The Legislature: means the lawmaker. In Ireland, the Oireachtas is our sole lawmaker (Article 15). It is composed of the Dáil, consisting of directly elected TDs, the Seanad, consisting of people who have been become members by a form of indirect popular vote, and the President, whose main function is to sign Bills into law, whereupon they become Acts. TDs and Senators are sometimes referred to as 'legislators'.

Cases Referred to

The references to the cases criticised in Chapter 8 and in the Appendix are listed separately. All cases otherwise mentioned appear in alphabetical order.

Cases criticised in Chapter 8:

C.C v. Ireland [2005] IESC48 and *C.C v. Ireland* [2006] IESC 33 (two judgments); *A v. Governor of Arbour Hill Prison* [2006] IESC 45; *Maguire & ors v. Ardagh & ors* [2002] 1 IR 385; *McKenna v An Taoiseach* [1995] IESC 11, [1995] 2 IR 10; *Damache v. DPP* [2012] IESC 11

Other cases referred to:

Blake v. Attorney General [1981] IESC 1; [1982] IR 117; [1981] ILRM 34 is the case in which the Supreme Court declared the Rent Restrictions Acts unconstitutional.

Brennan v. Minister for Justice [1995] 1IR 612 [1995] 2 ILRM 206

Buckley v. A.G [1950] IR. 67 Same (No. 2) [1950] 84 ILTR 9, known as the 'Sinn Féin funds case' is the case in which Judge O'Byrne spoke of 'the respect that one great organ of State owes to another'.

De Burca v. A.G. [1976] I.R. 38 [1977] III ILTR 37 is the case where the then current jury selection process was held to be unconstitutional

Donnelly (Dublin) Ltd v. Pigs Marketing Board [1939] [2000] IR 413 is the case in which the Supreme Court laid down the principle of 'presumption of constitutionality'.

Greendale Developments Ltd. (In liquidation) (no. 3) [2002] IR 514 & [2001] ILRM 361 is the case in which Judge Hamilton spoke of the finality of proceedings not being lightly breached.

Re Haughey [1971] IR. 217

Kenny v. Trinity College and another [2007] IESC 42 is the case where the Supreme Court set aside its previous decision on the ground of 'objective bias'.

Lloyds Bank Ltd v. Bundy [1974] WLR 501 [1974] EWCA CIV 8 - 'Old Farmer Bundy'

McMahon v. A.G [1972] IR 69, (1972) 106 ILTR is the case where the then current electoral process was held to be unconstitutional.

Murphy v. A.G. [1982] IR 241 is the case where the Revenue had collected tax they should not have. It is the case where Judge Griffin spoke about the egg that could not be unscrambled.

The following is a partial list of cases where judges have described how the Constitution is to be interpreted:

Pigs Marketing Board v. Donnelly (Dublin) Limited [1939] I.R. 413

NUR v. Sullivan & ors [1947] IR 77; (1947) 81 ILTR55

DPP v. O'Shea [1982] IR 384

A.G. v. Paperlink Ltd [1984] IEHC 1; [[1984] ILRM, 1983] 1984} ILRM 373

Murray v. Ireland [1985] IR 532; D.P.P. v. S. (M.) [2003] IESC 24, [2003] IR 606

Tormey v. Ireland [1985] IR 289, (1985) ILRM 375

Latin Phrases

Rather than baldly translate, I will explain the Latin phrases that appear in the text.

A fortiori: To a greater extent. If A is heavier than B and B is heavier than C, then A must be heavier than C. If the Constitution denies a right to a citizen, it certainly does not confer it on a non-citizen.

Actus non facit rea nisi mens sit rea: An action that would otherwise be a crime will not be if it was done with an innocent mind.

Audi alteram partem: Hear the other side. A judge should hear both (or all sides) in a dispute before deciding. As an extension of that principle, a judge should never make a decision that affects anybody adversely, even if that person is not formally a party to proceedings, without giving the person affected a right to argue against the decision.

Cassus omissus pro omisso habendum est: If something you might expect to see in legislation does not appear, assume its absence is intentional.

Certiorari: a form of legal process in which a judge is asked to review (and if appropriate amend) a decision of a lower court or body acting in a judicial capacity.

De jure and *de facto* mean, respectively, 'in accordance with law', and 'in reality'. Legally, the Westminster Parliament governed Ireland between 1916 and 1922, but in some parts of the country that was effectively no longer true.

Ejusdem generis: Of the same kind.

Ex parte: in the absence of one party in litigation. A judge may make an urgent order (e.g., to prohibit picketing that seems to be illegal) on the application of one party only, but will not decide the issues finally without giving both sides an opportunity to be heard. (See *Audi alteram partem*.)

Expressio unius exclusio alterius est: If a Section of a Statute lists a number of things but excludes another similar thing, assume the omission is intentional. This is similar to *Cassus omissus pro omisso habendum est*, mentioned above.

Fiat justitia ruat caelum: Let justice be done, though the Heavens fall. A judge should not allow possible consequences of a decision to prevent him from doing justice in the case before him.

Inter alia: Among other things.

Modus operandi: The way of going about one's business.

Nemo judex in causa sua: Literally, nobody should judge a matter where he is involved, but the concept goes further than that, and requires a judge not to hear a case in whose outcome he may have an interest, or may be thought to have an interest.

Noscitur a sociis: Words are to be interpreted in the context in which they appear.

Prima facie: 'at first sight', but again it means something more. For example, a Plaintiff must prove his case, but if a Plaintiff establishes a *prima facie* case, the burden of disproving it transfers to the Defendant.

Quia timet: Literally, 'because he fears'. Someone seeking an injunction must show that his rights are being infringed or are demonstrably about to be infringed, not merely that he is afraid this may happen.

Ubi jus ibi remedium: Literally, where is law, there is a remedy, but really this means that a legal system that fails to remedy injustice is not worthy of the name.

Ultra vires: An *ultra vires* act is one committed by someone who did not have the authority to do it.

Quotations from the Constitution

The following is the text of all provisions of the Constitution mentioned in this book.

Article 5

Ireland is a sovereign, independent, democratic state.

Article 6

1. All powers of government, legislative, executive and judicial, derive, under God, from the people, whose right it is to designate the rulers of the State and, in final appeal, to decide all questions of national policy, according to the requirements of the common good.

2. These powers of government are exercisable only by or on the authority of the organs of State established by this Constitution.

Article 15

2. 1° The sole and exclusive power of making laws for the State is hereby vested in the Oireachtas: no other legislative authority has power to make laws for the State.

2.2° Provision may however be made by law for the creation or recognition of subordinate legislatures and for the powers and functions of these legislatures.

4.1° The Oireachtas shall not enact any law which is in any respect repugnant to this Constitution or any provision thereof.

4.2° Every law enacted by the Oireachtas which is in any respect repugnant to this Constitution or to any provision thereof, shall, but to the extent only of such repugnancy, be invalid.

Article 16

1. 4° No voter may exercise more than one vote at an election for Dáil Éireann, and the voting shall be by secret ballot.

2. 1° Dáil Éireann shall be composed of members who represent constituencies determined by law.

Article 17

2. Dáil Éireann shall not pass any vote or resolution, and no law shall be enacted, for the appropriation of revenue or other public moneys unless the purpose of the appropriation shall have been recommended to Dáil Éireann by a message from the Government signed by the Taoiseach.

Article 28

2. The executive power of the State shall, subject to the provisions of this Constitution, be exercised by or on the authority of the Government.

4. 1° The Government shall be responsible to Dáil Éireann.

Article 34

1. Justice shall be administered in courts established by law by judges appointed in the manner provided by this Constitution, and, save in such special and limited cases as may be prescribed by law, shall be administered in public.

3. 1° The Courts of First Instance shall include a High Court invested with full original jurisdiction in and power to determine all matters and questions whether of law or fact, civil or criminal.

Article 40

1. All citizens shall, as human persons, be held equal before the law.

This shall not be held to mean that the State shall not in its enactments have due regard to differences of capacity, physical and moral, and of social function.

3. 1° The State guarantees in its laws to respect, and, as far as practicable, by its laws to defend and vindicate the personal rights of the citizen.

3. 2° The State shall, in particular, by its laws protect as best it may from unjust attack and, in the case of injustice done, vindicate the life, person, good name, and property rights of every citizen.

5. The dwelling of every citizen is inviolable and shall not be forcibly entered save in accordance with law.

Article 45

(The provisions of this Article relevant to the *C.C.* case have been underlined for ease of reference, and material not relevant to the argument made in relation to the *C.C.* decision has been omitted.)

The principles of social policy set forth in this Article are intended for the general guidance of the Oireachtas. The application of those principles in the making of laws shall be the care of the Oireachtas exclusively, and shall not be cognisable by any Court under any of the provisions of this Constitution.

3. 2° The State shall endeavour to secure that private enterprise shall be so conducted as to ensure reasonable efficiency in the production and distribution of goods and as to protect the public against unjust exploitation.

4. 2° The State shall endeavour to ensure that the strength and health of workers, men and women, and <u>the tender age of children shall not be abused </u>and that citizens shall not be forced by economic necessity to enter avocations unsuited to their sex, age or strength.

Article 49

1. All powers, functions, rights and prerogatives whatsoever exercisable in or in respect of Saorstát Éireann immediately before the 11th day of December, 1936, whether in virtue of the Constitution then in force or otherwise, by the authority in which the executive power of Saorstát Éireann was then vested are hereby declared to belong to the people.

Article 50

1. Subject to this Constitution and to the extent to which they are not inconsistent therewith, the laws in force in Saorstát Éireann immediately prior to the date of the coming into operation of this Constitution shall continue to be of full force and effect until the same or any of them shall have been repealed or amended by enactment of the Oireachtas.

Index